Latin American Identities
Race, Ethnicity, Gender, and Sexuality

SALALM Secretariat
Benson Latin American Collection
The General Libraries
The University of Texas at Austin

Latin American Identities:
Race, Ethnicity, Gender, and Sexuality

Papers of the Forty-Sixth Annual Meeting of the
SEMINAR ON THE ACQUISITION OF
LATIN AMERICAN LIBRARY MATERIALS

Tempe, Arizona
May 26–29, 2001

Víctor Federico Torres
Editor

SALALM Secretariat
Benson Latin American Collection
The General Libraries
The University of Texas at Austin

ISBN: 0-917617-72-X

Contents

Research Sources on Gender, Sexuality, and Ethnicity

Latin American and Latino Collections

Access and Bibliographic Control of Latin American Resources

Preface

In many ways the theme for SALALM XLVI was inspired by "Latin American Masses and Minorities: Their Images and Realities," the theme of one of the first conferences I attended. Reviewing the themes of past conferences, I realized that since 1985 we have not focused on the population of Latin America and the Caribbean, especially the segments of the population that have traditionally been ignored or misrepresented. The theme "Latin American Identities: Race, Ethnicity, Gender, and Sexuality" provided an opportunity to explore a number of identities including women, nipo-brasileiros, people of color, gays, and indigenous groups from multidisciplinary perspectives in areas such as art, music, cinema, literature, history, and gender studies. The theme also fostered the use of approaches and resources such as photographs, postcards, lyrics, serials, movies, and manuscripts to study the complex interrelations of race, gender, ethnicity, and sexuality.

SALALM XLVI was unique in many ways. Not only was this our first twenty-first-century conference, but it also paved the way for several initiatives such as the first joint conference with Reforma, the National Association to Promote Library Services to the Spanish Speaking. Fifty people attended the preconference, which addressed the needs of professionals at nonresearch institutions with responsibilities for Latin American collection development. During SALALM XLVI, the Presidential Travel Fund was also launched as part of our organization's effort to increase conference attendance, especially by librarians unable to attend due to economic restraints. The conference program was organized differently with committee meetings scheduled throughout the four-day conference. These changes responded to the concerns of many members as expressed in previous town hall meetings.

In spite of the heat and hectic schedule, SALALM XLVI was well received. This was partly due to the excellent organization provided by the Local Arrangements Committee, headed by Orchid Mazurkiewicz, and the support of Arizona State University and Sherrie Schmidt, ASU dean of University Libraries. Also contributing to the overall success were the panels organized by our members as well as the participation of several faculty members from Arizona State University and the University of Arizona who joined us as speakers.

I want to express my gratitude to several colleagues who offered their advice and assistance during the preparation of SALALM XLVI: Peter T.

Johnson, who provided valuable insights for the conference theme; Tom Marshall, who provided continuous support from the University of Arizona; and Molly Molloy and Rhonda Neugebauer, who did not hesitate to respond to our last-minute call for help. Finally, a special thanks to Darlene Waller, who devoted long hours working for the conference, to Manuel Nuño, who has accompanied me through this journey, and to Mark L. Grover and Shannon Thurlow, who worked on editing these papers.

Víctor Federico Torres

Identity and Ethnicity

1. Ethnicity, Race, and Class in Early Caribbean Postcards: A Preliminary Research Report

Darlene Waller

My work with postcards started in the summer of 2000 when I received a Library Research Fellowship, from the Caribbean Resource Center at the University of Puerto Rico, to study a collection of early-twentieth-century Puerto Rican postcards housed in the Colección Puertorriqueña of the Library System, UPR, Rio Piedras campus. My research has continued as I have studied private collections both in Puerto Rico and the United States. I have also attended a variety of postcard shows and have started to collect early-twentieth-century postcards from Puerto Rico as well as from other Caribbean islands.

In my research I view postcards as valuable testimonies of the past. Images are becoming increasingly important as valuable historical and cultural sources for the study of societies and cultures of the past. Included in this category of historic artifacts is the postcard, which can provide important cultural, historic, and anecdotal information about a particular people, place, and time. Since postcards were produced as a commercial product, and generally without editorial control or selection, they represent a unique contemporary pictorial representation of a society. Probably more than any other mass-media product, the picture postcard has been responsible for creating and disseminating images of places and peoples of the world. As stated by Malek Alloula in his book *The Colonial Harem:* "Postcard imagery is a major vehicle by which understandings of various cultures are constructed for a general mass audience of potential tourists."[1]

As demonstrated by a selective bibliography of works that I have consulted in my research, evidence shows that, in recent years, scholars have begun to make greater use of these visual materials for scholarly research. Some of these scholars argue "that the visual text holds as much power as the written text to construct and define social identities and relationships . . . as these are organized into historically generated conventions for realism, naturalism, classed, and gendered representations."[2]

As I approached my research at the University of Puerto Rico, which focused on a collection of approximately one thousand early-twentieth-century postcards of Puerto Rico, I attempted to answer several questions including: Could this collection be considered a discreet documentary body of "literature" that would offer valuable historical and cultural information as a source for the study of early-twentieth-century Puerto Rico? Do the cards represent a unified body of images that will provide information on the construction of society and national development? What do the postcards (images and correspondence) reveal about aspects of Puerto Rican society such as work, food, transportation, architecture, agriculture, landscapes, urbanization, urban life, rural development, racist images, local history, customs and manners, political and social events, popular images of the *jíbaro,* and representations of tourism—in other words, were the postcards designed to sell paradise? My research also involved investigating if the information found in the cards can be placed in a broader context by relating it to other work in the field. In short, I intended to investigate postcards and postcard collections for a wide range of information about life of a particular people, place, and time to study the collections as a patrimony of richness from historical, anecdotal, and cultural perspectives.

Despite my hopes of addressing this broad research agenda, I quickly realized that my month-long research trip in Puerto Rico would not allow me sufficient time to fully answer all the questions I had presented in my proposal. Hence, I was faced with selecting one category of images represented on the postcards for close analysis. I chose to focus on cards depicting ethnic subjects, specifically images of the jíbaro, and to relate analysis of these images in a broader context by connecting it to other work on ethnicity and race in Puerto Rico. As my research has expanded, I have continued to focus on representations of ethnicity and race in Puerto Rican postcards as well as in cards from other Caribbean islands.

Postcards first appeared in Germany in 1865, in Austria in 1869, and in England in 1870. In general, the heyday for postcards in Europe and other parts of the world was between 1900 and 1920. The first postcards in the period between 1865 and 1892 were not intended for souvenirs but for advertisements. During this period all U.S. privately printed cards required the regular two-cent letter rate postage, while government printed cards required only one cent. Starting in 1898, American publishers were allowed to print and sell cards bearing the inscription "Private Mailing Card, Authorized by Act of Congress on May 19, 1898." These private mailing cards were to be posted with one-cent stamps, thus significantly enhancing the use of postcards. Writing was limited to the front of the card until about 1902 in some parts of the world and until 1907 in the United States. After 1907 the divided back became almost universally used.

How quickly the craze might have caught on in a particular Latin American or Caribbean country that often depended on its ties to Europe. For many of these countries, as well as in other parts of the world, photographic postcards made up a significant part of the national iconography in the early 1900s, because these countries lacked popular illustrated magazines or other publications. In fact, for some parts of the world, such as several countries in Africa, picture postcards are virtually the only remaining imagery for that period because they were sent out of the country. Almost all images that remained in the country have been destroyed as a result of ongoing civil conflict.

The source of most images for early postcards was the work of photographers. Real photograph postcards are particularly useful to contribute to research on peoples, places, cultures, and societies of the past. Other categories of postcards include advertising cards, art cards, and colorized cards.

Regarding ethnic imagery represented in the Puerto Rican postcards I have studied, I can offer some general observations. Almost all cards presented a highly "exoticized" yet primitive view of traditional Puerto Rican culture portrayed in a pre–U.S. contact context, or precontact by industrialization and the movement away from rural and agricultural life. This view is different from the exotic and romantic view of a "paradise" often depicted in postcards of Hawaiian or Polynesian natives. The "exotic-primitive" view fully displays poverty and the harsh realities of peasant or jíbaro life. By placing the jíbaro almost exclusively in a work setting (for example, selling goods, cutting tobacco, washing clothes, or going to a market), with a sad and tired expression implies that these people had only a life of anguish and struggle.

Also important to point out is the common practice among several postcard producers to use or reuse photographs of an earlier period to perpetuate the exotic-primitive view. Even when one can identify this practice in individual cards or series of cards, it does not negate the obvious attempt to portray, construct, and "advertise" the culture in a deliberate and often backward way. Additionally, commercial photographers and postcard producers desired to provide the public with what they perceived the public wanted. In so doing they produced and reinforced the visual clichés believed to be true of Puerto Rico. In an article called "Postcards of Palestine: Interpreting Images," the authors suggest that the selection of images provided the vehicle for reinforcement of racial, ethnic, and cultural stereotypes. The images reinforced the feel-good belief of visitors of their superiority—that they came from a more civilized, modern, and democratic society. The choice of inclusion or exclusion is central to this analysis.[3] What is included or excluded from the photos is critical in interpreting representations of cultural identity in Puerto Rico. When analyzing an image one needs to consider whether the image represents a real or natural situation or whether the scene may have been staged to create the desired effect.

Most postcard images depicting rural Puerto Rican peasants are devoid of modern man-made objects or suggestions of modernity. What is being viewed is often placed in nature and is therefore conceived as a natural, common condition, which erases all evidence of change and therefore conveys timelessness. This, however, was not the general situation in the mountains of Puerto Rico by the end of the first decade of the twentieth century as U.S. contact and subsequent industrialization had significantly affected rural Puerto Rico. The postcard images also presented virtually all the rural ethnic people as black, which is not an accurate representation of the majority composition of the rural populace at the time. "Whitening" of the island had begun a century before with the provisions of the *Real Cedula de Gracias* in 1815, which encouraged white foreigners to move to the island with their capital and technical know-how in order to increase the island's involvement in the world sugar market, and to "whiten" the island in order to lessen fears of slave rebellions.

Census statistics of the time do not reflect such a heavy black population on the island. The 1899 census, the first conducted after U.S. occupation, indicates a total population of 953,000 of which only 59,400 or 6.2 percent are black. By the 1910 census, the numbers reflect a total population of 1,118,000 and a black population of a little over 50,000 or 4.5 percent. By 1920 the Puerto Rico census reveals an identified black population of only 3.8 percent of the total population.

Christin Mamiya points out in her article on Hawaiian postcards that given "the ritualistic nature of sending postcards while on vacation [or traveling] and the public nature of this medium [in other words, not enclosed in an envelope], the power of such visual representations to construct public perception and to encode specific values cannot be understated."[4] Or, in other words, the post-card images have power to construct and encode stereotypes.

The images selected and presented allow consumers to see Puerto Rican natives as the "other"—representations of what the tourist, traveler, or viewer from the developing world was not, the exotic-primitive other. Motivation to travel to these places is to escape from the normal and to go to the exotic. Mamiya states: "postcards exploit differences between the visited culture and the traveler's culture and establishes the visited as the other." The images are purposefully presented in a primitive, exotic fashion to construct a cultural image "that is enticing and readily recognized as distinct from that of the aver-age white [European or U.S. traveler]."[5] Interpreting from Said's *Orientalism,* Mamiya says that "when control over the mechanisms that determine represen-tation and understanding of a culture is maintained by an outside group, as is usually the case in ethnic tourism, the native population is denied the opportu-nity to construct a cultural identity that strengthens their self image and sover-eignty."[6] In the case of Puerto Rico this theory is reinforced by information and images found in a variety of other publications of the time such as the series of U.S. War Governor's Annual Reports from Puerto Rico submitted to the U.S. Congress from 1901 to the 1930s. These documents describe native popula-tions in extremely pejorative ways and, in many instances, set up an image of Puerto Ricans, as well as many immigrant groups from Latin America and the Caribbean, as lazy, poor, and dirty.

This early advertising and reporting of Puerto Rican people as backward and inferior established the historical context that has affected the social, eco-nomic, and political status of the society in the past, and maybe even today.

Because of images presented historically and perpetuated presently, the Puerto Rican, as well as other ethnic groups of Latin American and Caribbean origin, confronts history on a daily basis. Present social relations and interactions can imply information about the past and, conversely, histories of the past are evidence of the persistence of present-day stereotypes, prejudices, and resultant social interactions and relations. Postcards have contributed to establishing these stereotypes.

My brief study of postcards from other Caribbean islands that focus on ethnic subjects reveal similar observations and conclusions. As I have viewed and gathered these postcards I often wonder if I might, at some point, come across the same image being used for more than one island, an image representing the Caribbean ethnic subject of the early-twentieth century regardless of place.

Postcards from the Caribbean[7]

The following descriptions of postcard images illustrate some of the points discussed in this paper.

1. The first two postcards were produced by the Boletín Mercantil, Puerto Rico. These are some of the earliest cards produced in Puerto Rico and were published between 1898 and approximately 1901. These two cards actually depict the jíbaro at leisure. There are not many of these images that exist. These cards are provided courtesy of the Colección Puertorriqueña, Library System, University of Puerto Rico, Río Piedras.

2. The third card is similar in style to the first two, but it was produced by Arthur Livingston Publishers, New York, sometime between 1898 and 1901 and represents a market scene in Puerto Rico. Provided courtesy of the Colección Puertorriqueña, Library System, University of Puerto Rico, Río Piedras.

3. The next six cards (#4–9) are a selection I have made to illustrate the black jíbaro in a work setting. Card number 4, the "Native Fruit Stand," was produced sometime between 1907 and 1915. Card number 5, "Winnowing Upland Rice in Porto Rico," was issued in 1912 by the Waldrop Company of San Juan who regularly indicated copyright dates on their cards. Card number 6, "Lavanderas—P.R.," has a written message on the verso that reads: "Dear Mrs. Rose, These are the fancy lavanderas we have to wash our clothes. They are real 'fancy' in making holes in the washing. Joseph Barte." Card number 7, "Cargando tabaco," was published around 1920 by A. Moscioni, a Ponce-based photographer and postcard producer. Card number 8, "Quincalleros—P.R.," seems to document the speed with which these hardware merchants are traveling down the dirt road despite the loaded baskets of heavy ware on

their heads. Card number 9, "Carrying Fruit to Market in Porto Rico," represents a staged or posed shot. Cards #4–9 provided courtesy of the Colección Puertorriqueña, Library System, University of Puerto Rico, Río Piedras.

4. The next two cards (#10–11) represent work in an urban setting in San Juan. The "worker" has a lighter skin color. I find the card of the orange seller (#11) particularly interesting in terms of the image's ability to deliver a message in terms of clothing. The seller and buyer are clearly distinguished by wardrobe.

5. The next four cards (#12–15) show the jíbaro placed in his native rural setting represented as black, poor, etc., and often with children partially or completely unclothed.

6. On card number 16, "Porto Rico. A Bunch of Pickaninnies," the publisher, Waldrop Photo Company in San Juan, a U.S.-based company, uses the contemptuous term "pickaninnies" to describe the black children grouped together for this shot.

7. Card number 17, "A Cockfight in Porto Rico," presents the same photograph we saw earlier in the Boletín Mercantil card. I do not know when this photo was originally taken, but it is clearly a number of years before this later postcard was produced. This deliberate misrepresentation reinforces the primitive, timeless image of the Puerto Rican jíbaro.

8. The next two cards (#18–19) present work settings, which depict a "craft" as work and clearly present this type of work as reserved for a different class of women.

The remainder are cards from other Caribbean islands which, as I have indicated, offer similar representations and messages.

• Cards #20–23 are from Jamaica. The written message on card number 20 reads: "This is a queer old town," signed by Fred and sent from Kingston on March 10, 1905. Similar to cards #18–19, this Jamaican card (#23), representing craft as work, tells us that this type of work was reserved for a different class.

• Cards #24–27 are from Trinidad. By 1800 Trinidad was already quite a multicultural place. African slaves were followed by Madeirans, Chinese, and predominantly East Indians, all who have left their mark on the island.

• Card number 28 presents a "Vegetable Seller" in Barbados. Barbados has an interesting history in terms of slavery and its black population.

By 1807, when most of the British slave trade was coming to an end, Barbadian slaveowners had "embraced the practice of breeding slaves rather than importing new ones, [supposedly] improving conditions and encouraging slave women to bear children through incentives." They also exported "locally-born slaves to other colonies, claiming them to be more reliable and less prone to unrest than 'unseasoned' Africans."[8]

- Card number 29 is a "Native Woman Fish Vendor" in Curacao, N.W.I.

- Card number 30 is "A Native Hut, St Thomas, D.W.I." This island was then a part of the Danish West Indies at the time this card was printed. Transfer of power to the United States for St. Croix, St. Thomas, and St. John did not occur until 1917 when fear over German influence in ailing colonies prompted the United States to buy these islands from the Danes.

- Card number 31 is entitled "Three Natives, Nassau, Bahamas." The printed message is telling in its wording, grouping the black man and child in the same "natives" category as the donkey!

- The last cards (#32–37) are from Cuba. You will notice in cards #32–35 that there is not such a heavy representation of the black native in the work and rural settings, yet the themes of poor, primitive, and time-lessness prevail. Card number 36 is a "Cuban Street Carnival Scene." I have yet to study all the faces, costumes, and paraphernalia but it is fascinating. This last card (#37) is a bit more modern than the other cards I have presented. However, the sentiment expressed in the printed text as well as the message, "Visit Cuba—So near and yet so Foreign," perpetuate historic stereotypes.

NOTES

1. Malek Alloula, *The Colonial Harem* (Minneapolis: University of Minnesota Press, 1986), p. 15.

2. Catherine Preston and Anton Rosenthal, "Correo mítico: The Construction of a Civic Image in the Postcards of Montevideo, Uruguay, 1900–1930," *Studies in Latin American Popular Culture* 15 (1996): 233.

3. Annelies Moors and Steven Machlin, "Postcards of Palestine: Interpreting Images," *Critique of Anthropology* 7, no. 2 (1987): 69–70.

4. Christin J. Mamiya, "Greetings from Paradise: The Representation of Hawaiian Culture in Postcards," *Journal of Communication Inquiry* 16 (1992): 86.

5. Ibid., p. 87.

6. Ibid.

7. To access these postcard images and others presented at the conference contact the author at dhull@lib.uconn.edu.

8. Ferguson, p. 150.

BIBLIOGRAPHY

Albers, Patricia C., and William R. James. "Images and Reality: Postcards of Minnesota's Ojibway People, 1900–1980." *Minnesota History* 49 (1985): 229–240.

———. "Travel Photography: A Methodological Approach." *Annals of Tourism Research* 15 (1988): 134–158.

Alloula, Malek. *The Colonial Harem.* Minneapolis: University of Minnesota Press, 1986.

Baldwin, Brooke. "On the Verso: Postcard Messages as a Key to Popular Prejudices." *Journal of Popular Culture* 22, no. 3 (1988): 15–28.

Cohen, Erik. "The Study of Touristic Images of Native People: Mitigating the Stereotype of a Stereotype." In *Tourism Research: Critiques and Challenges,* edited by Douglas G. Pearce and Richard W. Butler. New York: Routledge, 1993. Pp. 36–69.

———. "Who Are the Chao Khao?: 'Hill Tribe' Postcards from Northern Thailand." *International Journal of Society and Language* 98 (1992): 101–125.

Corbey, Raymond. "Alterity: The Colonial Nude: Photographic Essay." *Critique of Anthropology* 8, no. 3 (1988): 75–92.

David, Philippe. "La Carte Postale Africaine (1900–1960)." *Revue Juridique et Politique Indépendence et Cooperation* 40 (1986): 166–177.

Evans, Eric J., and Jeffrey Richards. *A Social History of Britain in Postcards, 1870–1930.* London and New York: Longman, 1980.

Grant, Stephen. *Postales salvadoreñas del ayer* (Early Salvadoran Postcards: 1900–1950). San Salvador: Fundación María Escalón de Nuñez, Banco Cuscatlán, 1999.

Kearns, Séamus. "Picture Postcards as a Source for Social Historians." *Saothar* 22 (1997): 128–133.

Klamkin, Marian. *Picture Postcards.* New York: Dodd, Mead, and Company, 1974.

Levine, Robert M. "Faces of Brazilian Slavery: The Cartes de Visite of Christiano Júnior." *Americas* (Academy of American Franciscan History) 47, no. 2 (October 1990): 127–159.

Mamiya, Christin J. "Greetings from Paradise: The Representation of Hawaiian Culture in Postcards." *Journal of Communication Inquiry* 16 (1992): 86–101.

Mellinger, Wayne Martin. "Postcards from the Edge of the Color Line: Images of African Americans in Popular Culture, 1893–1917." *Symbolic Interaction* 15 (1992): 413–433.

———. "Toward a Critical Analysis of Tourism Representations." *Annals of Tourism Research* 21, no. 4 (1994): 756–779.

Moors, Annelies, and Steven Machlin. "Postcards of Palestine: Interpreting Images." *Critique of Anthropology* 7, no. 2 (1987): 61–77.

Peterson, Nicolas. "The Popular Image." In *Seeing the First Australians,* edited by Ian Donaldson and Tamsin Donaldson. Sydney: Allen and Unwin, 1985. Pp. 164–180.

Preston, Catherine, and Anton Rosenthal. "Correo mítico: The Construction of a Civic Image in the Postcards of Montevideo, Uruguay, 1900–1930." *Studies in Latin American Popular Culture* 15 (1996): 231–259.

Prochaska, David. "Fantasia of the Phototheque: French Postcard Views of Colonial Senegal." *African Arts* 24 (October 1991): 40–47, 98.

Samponaro, Frank N., and Paul J. Vanderwood. *War Scare on the Rio Grande: Robert Runyon's Photographs of the Border Conflict, 1913–1916*. Austin: Texas State Historical Association, 1992.

Schor, Naomi. "Cartes Postales: Representing Paris 1900." *Critical Inquiry* 18 (1992): 188–244.

———. "Collecting Paris." In *The Cultures of Collecting,* edited by John Elsner and Roger Cardinal. Cambridge: Harvard University Press, 1994. Pp. 252–302.

Stevens, Norman D. *Postcards in the Library: Invaluable Visual Resources*. New York: Haworth, 1995.

Vanderwood, Paul J. "The Picture Postcard as Historical Evidence: Veracruz, 1914." *Americas* (Academy of American Franciscan History) 45, no. 2 (1988): 201–225.

Vanderwood, Paul, and Frank N. Samponaro. *Border Fury: A Picture Postcard Record of Mexico's Revolution and U.S. War Preparedness 1910–1917*. Albuquerque: University of New Mexico Press, 1988.

Wilkinson, Billy R. "Library Postcards—The Messages." In *A Guide to Collecting Librariana,* by Norman D. Stevens. Lanham, Md.: Scarecrow Press, 1986. Pp. 68–73.

2. Pan-American Identity and Ethnicity: Buscando la América de Rubén Blades

Anne C. Barnhart-Park

Rubén Blades sings in the title track of his 1984 recording that he is in search of America. Through his music and lyrics, he explores a new definition of America, stretching traditional boundaries and encouraging new identities. Lyrically, he has done this both through the songs he has composed and through his selection of songs written by others. In this work, I examine the texts of several of Blades's songs and talk about their effect on listeners through a textual analysis.

The nation Blades calls America reaches across the continent, what he refers to as "América el continente."[1] In order to explore how he establishes this new nation, it is useful to examine Benedict Anderson's 1983 book, *Imagined Communities: Reflections on the Origin and Spread of Nationalism.* Anderson defines a nation as "an imagined political community," a definition he unpacks in the following manner:

> It is imagined because the members of even the smallest nation will never know most of their fellow-members, meet them, or even hear of them, yet in the minds of each lives the image of their communion. . . . In fact, all communities larger than primordial villages of face-to-face contact (and perhaps even these) are imagined. Communities are to be distinguished, not by their falsity/genuineness, but by the style in which they are imagined. . . . The nation is imagined as limited because even the largest of them, encompassing perhaps a billion living human beings, has finite, if elastic boundaries, beyond which lie other nations. . . . Finally, it is imagined as a community because, regardless of the actual inequality and exploitation that may prevail in each, the nation is always conceived as a deep horizontal comradeship.[2]

Anderson states that one of the ways in which the community is imagined is through the experience of "simultaneity"—the awareness that others whom one does not know personally exist and act at the same time as oneself. He further describes how print capitalism helped create nations, because through a novel, readers relate to the experiences of the protagonist. For instance, if the readers have walked down the same muddy streets described in the text, by reliving the event through the eyes of the narrator, the readers share an experience, thus creating the imagined community. Anderson argues that newspapers are slightly different because the events described happened to *actual people* so the connection is easier for the reader to make. According to Anderson, the very act of reading the newspaper has become an exercise in simultaneity.

Anderson can only be relied on to a certain extent since he limited his observations to print media. Unfortunately, he ignores oral tradition, failing to acknowledge that with the advent and spread of radio and public music performances, simultaneity could be experienced by much larger masses. Christopher A. Waterman applied Anderson's concepts of imagined community in his discussion of pan-Yoruba identity:

> Hegemonic values enacted and reproduced in musical performance portray the Yoruba as a community, a deep comradeship founded in shared language, political interests, ethos, and blood. . . . Yoruba popular music portrays an imagined community of some 30 million people—a sodality that no individual could ever know in entirety through first-hand experience—and embodies the ideal affective texture of social life and the melding of new and old, exotic and indigenous within a unifying syncretic framework.[3]

When considering Latin America, music might even be more important than print media because at various times throughout the colonial era, Spain discouraged literacy. Therefore oral traditions, especially music, remained popular vehicles of cultural expression.

Through the stories Blades sings, listeners experience simultaneity. As a musical newspaper or novel, Blades's songs tell the story of events in the daily lives of people all across America. Blades acknowledges and embraces this role as he stated in an interview in *Americas,* "I felt that popular music would play an important role in Latin America. I felt it was an effective way of stating cases, of presenting the truth, the people's side . . . what I am doing is creating not songs but a popular literature that is sung."[4] Several of Blades's songs include separate vignettes describing the actions of people who do not know each other, but who are acting simultaneously. Through his storytelling, Blades shapes the "imagined community" constructed in the minds of his listeners. He also juxtaposes the lives of various sectors, emphasizing the similarities of members of the community, regardless of national or class lines.

Blades was born in Panama City in 1948. In 1970, he went to New York and, with Pete Rodríguez, recorded his first album, *De Panamá A Nueva York.* He returned to Panama and finished his university education and later earned a law degree from Harvard. He has recorded over twenty albums, the latest being *Tiempos,* released in 1999. In addition to being a musician, he is an actor starring in movies and in ABC's "Gideon's Crossing."

The second track on the 1984 recording *Buscando América* is "G.D.B.D." While the liner notes for the recording do not mention this, in an article about Blades, "G.D.B.D." is said to stand for "gente despertando bajo dictaduras."[5] In this song, Blades lulls listeners with a hypnotic beat and short, choppy sentences as he describes the mundane morning routine of a man getting ready to go to work. The listeners relate to this man because they quickly recognize the pattern of their own morning rituals:

> Despiertas. No has podido dormir muy bien. Te levantas . . .
> Te vistes. No encuentras la correa . . .
> Vas a la cocina . . . [Tu esposa], sin contestarte, te recuerda que hay que pagar
> la cuenta de la luz.

Early in the song, Blades foreshadows that listeners might not share every aspect of this person's life, but he also implies that such differences are normal: "Cada uno tiene su lado de la cama. / Cada uno tiene su lado en todo." After the listeners have been comforted by their similarities with this man, they find out that this man who is a member of their imagined community, a member of their nation, is also a member of the secret police, and here is where his morning ritual dramatically differs from theirs:

> Suena el teléfono. Tu esposa lo contesta.
> Es para tí. De la oficina.
> Hoy van a arrestar al tipo. Va un carro a recogerte. Que lo esperes abajo . . .
> Sacas tu libreta y los lentes negros.
> Vas a la cama. Levantas el cochón y sacas tu revólver.

After establishing this man as someone often perceived as the enemy, Blades returns us again to the familiar: "Le das un beso al espacio, al lado de la mejilla, que ella no devuelve, o sí? / Abres la puerta y bajas por la escalera de madera, saltando los escalones de dos en dos." Blades has obligated listeners to relate to someone whom they would normally not; he, too, is a part of their nation whether they like it or not.[6]

The next song on that same recording has listeners relating to a different group of people—the families of the disappeared. First the listeners are introduced to the intimacies of the secret police agent, then they are faced with the victims left in his wake:

> Que alguien me diga si han visto a mi hijo.
> Es estudiante de Pre-Medicina.
> Se llama Agustín y es un buen muchacho.
> A veces es terco cuando opina.
> Lo han detenido. No sé qué fuerza.
> Pantalón blanco, camisa a rayas. Pasó anteayer.

Blades never tells the listeners which country is home to these voices. They could all be from one country, or they could be from scattered places throughout the Americas. The song begins with somber music and sporadic snare-drum sounds, imitating gunshots. Then over a reggae beat, Blades forces listeners to learn about the disappeared. The listeners hear the voices of the spouses, siblings, parents, and children of the disappeared giving the listeners information as if they were filling out missing-persons reports. The listeners know what the disappeared were wearing—now they too are armed with enough knowledge to be able to help in the search. In some cases the listeners get a vague idea of why the person might have been detained, but in other cases they are left wondering, as are their family members.

In 1992 Blades recorded the tongue-in-cheek "El apagón," in which he relates vignettes from a blackout in an unnamed city. He celebrates the diversity within this city as he brings together the experiences of different individuals during the same event, telling how some benefited from the blackout while others were inconvenienced:

> La electricidad, se interrumpió, y por el apagón, se suspendió
> la tortura de un subversivo por un empleado del desgobierno . . .
> A diez cuadras del interrogatorio protesta la gente, pués se canceló la versión
> local de un concurso de belleza de la "Miss Internacional" . . .
> Por el apagón, en otro lugar, alguien se alegró
> pues la oscuridad lo va a ayudar a desempeñar
> la muy popular función de robar.

By hearing these different people in the same city, the listeners again experience simultaneity upon recalling their own adventures during a blackout. In the chorus, Blades weaves together symbols and literary references from across the Americas, uniting them under the name "el Sub-D":

> Aquí en el Sub-D: La tierra de Sonia Braga.
> Aquí en el Sub-D: El que no la hace, la paga.
> Aquí en el Sub-D: De abuelas y dictadores.
> Aquí en el Sub-D: De santos y pecadores . . .
> Aquí en el Sub-D: El fin del imperialismo.
> Aquí en el Sub-D: La tumba del comunismo . . .
> Aquí en el Sub-D: Entre un Fidel y un Somoza . . .
> Aquí en el Sub-D: Del beso y de la tortura.

When he refers to the Brazilian actress Sonia Braga, Blades further extends the boundary of his America. Again, as a musical version of Anderson's print capitalism, as "popular literature that is sung," Colombia and Argentina are represented by references to their famous literature: "De abuelas y dictadores" (García Márquez's *Cien años de soledad*) and "Del beso y la tortura" (Puig's *El beso de la mujer araña*).

In 1996, Blades released *La rosa de los tiempos,* his first 100 percent Panamanian recording—all the music, musicians, and studio production are from his homeland. The track "En el semáforo" celebrates another typical city experience—traffic-light vendors. Like "G.D.B.D.," Blades humanizes the other and gets the listeners to relate to a social group different from their own; this time he focuses on the vendors. In "semáforo," he is not as deceitful as in "G.D.B.D."—the listeners are never tricked into thinking that they are just like the other. But, through personalizing the individuals who wash windshields and try to sell bananas, the listeners acknowledge their inclusion in their imagined community. Blades starts out by singing verses in the voices of the street vendors:

> Llévese, por favor, la flor marchita;
> y el pan que bajo el sol se fermentó;
> el maní dulce pa' darle al muerto su misa,
> plátano verde para pagarle al doctor.

After the verses, Blades calls out lines (that do not appear in the CD liner) and the chorus responds affirming, "En el semáforo." Now that he has made the listeners see the humanity of the vendors, he reminds them that they are not that different from the other classes, everyone must wait at the traffic light:

> espera el rico, espera el pobre, la clase media
> pensando en el Papá Egoró (En el semáforo) . . .
> hoy por tí, mañana por mí
> cuidado, quizás seas tú
> él que mañana esté allá afuera (En el semáforo).

Blades does add a political message as he states all classes think about Papá Egoró, the political party he helped to form and on whose ticket he unsuccessfully ran for president in 1994.

As mentioned above, Blades's America is not limited by state boundaries, nor by language. In 1988, realizing a long-standing dream, he released a recording in English called *Nothing But The Truth,* with guest artists Lou Reed, Elvis Costello, and Sting. While this recording was embraced by critics, it was not a commercial success. In English, Blades tackles social issues like AIDS, Oliver North, and violence in Latin America. Before recording the album, Blades explained the rationale behind recording one in English, "'the need to do social commentary about Latin American cities doesn't change with the language.'"[7] The one attempt at simultaneity on this album is "In Salvador," which places the listeners in the world of Central American political oppression:

> Better cross yourself before you leave your home.
> Don't forget to carry your I.D.
> Any time you walk the streets in Salvador, you can't tell what kind of eyes you'll meet.
> Cause when night comes they'll hunt you down, they'll take your life and leave you to be found.
> *Chorus:* No one can protect your life in Salvador.
> Judges that condemn you have no name. Could it be the gentleman that lives next door, or the guy who goes with you to work?

Like the *Buscando América* song "Desapariciones," "In Salvador" incorporates a reggae beat behind the lyrics. While in this essay I focus on the lyrics, not the music, Blades's use of reggae does merit a brief comment. Traditionally most of Blades's music has been salsa, with more recent experimentation with music from across the Americas.[8] In the liner notes from his English release,

Blades explains his use of reggae in his stream-of-consciousness introduction to the song "In Salvador":

> A follow-up to my Spanish song, "Father Anthony and His Altar Boy, Andrés" from the *Buscando América* album. It also completes "Desapariciones," from that same album. Went to the reggae rhythm because I associate it with political consciousness and it's very basic, doesn't get in the way of the lyrics. [*sic*]

While the use of reggae probably does create the overall effect Blades mentions in the above quote, the song as a whole falls flat when compared to the images he creates in Spanish. This could be because the tone is more preachy than engaging—the listeners can sympathize with the terrifying conditions, but they are never forced to actually relate to the situation.

Blades not only wants to establish the listeners as citizens of the same imagined community, he wants them to be *responsible* members of this pan-American nation. In several of his songs, *Siembra,* he admonishes listeners for failing to become involved, failing to fight injustices. The 1978 recording, *Siembra,* produced with Wille Colón, contains "Plástico," in which Blades urges people to reject materialism and to be proud of their heritage: "Oye latino, oye hermano, oye amigo / Nunca vendas tu destino por el oro / Ni la comodidad." The same recording also contains "Pedro Navaja," a song that criticizes members of a community for failing to act after witnessing a crime. Jorge Duany provides a rich analysis of this song:

> The song is narrated in the third person by an observer who stands by ("I saw him passing" [Lo vi pasar]) but, who like the rest of the *barrio* does not get involved in the action of the story; hence, the point of view is testimonial but detached. The narrator sees with the eyes of his peers and thus becomes their accomplice in keeping crime quiet. . . . The song condemns social indifference and collective anomie and, conversely, incites slum dwellers to organize and commit themselves to the welfare of their community.[9]

Blades does not hide his anger with community apathy and he openly discusses in interviews his disappointment: "Behind every military coup in Latin America, behind every civilian dictatorship, lies civilian responsibility. We allowed it to happen. We did not look inside, we did not act from within. We voted and then went home."[10] This attitude is seen in the song "Desapariciones" where after introducing listeners to the families of the disappeared, Blades admonishes them as witnesses who refused to get involved:

> Anoche escuché varias explosiones. [*vocalizations which represent gunfire*]
> Tiros de escopeta y de revólver.
> Carros acelerados, frenos, gritos.
> Eco de botas en la calle.
> Toques de puerta. Quejas. Por Dioses. Platos rotos.
> Estaban dando la telenovela.
> Por eso nadie miró pa' fuera.

Blades continues the theme of oppression under dictatorships in a later release, "Prohibido olvidar" (1991). Again, without telling listeners a specific setting for the story, in each verse he sings a litany about the activities prohibited under the regime, then he asks listeners to take action:

> Prohibieron ir a la escuela e ir a la Universidad.
> Prohibieron las garantías y el fin constitucional.
> Prohibieron todas las ciencias, excepto la militar.
> Prohibiendo el derecho a queja,
> Prohibieron el preguntar.
> Hoy te sugiero, mi hermano,
> Pa' que no vuelva a pasar,
> ¡Prohibido olvidar!

The song ends with a more direct challenge to the listeners, challenging them not to forget past oppression. And, through listing the ways in which people are oppressed, they are forced to bear witness to experiences that they had not previously shared.

Blades forces listeners to identify with the victims and to recognize that they are also passive participants in the injustice through their inaction. His music is an attempt to make people aware of their new community and their role in it. His storytelling allows listeners to explore the outer limits of their imagined community. This community is not one defined by geopolitical boundaries. He attempts a definition of this nation in the 1988 "Patria":

> Hace algún tiempo me preguntaba un chiquillo
> por el significado de la palabra "patria" . . . le dije así:
> . . . no memorices lecciones de dictaduras o encierros;
> la patria no la definen los que suprimen al pueblo.
> La patria es un sentimiento en la mirada de un viejo,
> Sol de eterna primavera, risa de hermanita nueva;
> te contesto, hermanito: patria son tantas cosas bellas!

But, as the song explains, "patria," community, is a sentiment—it cannot be confined by a singular definition of words because it is so many beautiful things. The definition is ever evolving and the listeners, as its residents, have the responsibility of defining and redefining their nation, their "patria."

Blades helps his listeners work this definition. Through his songs he creates simultaneity because through listening to the events in the lives of others, listeners become aware of their presence. These people whose lives share similarities with the listeners' are part of their imagined community. The irony of everyone living together is not lost on Blades; he intentionally juxtaposes the humanity of the secret police agent in "G.D.B.D." and the victims of the disappeared in "Desapariciones." On the *Live!* CD he comments on this incongruity: "we have to deal with the fact that we're all here, nobody's gonna leave and we might as well make the best of it. Let's, let's play our strengths as opposed to our differences. With respect. And, we'll get somewhere, ah?"[11]

Blades reuses the line "patria son tantas cosas bellas" in several songs, reminding his listeners that they are constantly reimagining their community as they become aware of new, perhaps previously invisible members and sectors. Then, after establishing whom to include, he challenges them, his audience, to become involved in politics at local, national, and international levels.

NOTES

1. In the live version of "Buscando América," Blades introduces the song and speaks to the audience, switching from Spanish to English:

> Dentro del trabajo que hablamos anteriormente esta canción también formó parte de un album titulado *Buscando América.* This song was part of an album titled *In Search for America.* Y me permito decir una cosa. Acuérdense siempre de algo y esto es, sin ánimo de ofender a nadie, pero acuérdense de una cosa—que América e' un continente. Y todo lo que nace en América es americano. No solamente un grupo. Todo lo que nace en el continente americano es americano. Igual que todo que nace en el continente europeo es europeo. Así que when I'm talking about America, I'm talking about the continent and anybody, everybody who's born in the continent of America is an American. And, if we, the more we think about it the more sense it makes. Because we should be working together as opposed to against each other, you know. And we have to talk and we have to deal with the fact that we're all here, nobody's gonna leave and we might as well make the best of it. Let's, let's play our strengths as opposed to our differences. With respect. And, we'll get somewhere, ah?

2. Benedict Anderson, *Imagined Communities: Reflections on the Origin and Spread of Nationalism,* rev. ed. (New York: Verso, 1991), pp. 6–7.

3. Christopher A. Waterman, "'Our Tradition is a Very Modern Tradition': Popular Music and the Construction of Pan-Yoruba Identity," *Ethnomusicology: Journal of the Society for Ethnomusicology* 34, no. 3 (fall 1990): 376.

4. Robert A. Parker, "The Vision of Rubén Blades," *Américas* (March–April 1985): 16, 17.

5. Quoted in Sergio A. Santana, *Yo, Rubén Blades: confesiones de un relator de barrio* (Medellín: Ediciones Salsa y Cultura, 1997), p. 61. Interestingly, on the same album, in the song "El Padre Antonio y su monaguillo Andrés," a song about the murder of a Central American priest (paralleling Archbishop Romero), Blades celebrates "gente despertando."

6. Blades might have a more personal reason for including the secret police in his imagined community since his father was a member of the secret police (having been recruited to play basketball for them).

7. Parker, "Vision of Rubén Blades," p. 19.

8. A completely different study could be done on how Blades attempts to create a pan-American identity through his music, lyrics aside. His latest release, *Tiempos,* would be difficult to classify as salsa.

9. Jorge Duany, "Popular Music in Puerto Rico: Toward an Anthropology of Salsa," *Revista de Música Latino Americana* (Latin American Music Review) 5, no. 2 (fall/winter 1984): 202. Here Duany is also referring to the last stanza of the song, which tells of the *barrio's* indifference to the double murder which was just recounted in the song: "Y créanme gente, que aunque hubo ruido, nadie salió. No hubo curiosos, no hubo preguntas, nadie lloró." (In this same article, Duany also analyzes Blades's songs "Juan Pachanga" and "Pablo Pueblo.")

10. Rubén Blades quoted in David Fricke, "Rubén Blades's Latin Revolution," *Rolling Stone* (April 23, 1987): 38.

11. See note 1.

BIBLIOGRAPHY

Anderson, Benedict. *Imagined Communities: Reflections on the Origin and Spread of Nationalism*. Rev. ed. New York: Verso, 1991.

Blades, Rubén. *Nothing But the Truth.* Elektra compact disc 60754-2. 1988.

———. *La rosa de los tiempos.* Sony compact disc CDT-81992. 1996.

Blades, Rubén con Seis del Solar. *Buscando América.* Elektra compact disc 60352-2. 1984.

Blades, Rubén con Son del Solar. *Amor y control.* Sony compact disc CDZ-80839. 1992.

———. *Antecedente.* Elektra compact disc 60795-2. 1988.

———. *Caminando.* Sony compact disc CD-80593. 1991.

———. *Live!* Elektra compact disc 60868-2. 1990.

Cedeño, Roberto. *Blades: la calle del autor.* Caracas: Fondo Editorial Tropykos, 1992.

Duany, Jorge. "Popular Music in Puerto Rico: Toward an Anthropology of Salsa." *Revista de Música Latino Americana* (Latin American Music Review) 5, no. 2 (fall/winter 1984): 186–216.

Fricke, David. "Rubén Blades's Latin Revolution." *Rolling Stone* (April 23, 1987): 36–39, 158.

Parker, Robert A. "The Vision of Rubén Blades." *Américas* (March–April 1985): 15–19.

Santana, Sergio A. *Yo, Rubén Blades: confesiones de un relator de barrio.* Medellín: Ediciones Salsa y Cultura, 1997.

Waterman, Christopher A. "'Our Tradition is a Very Modern Tradition': Popular Music and the Construction of Pan-Yoruba Identity." *Ethnomusicology: Journal of the Society for Ethnomusicology* 34, no. 3 (fall 1990): 367–379.

3. Nipo-Brazilian Return Migration to Japan: A Review Essay and Annotated Bibliography

Roberta Astroff

As anyone who has conducted research into U.S. Latino issues knows, subject access to such materials is made difficult by differences and shifts in naming. The use of ethnic labels and even the constitution of an ethnic group change over time. The pattern of these namings and the history of ethnic labels, when traced back to their discursive communities, provide a schematic of the speakers, the participants, their concerns, and the frames within which they see, analyze, and act on social issues (Oboler 1995; Astroff 1997).

This study of the patterns of ethnic and national labels grew out of a bibliographic study. The original intent was to compile an annotated bibliography of materials published since 1967 on Japanese-Brazilians.[1] A significant percentage of the material published in the 1990s and later focuses on a recent phenomenon: since the late 1980s, a growing number of Brazilians of Japanese descent have gone to Japan to work. In 1990 the Japanese government in fact created a special visa category for the people they call *nikkeijin,* overseas Japanese, emigrants and the children and grandchildren of Japanese emigrants. Wayne Cornelius, a preeminent specialist on Mexican migration to the United States, and founding director of the Center for U.S.-Mexican Studies at the University of California, San Diego, describes this moment in Japan as "perhaps the most intriguing and important laboratory in the world today for studying the interplay among private market forces, cultural tolerance for immigration, and government attempts to regulate it."

The Center for U.S.-Mexican Studies is also a rich site for researchers interested in ethnic, racial, and national identity; cultural and economic globalization; and hybridity. A bibliographic search using the ethnic labels used in this case makes explicit how race and ethnicity are produced in discourse. The ethnic classifications used by the Japanese government, the Japanese people, the Japanese-Brazilians, other Brazilians, and the social scientists also provide a useful device for analyzing the social phenomenon and the literature developing around it. This critical review essay describes the "return migration" and focuses on the frameworks being established in the growing academic literature available in English, Spanish, and Portuguese on Japanese-Brazilian labor migration to Japan. The disciplinary homes of the researchers and journals providing materials in this area include history, sociology, anthropology, economics, political science, and women's studies. These academic frames at times analyze and at times adopt the public discourses about Japanese-Brazilian labor migration to Japan.

Japanese-Brazilians

The perception of the Latin American population by people outside Latin America generally puts the emphasis on the Latin or Spanish heritage and on the indigenous or Indian populations and their combination. National self-perceptions throughout Latin America tend to emphasize the same origins. However, the populations of Latin American countries are considerably more diverse than that. In addition to African populations brought to the Americas through the slave trade, Latin America has absorbed major waves of immigration from Italy, China, India, Syria, Lebanon, Great Britain, and Germany, among others (Ferreira de Olivera 1992). There was also Japanese migration to Peru, Argentina, Bolivia, Paraguay, Mexico, and especially Brazil.

Some claim that the population of Japanese origin in Brazil is the largest such community outside of Japan itself (Yamanaka 1996). Beginning in 1908, the state government of São Paulo, the Japanese government, the plantation owners, and the nascent agribusinesses of Brazil subsidized the immigration of Japanese farmers to the coffee plantations of Brazil.

The end of slavery in Brazil in 1888 meant a labor shortage for the coffee plantations. While Italian and German workers went to work on the plantations, working conditions were so poor that the Prussian and Italian governments prohibited migration to Brazil (Mita 1995). So agriculture, especially the coffee industry, was short on laborers.

Japan at this point was industrializing and going through significant land reforms. As Japan industrialized, there was an increase in population, aided by a declining mortality rate and the prohibition of abortion. At the same time, a drop in the price of rice and an increase in taxes combined with the extension of primogeniture codes beyond the samurai class produced many landless peasants, a situation the Japanese government recognized had real political dangers (Woortmann 1995; Yamanaka 1996). The government promoted and supported the emigration of Japanese citizens to Hawaii, the Philippines, Canada, and the United States. Despite earlier restrictions in Brazil that prohibited Asian immigration, the needs of Brazilian agriculture and the changing Japanese economy led to immigration agreements.

Japanese immigration to Brazil can be divided into three broad stages. The first stage (1908–1924) was subsidized by the Paulista government trying to find workers for the coffee plantations (see Rocha Nogueira 1995). Japanese workers were supposed to stay on the plantations for three or four years in return for their passage to Brazil. However, working conditions were still very poor, and most immigrants left the plantations as soon as possible. The Paulista government ended its subsidies in 1924 (Mita 1995).

During the second stage (1925–1941), immigration to Brazil was subsidized by the Japanese government and organized by the Kaigai Kogyo Gaisha Company, known as Kaiko, a publicly funded organization. They specialized in sending immigrants to Brazil. By 1933 the majority of immigrants entering Brazil were Japanese (Mita 1995).

After the crash of 1929, however, the Brazilian government passed laws that restricted immigration and required the hiring of local workers. The nationalist government of Getúlio Vargas (1930–1945) continued to restrict immigration, instituted quotas, prevented the organization of immigrant groups, and emphasized the assimilation of immigrants into Brazilian culture (Leão 1989; Mita 1995). Since migration from Japan was at its height when the quotas were instituted in 1934, some argue that the law affected only Japanese immigration. The Japanese in Brazil called the law *anti-nipona* and said that it was responsible for creating "a crisis in Japanese immigration to Brazil" (Leão 1989; Mita 1995).

With the establishment of additional anti-immigrant laws that closed foreign-language schools and prohibited foreign-language newspapers, a significant number of Japanese immigrants returned to Japan. Brazil broke off diplomatic relations with Japan in January 1942, after the start of World War II, and immigrants who wanted to return to Japan found themselves stranded in Brazil and subject to increasing restrictions as citizens of an enemy state.

The postwar phase (1952–1970) began with the normalization of relations in 1952. Immigration from Japan to Brazil started up again, with agricultural-labor immigration peaking between 1953 and 1961. There was an increase in skilled-labor migration, but as the Japanese economy improved, the increase in the quality of life and the new shortage of manual labor in Japan led to a decrease in migration. At the same time, the improving economy in Brazil meant that Japanese-Brazilians could travel to Japan to visit family, often with the intent of announcing their permanency in Brazil (Mita 1995). Their children, brought up during the nationalist era, had been educated as Brazilians.

Within two generations, significant occupational and class mobility could be seen by a decreasing percentage of *issei* (Japanese immigrants) and *nisei* (first-generation born in Brazil) Japanese-Brazilians working as farmers (Saito and Maeyama 1973; Suzuki 1976; Yamanaka 1996). The Japanese-Brazilian, or *nipo-brasileiro,* population now has one of the highest education rates among Brazilians and is primarily urban.

The figures for the ethnic Japanese population in Brazil are somewhat controversial. The Brazilian government's Immigration Department of the Ministry of Foreign Affairs' Consular Section states:

counted the number in 1986 of first generation Nikkeijin who had taken Brazilian citizenship, as well as second, third, and higher-generation Nikkeijin, and found that there were 520,000 such people. In addition, it found that as

of 1989 there were approximately 109,000 Japanese citizens living in that
country. (Komai 1995)

In contrast to these estimates, a survey of the nikkeijin population in Brazil
conducted by the Japan-Brazil Cultural Study Center found that, as of 1988,
there were roughly 1,280,000 people in Brazil with "some Japanese blood"
(Centro de Estudos Nipo-Brasileiros 1990; Komai 1995; Yamanaka 1996).
This is the figure accepted by the Japanese government (Cornelius 1994).

The end of the "Brazilian miracle" and the development of recession and
hyperinflation changed migration patterns in Brazil. By 1985 more people
were leaving Brazil than entering it (Mita 1995). The middle class migrated to
Portugal, Canada, France, Spain, Italy, Australia, the United States, and New
Zealand. In 1987 a poll indicated that 60 percent of those questioned in São
Paulo and 65 percent of those questioned in Rio de Janeiro wanted to leave the
country (Mita 1995). Estimates now indicate that more than 10 percent of the
nikkei people in South America have gone to Japan to work. More than 90 percent of these workers are from Brazil (de la Flor Belaúnde 1991; Mori 1994).
Peruvian migration has been restricted by rumors that Peruvian nikkeijin are
selling the documentation proving their Japanese ancestry to non-nikkeijin
who want to work in Japan. Unlike foreign workers from other Asian countries, the Brazilians, working legally in Japan for extended periods of time,
tend to bring their families.

Naming

Despite the use of the term "return migration," the social phenomenon
under study here is *not* primarily the return to the country of origin by immigrants to Brazil. It is not for the most part the Japanese immigrants to Brazil
who are returning to Japan, but rather their children and grandchildren. That is,
second- and third-generation Japanese-Brazilians, mostly those with Japanese
parents and grandparents who migrated to Brazil, are moving to Japan to work.

The terms used to name Brazilians of Japanese descent vary with the
generation and the nationality of the speaker, and reveal, as all ethnic labels
do, ideologies of identity. The literature in Portuguese and Spanish often uses
the term "nikkei" (at times spelled "nikkey") from the Japanese term "nikkeijin" (Onitsuka 1992; Tahima 1995; Toda 1992). While the term "nikkeijin" is
widely used in Japanese to refer to overseas Japanese, the author of a recent
dissertation (Roth 1999) notes that the term is not clearly defined. While the
term means "Japanese," it is not used to refer to ethnically Japanese people
residing in Japan, who are called *nihon-jin*. "Nikkeijin," Roth says, "is a category without reference to a specific place." It is not used to refer to Japanese
students, tourists, or businessmen outside of Japan. A different term *(ijuusha)*
refers to Japanese emigrants. "Nikkeijin" is used to refer to the descendents
of Japanese emigrants. The generational term "issei" refers to the migrants

themselves, while their children are nisei, their grandchildren *sansei,* and the fourth generation *yonsei.*

It is important to note that this is the language used by the Japanese and the issei when speaking in Japanese and talking about the descendents of Japanese emigrants. Brazilians use a different terminology. Japanese-Brazilians born in Brazil refer to the immigrant generation as issei or *japonês,* to themselves as nisei, *brasileiro,* nipo-brasileiro, and *decendente,* and to non-nikkei Brazilians as brasileiros, or at times, *gaijin.* Note that "decendente" is an accurate translation for "nikkeijin." Non-nikkei Brazilians refer to both immigrants and the children and grandchildren of immigrants as japonês, not as nipo-brasileiro or Brazilians (Tsuda 1997).

Naming Japanese-Brazilians

People Categorized	Japanese Migrant Speakers (Born in Japan)	Nikkeijin Speakers (Born in Brazil)	Non-Nikkei Brazilian Speakers
Japanese Migrant	nippon-jin, issei	japonês, issei	japonês
Nikkeijin	nisei, sansei, yonsei, nikkeijin	nisei, nihon-jin, brasileiro, decendente*	japonês
Non-Nikkei Brazilian	gaijin, burajiru-jin**	gaijin, brasileiro	brasileiro

(Roth 1999)
(*added from Roth 1999)
(**Burajiru is the Japanese word for Brazil)

The categories are based on an implicit definition of "Japanese" as either racial or national, that is, second- and third-generation Japanese-Brazilians insist on their Brazilian nationality by referring to themselves as nisei rather than japonês. In Japan, Japanese-Brazilians use either the Latinized nikkei or brasileiro when referring to themselves. The youngest generation of Japanese-Brazilians in Brazil has turned the naming issue into a joke: when asked for their generational label (for example, nisei, sansei, yonsei, etc.), they replied, "nisei, sansei, não sei" (Roth 1999).

Japanese Immigration Policies and the Nikkeijin

As the world economy changed, Japan found itself with a shortage of manual laborers. In the immediate postwar years, migrant workers from the countryside *(dekassegui)* and women entered the urban job market. But by the 1980s, the prosperous native Japanese refused to work in what are referred to as "3-K" jobs (from the Japanese words *kitsui, kitanai,* and *kiken;* or difficult, dirty, and dangerous), and the Japanese government was reluctant to allow in the many Asian workers (from China, Thailand, the Philippines, Malaysia, and South Korea) who wanted to work in Japan but who were considered racially different and "impure" (Mori 1994; Cornelius 1994; Komai 1995; Yamanaka

1996). For years Japan has denied even the existence of minority populations
in Japan (H. Smith 1995). During the discussions about the Immigration Control Law of 1990, lawmakers made explicit their belief that social unrest in
other countries often had to do with the multicultural and multiracial makeup
of their populations, and that to let in people from other cultures and races
would bring disharmony and social conflict to Japan. A significant public
debate ensued on whether Japan should be "open" or "closed," its intensity
seemingly out of proportion to a relatively small number of foreign workers
(Komai 1995; Lie 1997). One solution was to allow nikkeijin, particularly
Latin Americans of Japanese ancestry, open access to the Japanese job market. With the passage of the 1990 immigration law (Mori 1994), the nikkeijin
became the one category of unskilled foreign labor allowed to work legally in
Japan (Bornstein 1992).

Their solution appears to be based on a conflation of culture and race: the
grandchildren of Japanese emigrants to other countries are, in their perception, Japanese (see Tsuda 1997; Yamanaka 1996). Therefore there appeared
to be an elegant solution to the labor problem: bring these supposed Japanese
workers back to Japan. The 1990 immigration law gives issei, nisei, and sansei
Latin Americans of Japanese ancestry unrestricted access to the Japanese labor
market.[2] While work visas are issued for three years, nikkeijin can renew the
visa an unlimited number of times. They are de facto permanent residents if
they so choose (Yamanaka 1996). The result of this special status is that an
estimated 10 percent, about 230,000, of the Brazilian nikkeijin population is
now in Japan.

This policy fits in with the political desire for or fantasy of racial homogeneity in Japan. In fact, most nisei and sansei speak little or no Japanese,
are culturally Latin American, and rely on labor brokers rather than family
ties to find work (Bornstein 1992). Rather than coming "home" to Japan, they
found themselves included in the public debate about the "problem" of foreign
workers. While the Latin American literature on this subject uses the word
"dekassegui," a term that originally meant seasonal contract labor, to mean
Latin Americans of Japanese ancestry working in Japan (Lie 1997; Ninomiya
1992), the social science literature being written in Japan and the common
political discourse uses *gaikokujin rodosha* or foreign workers. The debate
focuses on selected segments of the foreign-worker population, particularly
manual and service workers from Asian countries other than Korea and China,
and the nikkeijin from South America (Komai 1995; Lie 1997, 288; Mori 1994,
7; Morita and Sassen 1994; Oka 1994). Since the 1990 immigration law was
passed, the term "foreign workers" has been defined in four ways in the literature: those who entered the country illegally; the visa "overstayers"; unauthorized laborers (working in ways not permitted by their visas); and "people of
Japanese descent from Latin America who have been given the legal right to
work as unskilled laborers" (Komai 1995; Friman 1996; Lie 1997; Mori 1994;

Morita and Sassen 1994; Sassen 1994; Shimada 1994). There is some concern that this ignores other legal foreign workers and equates "foreign worker" with unskilled workers. The immigration law also includes provisions for visas for international specialists, instructors, engineers, investment/business managers, and skilled workers, who are not generally discussed in the debates over opening Japan.

The implications of this perceptual frame can be seen in a number of articles and books on the subject. Komai's *Migrant Workers in Japan* (1995) limits the definition of foreign workers to unskilled workers divided into four groups: illegal immigrants, visa overstayers, unauthorized workers, and nikkeijin. Haruo Shimada's *Japan's "Guest Workers": Issues and Public Policies* (1994) also similarly limits the definition of foreign workers, despite sympathetic chapters on "The Foreign Workers and their Problems" and "Foreign Workers and Human Rights." While Mori (1994) provides a series of schema for classifying foreign workers in Japan by residency status, work permits, and the categories of the immigration control system; the conflation of illegal workers, unskilled workers, and nikkeijin is persistent in the literature. The same conflation can be seen in Japanese public discourse to the detriment of Japanese-Brazilians.

The Dekassegui Experience

The so-called Japanese workers brought "back" to Japan were second- and third-generation Brazilians. It is hard to imagine two more different cultures. The culture shock, on both sides, caused considerable disruption in various communities in Japan. The nikkejin spoke little or no Japanese. The local Japanese complained that the nikkeijin had loud parties at night, played music outdoors, drank, and danced on the streets. All this shocked and offended their Japanese neighbors. In addition, if they did not like their bosses or their working conditions, they quit and moved to other jobs, which also seemed shocking and disruptive to the Japanese. The Brazilians complained if treated badly. And they did of course run into a variety of conflicts (Inoue 1992). Though Takeyuki Tsuda (1998) found that Japanese rule of polite behavior tended to prevent overt discrimination toward the nikkeijin, except in housing, there are visible signs of Japanese discomfort with the nikkeijin.

It is important to recognize that their alien status in Japan was a shock to the nikkeijin as well. In Brazil, after all, they were japoneses. Their issei parents and grandparents had been angered by the bureaucratic obstacles placed in the way of nikkeijin interested in working in Japan, their putative homeland, before the 1990 law (Yamanaka 1996). Nikkeijin politicians from São Paulo lobbied the Japanese government ministries to make Japanese-Brazilian employment in Japan easier to obtain legally. They lobbied the Brazilian government to change laws that restricted Brazilian employment in other countries (Böhning 1992; Harada 1992; Yamanaka 1996). The nikkeijin had attributed their relative success in Brazil to their supposed Japanese cultural traits of responsibility, hard work, and support of education. Now while working in Japan, they discovered they were Brazilians, and that they were frequently seen as lower-class, unsuccessful, ill-behaved aliens from the Third World. While they have higher education levels than other Brazilians (Yamanaka 2000; Centro de Estudos Nipo-Brasileiros 1990), in Japan they work primarily on factory assembly lines in jobs the Japanese often refuse to do (Mori 1994; Tsuda 1997). Since emigration from Japan holds a negative connotation in the discourse of "Japanese-ness" *(nihonjinron)* of failure and of abandoning Japan, the Brazilian nikkeijin are doubly marked: they are the grandchildren of Japanese failures, and must now come to Japan to work in low-level jobs, thus indicating failure in Brazil as well (Lie 2000; Tsuda 1998).

Tsuda (1998) concludes that while a common ethnic "consciousness" is what directed migration specifically to Japan, the actual ethnic encounter has in fact strengthened separate national identities as Brazilian and as Japanese. The Nipo-Brazilians had always been called japoneses in Brazil, by both the Brazilians and by the Japanese government. Their experience in Japan destabilized their identity. In Japan, their racial identity was filtered through Brazilian cultural mores and education, a stereotype of the Third World, their occupational status, their own emigrant status and that of their parents or grandparents, and regional identities (most discovered their families had actually emigrated from Okinawa). As a result, the local Japanese found the nikkeijin to be not Japanese enough, inadequate as Japanese, and even "false Japanese." At the same time, the Brazilians found Japanese culture to be rather cold and unfriendly.

Tsuda (1997) and Yamanaka (1997, 2000) found that those dekassegui who returned to Brazil, as all say they want to do, went from being "inadequate Japanese" and brasileiros back to being japoneses. Yamanaka found that nikkeijin women, once back in Brazil, went back to asserting that Japanese cultural characteristics made them more successful than other Brazilians in their professions and education. Their attempts at identity construction are further destabilized by the continued economic crisis in Brazil, which has helped create a pattern of "circular migration": the nikkeijin work in Japan for two to three years, go back to Brazil with the hopes of using their savings to start a business in Brazil, and are then forced by the economy to return to Japan to work. Those who stay in Japan continue to identify themselves, and be identified, as Brazilians, but their children are being educated in Japanese schools with strong assimilationist policies.

Wayne Cornelius describes the Nipo-Brazilian labor migration to Japan as a laboratory for the study of how market forces, cultural forces, and government regulation interact. The academic writings discussed in this essay also recognize the phenomenon as a locus of constant challenges to and the reinvention of national identities. The process of invention and reinvention of national identities takes place at a number of sites. The experience of being called japonês in Brazil and Brazilian in Japan made issues of identity visible at a personal level (Yamanaka 1997; Roth 1999). At the level of government, the Japanese Immigration Control Law of 1990 codified a nikkeijin identity. Local institutions in Brazilian neighborhoods in Japan, such as Brazilian cultural clubs, become sites of "Brazilianization" in which, for example, Brazilian nikkeijin participate in samba festivals for the first time (Roth 1999). Academic articles and studies participate, when, for example, the experiences of female dekassegui are analyzed by comparing "senior *nikkeijin* women" and "junior *nikkeijin* women" to "Brazilian [*sic*] wives" (Yamanaka 1997). The joke mentioned earlier ("Are you nissei, sansei, or yonsei?" "Não sei.") is one that will also speak to the Brazilian children now growing up in Japan.

NOTES

1. There is an extensive bibliography about the Japanese-Brazilian population in Brazil. In 1967, Smith et al. published *The Japanese and Their Descendants in Brazil: An Annotated Bibliography.* Though obviously dated, this is a very rich resource of material, containing 408 items in Japanese, 169 in Portuguese, 121 articles in other languages, and lists of cited Japanese organizations. The introduction provides a short and very useful history of the study of Japanese-Brazilians until 1967, a list of libraries containing the materials in Brazil and in Germany, and clear notes.

2. Note that the yonsei or fourth generation must apply for work visas like any other non-Japanese national.

REFERENCES AND ANNOTATED BIBLIOGRAPHY

Astroff, Roberta J. 1997. "Capital's Cultural Study." In *Buy this Book: Studies in Advertising and Consumption,* edited by Mica Nava. New York: Routledge.

Böhning, Wolf-Rudiger. 1992. "Formas e funções de relacionamentos internacionais no campo da migração para fins de emprego." In *Dekassegui: palestras e exposições do simpósio sobre o fenômeno chamado dekassegui,* by Masato Ninomiya et al. São Paulo: Estação Liberdade. Pp. 31–46.

The intent of the author is to establish a model of the different relations that can exist between two countries whose citizens migrate from one to the other for employment, in the context of international labor standards, or the Conventions and Recommendations of the ILO. The goal is to indicate a series of options and functions that can be examined to deal with problems, such as the regularization of temporary work for Brazilians in Japan. The internal question for Brazil is emigration for work, while the internal question for Japan is that of the admission, employment, and residency of migrants. Both governments and the private sector in both countries can be involved in complex relationships in the context of labor migration.

Bornstein, Lisa. 1992. "From *carioca* to *karaoke:* Brazilian Guestworkers in Japan." *Berkeley Planning Journal* 7, 48–75.

A relatively early article, this study details the use of both personal contacts and labor brokers (often "travel agencies" in Brazil) by nikkeijin going to Japan to work. Despite the inaccuracies in the cute title (most Brazilian nikkeijin live in São Paulo, not Rio), this is a useful and serious study of the institutions involved in labor migration.

Centro de Estudos Nipo-Brasileiros. 1971. *O Japonês em São Paulo e no Brasil.* Relatório do Simpósio realizado em junho de 1968 ao ensejo do 60º Aniversário da Imigração Japonêsa para o Brasil. São Paulo.

An anthology of twenty-three papers presented at the symposium in honor of the sixtieth anniversary of the beginning of Japanese migration to Brazil, this collection covers history, demographics, economics, rural development, society, and culture. Some articles have notes and references; others are essays.

————. 1990. *Pesquisa da população de descendentes de japoneses residentes no Brasil.* São Paulo: São Paulo Jinbun Kagaku Kenkyûsho.

Result of very extensive research on Japanese Brazilians conducted by Japan's Institute of Japanese-Brazilian Studies (1987–88), using sample methods. Provides highest estimate so far of Japanese descendents in Brazil (1,280,000 as of July 1988). Also analyzes regional, sexual, educational, vocational and social distribution of Japanese Brazilians. Edition also available in Japanese. (HLAS, vol. 51, item# bi91002022)

Cornelius, Wayne A. 1994. "Japan: The Illusion of Immigration Control." In *Controlling Migrations: A Global Perspective,* edited by W. A. Cornelius, P. L. Martin, and J. F. Hollifield. Stanford: Stanford University Press. Pp. 375–410.

Written by one of the preeminent specialists on Mexican migration to the United States and founding director of the Center for U.S.-Mexican Studies at the University of California, San Diego, this article presents Japan as "perhaps the most intriguing and important laboratory in the world today for studying the interplay among private market forces, cultural tolerance for immigration, and government attempts to regulate it" (375). Like other articles on this subject, Cornelius critiques the Japanese myth of racial homogeneity and reviews the labor shortage. His statistics on foreigners registered in Japan provide figures for Brazilians and other Latin Americans for over seventy years. With footnotes and references to sources, many in Japanese.

de la Flor Belaúnde, Pablo. 1991. *Japón en la escena internacional: sus relaciones con América Latina y el Perú.* Lima: Centro Peruano de Estudios Internacionales.

Peru has the second largest nikkei population in Latin America, after Brazil. The author devotes pages 45–49 to *la inmigración revertida,* or reverse immigration of Latin American nikkeis. The *decasegui* [*sic*] number about 8,000 to 12,000 Peruvians and about 800,000 Brazilians. In addition to describing the labor situation in Japan, the author notes that many of the *decasegui* are young professionals unable to find work in Brazil and Peru and willing to work at less-skilled jobs in Japan. No notes or references.

Ferreira de Olivera, Jadiel. 1992. "Os trabalhadores nipo-brasileiros no Japão—uma reflexão de natureza política." In *Dekassegui: palestras e exposições do simpósio sobre o fenômeno chamado dekassegui,* by Masato Ninomiya et al. São Paulo: Estação Liberdade. Pp. 49–58.

The author, a former *ministro conselheiro* at the Brazilian Embassy in Tokyo, places Japanese-Brazilian labor migration to Japan within the context of the Brazilian economy of the 1980s and ethnic Brazilian return labor migration to Germany, Italy, Portugal, and Spain.

Friman, H. Richard. 1996. "*Gaijinhanzai:* Immigrants and Drugs in Contemporary Japan." *Asian Survey* 36 (10), 964–978.

Opponents to immigration have pointed to increased drug use in Japan as the price of greater openness to foreigners. A systematic analysis of the situation indicates however that the collapse of the "bubble economy," changes in the immigration law, and the anti-gang legislation of 1992 have contributed to the increase in the number of foreigners committing drug crimes. The author also questions the way drug arrest data is analyzed and examines the history and characteristics of the drug trade in Japan. Finally, potential solutions are assessed. Five tables of statistics, references.

Harada, Kiyoshi. 1992. "Aspectos políticos e jurídicos do fenômeno dekassegui." In *Dekassegui: palestras e exposições do simpósio sobre o fenômeno chamado dekassegui,* by Masato Ninomiya et al. São Paulo: Estação Liberdade. Pp. 85–92.

An examination of Brazilian laws that address the treatment of Brazilian workers contracted to work in foreign countries reveals that there are no sanctions possible if the laws are broken. The author argues that the laws should be repealed and could be replaced by bilateral treaties with Japan that would protect the interests of the workers.

Inoue, Ryuzaburo. 1992. "Prestação de serviços aos *dekassegui* pela muncipalidade: Caso da cidade de Hamamatsu." In *Dekassegui: palestras e exposições do simpósio sobre o fenômeno chamado dekassegui,* by Masato Ninomiya et al. São Paulo: Estação Liberdade. Pp. 67–75.

The city of Hamamatsu is home to companies such as Yamaha, Kawai, Honda, and Suzuki. It is estimated that as many as 30,000 inhabitants out of a total of 550,000 are foreign workers. Of those legally registered, the majority are Brazilian nikkei. The city of Hamamatsu provides language classes and information in Portuguese about housing, medical services, and utilities. Other programs are intended to help Brazilian nikkei understand the Japanese systems of social services and education.

Komai, Hiroshi. 1995. *Migrant Workers in Japan.* Translated by Jens Wilkinson. London: Kegan Paul International.

Written by a Japanese researcher concerned with human rights and international labor migrations, this book limits the definition of foreign workers to unskilled workers divided into four groups: illegal immigrants, visa overstayers, unauthorized workers, and nikkeijin. The author provides a solid context (changes in immigration law, economic recession, manner of entry, different industries, housing) and devotes one chapter, chapter 4 in part 4, "The Third World's Structuralized Labor Exports," to Latin America. This chapter is too short, but provides one of the most detailed descriptions of the impact on Japanese-Brazilian communities of labor migration to Japan found for this bibliography. The author reviews the economic difficulties of Brazil, its impact on nikkei populations, the size of the Japanese-Brazilian community, and the impact on the nikkei communities of the exodus to work abroad. A survey of the nikkei community of Moji das Cruzes is included. The bibliography is primarily of Japanese-language sources.

Leão, Valdemar Carneiro. 1989. *A crise da imigracão japonesa no Brasil, 1930–1934: contornos diplomáticos.* Brasilia: Fundacão Alexandre de Gusmão, Instituto de Pesquisa de Relacões Internacionais.

A thorough historical study of the impact the nationalist regime in Brazil had on Japanese migration to Brazil in the 1930s.

Lie, John. 1997. "The 'Problem' of Foreign Workers in Contemporary Japan." In *The Other Japan: Conflict, Compromise and Resistance Since 1945,* edited by Joe Moore. Armonk, N.Y.: M. E. Sharpe. Pp. 288–300.

A critical analysis of the debate about opening Japan to foreign workers. Lie places the debate in the context of the historical discourse of "Japaneseness."

———. 2000. "The discourse of Japaneseness." In *Japan and Global Migration: Foreign Workers and the Advent of a Multicultural Society,* edited by Mike Douglass and Glenda S. Roberts. New York: Routledge. Pp. 70–90.

This article analyzes the discourse of Japanese-ness *(nihonjinron)* in the post–World War II era, focusing particularly on its assumptions about class, culture, and ethnicity. Despite the existence of educational inequality, income inequality, and occupational hierarchies, this discourse presents Japan as classless. It also equates nation-state and national culture, and represents Japan as culturally homogenous. The new foreign workers are considered to be class, cultural, and ethnic others.

Mori, Hiromi. 1994. "Migrant Workers and Labor Market Segmentation in Japan." *Asian and Pacific Migration Journal* 3 (4), 619–638.

The author examines how the 1990 immigration law has determined the segmentation of the migrant work force. He notes that nikkeijin migration to Japan started as illegal labor though this changed with the new immigration law. Nikkei workers largely work on production lines in the factories, though there has been some spillover into service industries. This concentration in manufacturing jobs holds for nikkei women workers as well. The nikkei are also concentrated in mid- to large-sized firms, who can afford to hire legal workers. Their legal status improved salaries and working conditions, even though their proficiency in Japanese is fairly low compared to the Pakistanis and Bangladeshis working illegally in Japan. Includes charts, statistics, and references.

Morita, Kiriro, and Saskia Sassen. 1994. "The New Illegal Immigration in Japan." *International Migration Review* 28 (1), 153–164.

Typical of the articles evaluating the alien labor in Japan, this article concentrates on illegal immigrations, usually those who stay past the time allowed on temporary work visas. It provides some basic statistics, and the identical paragraph (in Sassen 1994) about the descendents of Japanese emigrants as legal foreign workers. The print version contains several tables of statistical data, and fourteen references.

Ninomiya, Masato et al. 1992. *Dekassegui: palestras e exposições do simpósio sobre o fenômeno chamado dekassegui.* São Paulo: Estação Liberdade.

A collection of twenty papers and speeches presented as a symposium sponsored by Japanese-Brazilian organizations in November 1991. It includes political, economic, legal, psychological, and cultural analyses, as well as presentations by the consul general of Japan in São Paulo and the head of the department of International Labor Migration of the ILO. Many of the papers are listed separately here.

Oboler, Suzanne. 1995. *Ethnic Labels, Latino Lives: Identity and the Politics of (Re)presentation in the United States.* Minneapolis: University of Minnesota Press.

Oka, Takashi. 1994. *Prying Open the Door: Foreign Workers in Japan.* Washington: The Carnegie Endowment for International Peace.

The first two chapters describe the economic, demographic, and ideological context within which the Japanese debate about foreign workers is taking place. Chapter 7, "Reverse Immigration: Ethnic Japanese from Latin America," describes how second- and third-generation Japanese immigrants to Latin America have come to Japan as workers ever since the 1990 immigration law exempted them from work restrictions. Since these workers are in Japan with their families, legally and without work restrictions, the local governments have had to provide language teachers, social workers, and health professionals who can work cross-culturally. Though the motivation behind allowing nikkeijin to return to Japan to work was to maintain ethnic homogeneity, Japanese-Brazilians and Japanese-Peruvians, often racially mixed, still run into discrimination. Still, in the ethnically determined labor stratification of Japan, "ethnic Japanese" from Latin America occupy a middle rung, doing factory work rather than the more unskilled, dangerous, and dirty work of the Pakistani workers. Local Japanese, however, have had to recognize that culturally the nikkeijin are Latin American. Notes.

Onitsuka, Tadanori. 1992. "As condições de emprego dos nikkey brasileiros no Japão e os problemas pertinentes." In *Dekassegui: palestras e exposições do simpósio sobre o fenômeno chamado dekassegui,* by Masato Ninomiya et al. São Paulo: Estação Liberdade. Pp. 79–92.

A Japanese lawyer reviews the different ways Japanese-Brazilians can obtain jobs in Japan. Problems have arisen when workers are actually employed by agencies rather than directly by the companies in which they work. These agencies take commissions from workers' wages and some are associated with organized crime in Japan. Other problems result from vague contracts, poor training, work-related injuries, and forced labor. These problems can be resolved if these for-profit intermediaries are replaced by public agencies. It is also necessary to educate the nikkey [*sic*] about Japanese labor laws and to ensure that these laws are equitably enforced.

Rocha Nogueira, Arlinda. 1984. *Imigração japonesa na história contemporânea do Brasil.* São Paulo: Centro de Estudos Nipo-Brasileiros.

A summary and updating of the author's *A Imigração Japonesa para a Lavoura Cafeeira Paulista (1908–1922),* this book also contains photographs of early migrants, notes, and a long and useful bibliography.

———. 1995. "Início da imigração: chegada da primeira leva." *Revista do Instituto de Estudos Brasileiros* 39, 41–56.

Originally published in 1973 as chapter 7 in *A imigração japonesa para a lavoura cafeeira paulista (1908–1922)* (São Paulo: IEB, 1973, pp. 87–105), and based on primary archival sources, this chapter traces the history of corporate decisions to import Japanese labor to resolve the shortage of agricultural workers. The author notes the two governments' decision to proceed in the face of opposition from Brazilians concerned about "opening the door" to Japanese influence. Rocha Nogueira's footnotes provide an excellent source to original documents.

Roth, Joshua Hotaka. 1999. "Defining Communities: The Nation, the Firm, the Neighborhood, and Japanese Brazilian Migrants in Japan." Ph.D. diss., Cornell University.

This carefully nuanced study of identity confusions and formation relies on an ethnographic study of nikkeijin workers in Japan. Considerable attention is paid to questions of identity for mixed race nikkeijin and the varied interpretations of ethnic labels, as well as personal interactions between Brazilians and Japanese in work and social environments.

Saito, Hiroshi, and Takashi Maeyama. 1973. *Assimilação e integração dos japoneses no Brasil.* São Paulo: Editora de Universidade de São Paulo.

This anthology contains twenty-four articles about all aspects of Japanese immigrant life in Brazil, including the migratory process, history, socioeconomic structure, symbolic structure, acculturation and mobility, and some comparative studies (German and Japanese immigrants to Brazil, Japanese immigrants in Brazil and Peru, and generational comparisons). All articles are in Portuguese, with notes, references, charts, and tables.

Sassen, Saskia. 1994. "Economic Internationalization: The New Migration in Japan and the United States." *Social Justice* 21 (2), 62–83. Full text available: Expanded Academic ASAP (A16654708).

Written by a prominent researcher on international labor migration flows, this article discusses the changes wrought by the 1990 immigration law in Japan in the context of international economic, social, and political processes. It provides a useful history of the underlying conditions that have created immigration to a closed society, though unfortunately (and oddly, given the author's long history of Latin American research) devotes no more than a paragraph to the legal short-term labor migration to Japan of the descendents of Japanese migrants to Brazil. The focus of the article instead is on unauthorized "visa-overstayers." One table of statistics, footnotes, and references.

Shimada, Haruo. 1994. *Japan's "Guest Workers": Issues and Public Policies.* Translated by Roger Northridge. Tokyo: University of Tokyo Press.

Shimada attempts to define "the foreign worker problem" in Japan and propose guidelines toward a humane official policy toward foreign workers and a more open nation. A good brief discussion of the shortage of unskilled labor in Japan, the 1990 immigration law, and the beginnings of worker training programs starts the book, which then describes the various political positions taken in Japan about foreign workers. Most usefully, this section lists proposals, reports, and party statements (pp. 50–54). The rest of the book concentrates on labor conditions, the development of basic and intermediate skills training programs, and possible paths Japanese policy might take. While no one chapter is devoted exclusively to Japanese-Brazilians, references to their entrance to Japan and data about their socioeconomic status there can be found throughout. Unfortunately, the index lists only two of these references, one under "Brazil" and the other under "Latin American workers." The book reproduces the rhetoric of the debate by limiting discussion of foreign workers to unskilled and illegal immigrants.

Smith, Herman W. 1995. *The Myth of Japanese Homogeneity: Social-Ecological Diversity in Education and Socialization.* Commack, N.Y.: Nova Science Publishers.

The Japanese belief in the homogeneity of their culture appears to be based on the exclusion of those who do not fit into that picture. The so-called Korean community in Japan, most of whom were born in Japan, are denied Japanese citizenship and must deal with other forms of discrimination as well. The book also reviews the condition of other minority populations in Japan.

Smith, Robert J. et al. 1967. *The Japanese and Their Descendants in Brazil: An Annotated Bibliography.* São Paulo: Centro de Estudos Nipo-Brasileiros.

Though obviously dated, this is a very rich resource of material, containing 408 items in Japanese, 169 in Portuguese, 121 articles in other languages, and lists of cited Japanese organizations. The introduction provides a short and very useful history of the study of Japanese-Brazilians until 1967, a list of libraries containing the materials in Brazil and in Germany, and clear notes.

Suzuki, Teiiti. 1969. *The Japanese Immigrant in Brazil: Narrative Part.* Tokyo: University of Tokyo Press.

The now classic census of the Brazilian-Japanese. *HLAS* describes this work as "a splendid contribution of rigorously gathered and analyzed data" (HLAS, item# re675412a). The work provides tables of data on the population itself, economic aspects, social life, and acculturation. It also provides extremely useful information of a similar type about the immigrants in Japan before their emigration, data about them upon their arrival in Brazil, and their social and occupational mobility (see Suzuki 1976). State-of-the-art study only recently supplemented by Centro de Estudos Nipo-Brasileiros (1990).

———. 1976. "Occupation and Status Mobility of Japanese Immigrants in Brazil." In *Asiatic Migrations in Latin America. Proceedings of the XXX International Congress of Human Sciences in Asia and North Africa.* México, D.F.: El Colegio de México. Pp. 59–69.

With statistics drawn from his classic study (Suzuki 1969), the author examines social and occupational mobility of Japanese immigrants to Brazil fifty years after the beginning of this immigration. The information is based on a 1958 census. This article focuses only on those Japanese immigrants who arrived in Brazil before World War II and "who continue to be the head of their family (about 18,000 people)." The study shows a high level of occupational mobility away from farming. Statistics and notes from the 1958 census and other Brazilian censuses.

———. 1995. "A imigração japonesa no Brasil." *Revista do Instituto de Estudos Brasileiros* 39, 57–65.

This historical review identifies three phases of Japanese migration to Brazil. The article reviews the early sociology of the immigrants and provides basic statistics, though unfortunately does not provide sources for this data. Originally published in *Vida e arte dos japoneses no Brasil* (São Paulo: MASP/ Banco América do Sul, 1988).

Tahima, Hisatoshi. 1995. "The Case of Brazilian, Peruvian, Argentine, Bolivian, and Paraguayan Dekasegui Nikkeis in Japan" (El caso de los nikkeis dekaseguis brasileños, peruanos, argentinos, bolivianos y paraguayos en Japón). *Estudios migratorios latinoamericanos* 10 (30), 403–429.

Examines the recent migration of Latin American workers *(dekasegi nikkeis)* to Japan in the face of worsening economic conditions in Latin America and new immigration laws in Japan. Though the migration began in 1988, only recently are Latin American workers beginning to form permanent communities with their own institutions and associations. Problems encountered by these communities include lack of information about job opportunities, cultural and linguistic differences, and medical problems. It remains to be seen how successful their long-term transition and incorporation into Japanese society will be. 4 tables. (Copyright 1997, Sociological Abstracts)

Toda, Masanori. 1992. "Resumo da apresentação sobre aspectos políticos e jurídicos dos dekassegui." In *Dekassegui: palestras e exposições do simpósio sobre o fenômeno chamado dekassegui,* by Masato Ninomiya et al. São Paulo: Estação Liberdade. Pp. 59–65.

An official in the Division of Emigration Policy of the Consular Department, Ministry of Foreign Business Affairs in Japan, presents the position of the Japanese government toward "dekassegui nikkey." At the same time that the Japanese government claims a neutral position toward dekasseguis, neither encouraging nor restricting them, they recognize that there is a "feeling of trust and familiarity with the *nikkey.*" The government and other organizations have developed various initiatives to deal with both the problems the dekassegui nikkey confront and the problems they cause. The first dekassegui nikkey were first and second generation (issei and nisei) who spoke Japanese. With the arrival of the third generation or sansei, employers have complained that the Japanese-Brazilians do not speak Japanese nor do they behave in Asian ways. In addition, instances of fraud have arisen in which Latin Americans falsely claim Japanese heritage or marry nikkey only to get work visas in Japan. These problems, and a growing crime rate involving nikkey, are contributing to a growing distrust of the nikkey in Japan.

Tsuda, Takeyuki. 1997. "Ethnic Transnationalism and the Channeling of Migrant Flows: The Return Migration of Japanese-Brazilians." In *Beyond Boundaries,* edited by Diane Baxter and Ruth Krufeld. Arlington Va.: American Anthropological Association. Pp. 35–63.

Tsuda examines a common transnational ethnic consciousness that led to both the migration of Japanese-Brazilians to Japan, and to the Japanese government's establishment of a special nikkeijin immigration status. The actual experience of the nikkeijin and the Japanese has challenged this common identity, with the nikkeijin forming a stronger Brazilian identity and the Japanese seeing them as "false" or "inauthentic" Japanese.

———. 1998. "The Stigma of Ethnic Difference: The Structure of Prejudice and 'Discrimination' Toward Japan's New Immigrant Minority." *Journal of Japanese Studies* 24 (2), 317–359.

The author examines Japanese attitudes toward Japanese-Brazilian labor migrants. Those attitudes appear to be based on negative perceptions of those who emigrated from Japan, and of the Third World, factory labor, and Brazilian culture. Japanese concerns about purity make it particularly difficult to establish cross-cultural friendships. These concerns about purity of the household have resulted in discrimination in housing, the only overt form of discrimination Tsuda finds.

———. 1999. "The Motivation to Migrate: The Ethnic and Sociocultural Constitution of the Japanese-Brazilian Return-Migration System." *Economic Development and Cultural Change* 48 (1), 1–31.

The author focuses on transnational ethnic and sociocultural dynamics that shaped Japanese-Brazilian labor migration to Japan. In addition to the economic conditions that constituted both push factors (the poor economy in Brazil) and pull factors (the availability of jobs in Japan), Tsuda argues that perceived shared ethnicity, a Japanese-Brazilian "culture of migration," and transnational migrant networks shaped the size, destination, and ethnic makeup of the migrant flow.

Woortmann, Ellen F. 1995. "Japoneses no Brasil/brasileiros no Japão: tradição e modernidade." *Revista de Antropologia* 39 (2), 7–36.

A study of the influence traditional Japanese values have had on decisions by Japanese to migrate to Brazil, as well as decisions by Japanese-Brazilians to migrate to the *Distrito Federal* or to Japan. Most of the data focuses on internal migration within Brazil. The author identifies conflicts between traditional and modern identities and ambiguities in nipo-brasileiro identity.

Yamanaka, Keiko. 1996. "Return Migration of Japanese-Brazilians to Japan: The *Nikkeijin* as Ethnic Minority and Political Construct." *Diaspora* 5 (1), 65–97.

Using a migration systems approach, the author examines the reasons nikkeijin seemed most acceptable in Japan as low-skilled labor as well as the possibility that nikkeijin will stay in Japan and form communities there. The article is based on field research done in the Japanese-Brazilian community in the industrial city of Hamamatsu.

———. 1997. "Return Migration of Japanese-Brazilian Women: Household Strategies and Search for the 'Homeland.'" In *Beyond Boundaries,* edited by Diane Baxter and Ruth Krufeld. Arlington Va.: American Anthropological Association. Pp. 11–34.

Focusing on the experiences of women in migration between Japan and Brazil, the author compares two generations of nikkeijin and "Brazilian" or non-nikkeijin women, who went to Japan to work. The women who fell into her category of "senior *nikkeijin* women," who spoke Japanese and had grown up in families with strong Japanese cultural traits, were accepted in places other foreign women were not, particularly in hospitals and as caregivers to elderly Japanese. "Junior *nikkejin* women," educated as Brazilians, worked primarily on assembly lines. The author compares the linguistic skills, work experience, and identity issues of the three groups.

————. 2000. "'I Will Go Home, but When?': Labor Migration and Circular Diaspora Formation by Japanese Brazilians in Japan." In *Japan and Global Migration: Foreign Workers and the Advent of a Multicultural Society,* edited by Mike Douglass and Glenda S. Roberts. New York: Routledge. Pp. 123–152.

A detailed sociological analysis of the migration from Japan to Brazil, the nature of the Japanese-Brazilian population, and of the migration of nik-keijin to Japan. The article provides a useful summary of information about the nikkeijin in Brazil and in Japan, and identifies the growth of a circular migration, that is, the pattern of repeatedly going to Japan, staying a few years to work and save money, and then return to Brazil. Poor economic conditions in Brazil tend to motivate the nikkeijin to return to Japan.

Identity and Race

4. And When the Slaveowners Were Not "White"?: "Black" and "Brown" Slaveholders in Early-Nineteenth-Century Bahia

B. J. Barickman

As its title suggests, this paper deals with non-white slave-holding—that is, the ownership of African and Afro-Brazilian slaves by freeborn and freed Afro-Brazilians—in Brazil in the early-nineteenth century, and even more specifically in the northeastern province (now state) of Bahia.[1]

Slave-holding by free Afro-Brazilians has received only scant attention from historians interested in Brazil. That is perhaps not surprising since it is, in many ways, a disturbing topic. The idea that free blacks and other free Afro-Brazilians owned both Africans and other Afro-Brazilians as slaves runs counter to the common view that racial difference was the main motive for enslavement and that therefore race can somehow explain slavery. But, ignoring the topic simply because it is disturbing does not help when trying to understand Brazilian slavery and the connections between slavery and race in Brazil.[2]

Indeed, whether talking about Brazil, some other area of Latin America, or the United States, it is too easy today to look back at slavery and assume that, from the very start, it was a white-black relationship; in other words, a relationship where race was the fundamental dividing line between slaveowner and slave. But, if that assumption is made, then questions about how racism and notions of race became linked to slavery cannot be asked. By contrast, the topic of non-white slave-holding forces people to consider such questions.

To investigate non-white slave-holding in Brazil, I have relied mainly on two rare and unpublished household-by-household censuses, both dating from 1835.[3] The censuses are for two rural parishes in a region known as the Recôncavo in the northeastern province of Bahia. They thus come from an area that, by the early-nineteenth century, ranked as one of the oldest and most important slave-holding regions in the Americas.[4]

The censuses reveal that freeborn and freed non-whites made up a surprisingly large share of the slave-holding population in those two parishes. Yet, at the same time, the censuses also suggest that the pattern of non-white slave-holding largely mirrored the racial and color hierarchies that permeated Brazilian society in the first half of the nineteenth century. Furthermore, the results of the two censuses also help reveal the complex terrain that Brazilians in Bahia and elsewhere had to negotiate as they tried to construct racial identities in the early-nineteenth century and to sort for themselves the ideological link between slavery and color.

On that matter, the evidence presented here also points to some of the advantages and the limits of quantified census-based research on race, whether that research focuses on the past or the present. Quantified census-based research can direct attention to questions that might otherwise be missed, but often those are questions that cannot be answered with census data alone.

The two censuses on which my research is chiefly based are among the few surviving results of a failed attempt to carry out a general population count in the northeastern province of Bahia in 1835. Organized by *fogo* (hearth, that is, household), the censuses provide a range of individual-level information about the inhabitants of two neighboring and predominantly rural parishes: Santiago do Iguape (or simply Iguape) and São Gonçalo dos Campos, both located in the township of Cachoeira and fifty to ninety kilometers from Salvador, Bahia's capital, largest city, and main port.[5] Santiago do Iguape stood out as one of the wealthiest sugar-producing parishes in Bahia at the time; likewise, the sugar plantations *(engenhos)* found in the parish were amongst the largest not only in Bahia, but in all Brazil in the early-nineteenth century. In 1835, the average sugar planter *(senhor de engenho)* in Iguape owned fewer than 123 slaves. The parish was home not only to wealthy slave-owning sugar planters, but also to sharecropping cane farmers *(lavradores de cana),* who often owned slaves. Among cane farmers, the average holding in 1835 stood at approximately 14 slaves. Also living in Iguape were numerous free artisans, fishermen, seamstresses, and small farmers who grew food crops.

By contrast, tobacco, not sugarcane, was the main crop in the neighboring parish of São Gonçalo dos Campos.[6] São Gonçalo dos Campos in fact lay in the very heart of "the fields of Cachoeira *(os campos da Cachoeira),"* an area of light, sandy soils, and a little forest cover that, since at least the early-seventeenth century, produced the bulk of all tobacco exported from Brazil. Tobacco grown in São Gonçalo dos Campos and other nearby parishes was shipped to markets in Europe and Africa, where merchants used it in acquiring slaves for the transatlantic slave trade. Because tobacco could be grown almost efficiently on a few acres as on a large estate, this export staple was produced by a variety of rural establishments, ranging from peasant holdings that relied on family labor to large farms that employed 30 or more slaves. By the 1830s, tobacco, generally in combination with food crops, was cultivated in São Gonçalo dos Campos on more than five hundred small and large *fazendas* and *sítios* (farms).

The 1835 household censuses of these two Bahian parishes provide various types of individual-level information, including name (which makes it possible to determine sex), age, place of birth, occupation, legal status, and so forth. The censuses also record *qualidade,* which literally means color. Now Brazilians are notorious for using a large number of different terms to classify individuals by color. One study in the early 1970s recorded more than 130 color terms.[7]

Yet the number of color terms found in official documents and censuses has always been much smaller. And that is also true in the case of the 1835 censuses from Bahia. The 1835 census-takers used only 4 terms when it came to classifying the free and the slave population by color, or more precisely "quality." The first of those 4 is *branco,* or "white." The second is *preto,* or "black"; individuals classified as pretos included both African-born blacks as well as those born in Brazil. Third is *pardo,* which literally means "brown," but which is conventionally translated into English as "mulatto." "Pardo" was in fact the term most widely used in Brazil at the time to indicate some mixture of European and African ancestry.[8] The fourth term used for quality (color) by the 1835 census-takers was *cabra,* meaning literally "she-goat." But a far better translation would be "faded black," since it designated a color perceived as being between pardo and preto. At least in principle, cabras had one black and one pardo parent, or they were the children to two cabras. Perhaps because "cabra" carried clearly derogatory connotations, it was the least used term in the censuses.[9] It seems safe to assume that the census-takers classified as "pretos" or "pardos" many individuals whose parentage would have made them cabras.

Although definitely not meaningless, the 4 terms used in the 1835 censuses to designate color should not be taken at face value. They most certainly are not an infallible guide to either ancestry or pigmentation. And perhaps, for that matter, nor do they necessarily reflect the way people identified themselves on a daily basis or the way that their neighbors identified them. Instead, the 4 terms should be taken for what they are, namely, categories used by the 1835 census-takers to classify people according to a *preconceived* four-way and, in most cases, three-way color scheme—a preconceived scheme that allowed only four possible answers.

In any event, census-takers registered for the two parishes a combined total population of just over 18,800 inhabitants. Slaves made up 42 percent of that total population. And, as might be expected, slaves were proportionately more numerous in the sugar-producing parish of Iguape than in the neighboring tobacco parish.[10] Within the free population, whites represented a minority, accounting for only one fourth of all free residents. The rest of the free population (75 percent) consisted of freeborn and freed pardos, pretos, and cabras.[11]

Most, and in fact over 90 percent, of those free men and women of color were free by birth and not freed former slaves. Thus, they personally had no direct experience with enslavement. Here it is important to recall that the first enslaved Africans were introduced into Bahia in the mid- and late-sixteenth centuries. As a result, by 1835, it was entirely possible that as many as eight generations might have separated a freeborn person of color in Bahia from his or her nearest slave relative. Likewise, in both parishes, roughly 70 percent of free non-whites were classified by the census-takers as pardos. Both parishes were part of a slave-holding region where free people of color outnumbered whites.

The 1835 censuses also indicate that 813 of the more than 2,700 households in the two parishes owned slaves. Of those 813 slave-owning households, 278 or fully one-third were headed by individuals classified as pardos, pretos, and cabras. In the tobacco parish of São Gonçalo dos Campos, non-whites accounted for 29.8 percent of all slaveowners, while in the neighboring sugar parish of Santiago do Iguape almost one half (46.5 percent) of all slaveowners were free non-whites. Collectively, the 278 non-white slaveholders in the two parishes owned a total of 1,134 slaves. Most of these non-white slaveowners were, as might be expected, free by birth. But their number also included 31 freed slaves.

Now few historians of Brazil would be surprised to learn that free blacks and free Brazilians of mixed African and European ancestry sometimes owned slaves. After all, free African Americans in the pre–Civil War South in the United States sometimes owned slaves. Likewise, research has also uncovered slaveholders within the free population of color in the French and British Caribbean.[12]

But what might come as a surprise is the high proportion of non-white slaveowners found in these two Bahian parishes. Nothing in the available literature even remotely suggests that, in any area of Brazil in any period, nearly 1 out of every 2 or 3 slaveowners might have been black or mulatto. Indeed, it is quite possible that these two parishes may have displayed one of the highest rates of non-white slave-holding to be found anywhere in the Americas.

At the same time, although the proportion of non-white slaveowners was certainly high in São Gonçalo dos Campos and Santiago do Iguape, the two parishes were probably not, within the Brazilian context, exceptional cases. Scattered here and there in the research on other well-settled areas in early-nineteenth-century Brazil are hints that also point toward widespread ownership of slaves by free blacks and other free Afro-Brazilians.

In any event, several factors help explain the pattern of fairly widespread non-white slave-holding in these two Bahian parishes and elsewhere in Brazil by the early-nineteenth century, among them the long history of slavery and manumission in Bahia. By 1835, that history stretched back two and a half centuries. Another factor would be the very vigorous and ongoing slave trade that continued to supply Brazil with literally tens of thousands of captive Africans every year. And Salvador, Bahia's capital, was a major port in the transatlantic slave trade.

Furthermore, it is worth stressing that, in contrast with the U.S. South, there were no legal barriers to manumission in Brazil. If the non-white slaveowners in the two Bahian parishes had wanted to free their slaves, nothing at all prevented them from doing so. But they did not free them; instead, they chose to keep their slaves as slaves. The 278 free slaveowners of color in Santiago do Iguape and São Gonçalo dos Campos should therefore be regarded as slaveowners and, at least in their ownership of slaves, as not being different from their white neighbors who held slaves.

In fact, white and non-white slaveowners in both parishes shared several common features. For example, they tended to be middle-aged, they generally held similar occupations, and they were more likely to be formally married than household heads who did not own slaves. Likewise, most slaveowners of whatever color were men. Even so, women made up a substantial share of both the white and the non-white slave-owning population; in fact, about one fourth of all free slaveowners of color were women.

Yet, whatever similarities white and non-white slaveowners in these parishes may have shared, the two 1835 censuses hardly suggest that slave-holding was in any way color-blind or "racially democratic." As can be seen in the table, by the numbers of slaves owned and the frequency of slave-holding, a clear hierarchy based on color and place of birth emerges.

Non-whites made up fully one third of all slaveholders in Santiago do Iguape and São Gonçalo dos Campos, but they owned only a small share of the slaves living in the two parishes—no more than about 14 percent. By a wide and disproportionate margin, the great majority of those slaves belonged to white slaveowners. Likewise, nearly three-quarters of all white households owned at least 1 slave.

The same disparity also appears in the average number of slaves owned. Non-white slaveholders in the two parishes owned an average of about 4 slaves each. That average correctly suggests the generally small scale of non-white slave-holding in the two parishes; indeed, over half of all slaveowners of color could claim ownership of no more than 1 or 2 slaves. By contrast, the average holding among white slaveowners stood at over 11 slaves, or more than double the average for their non-white neighbors. And the disparity becomes even more striking when looking at the top end of the scale. As might be expected, sugar planters, who were all white, constituted the single wealthiest group of slaveowners in the two parishes. Sugar planters owned 100, 150, and sometimes more than 200 slaves. Not even the most prosperous slaveholders of color in either parish came remotely close to owning a comparable number of slaves.

A hierarchy in slave-holding also appears when focusing on non-white slaveowners. As might be expected, at the top of that hierarchy were individuals classified as "pardos." Pardos were substantially more likely to own slaves than their black neighbors, and, on average, they also owned more slaves than black slaveholders. Likewise, pardos also owned the majority (94 percent) of all slaves owned by non-whites in the two parishes.

Measures of Slave-Holding within the Free Population of Household Heads by Color: Parishes of Santiago do Iguape and São Gonçalo dos Campos, Bahia (Brazil), 1835

Slaveowners by Color	Slave-Holding Rate[a]	Number of Slaveowners[b]	Average Slaves Owned[b]	Total Slaves Owned[b]
Whites				
Santiago do Iguape	56.5%	108	26.9	2,906
São Gonçalo dos Campos	77.8%	410	7.3	3,005
Both parishes	72.1%	518	11.4	5,911
All non-whites				
Santiago do Iguape	12.9%	99	3.9	393
São Gonçalo dos Campos	14.6%	179	4.1	741
Both parishes	14.0%	278	4.1	1,134
Pardos				
Santiago do Iguape	18.4%	89	4.3	379
São Gonçalo dos Campos	18.4%	155	4.4	686
Both parishes	18.4%	244	4.4	1,065
Cabras				
Santiago do Iguape	33.3%	1	1.0	1
São Gonçalo dos Campos	9.5%	9	2.0	18
Both parishes	10.2%	10	1.9	19
All blacks/pretos				
Santiago do Iguape	3.2%	9	1.4	13
São Gonçalo dos Campos	5.2%	15	2.5	37
Both parishes	4.2%	24	2.1	50
Native Bahian-born blacks				
Santiago do Iguape	3.3%	8	1.5	12
São Gonçalo dos Campos	5.4%	14	1.9	27
Both parishes	4.4%	22	1.8	39
African-born blacks				
Santiago do Iguape	2.4%	1	1.0	1
São Gonçalo dos Campos	3.6%	1	10.0	10
Both parishes	2.9%	2	5.5	11

a. Defined here as the percentage of all households that owned slaves. For example, the figure 56.5% for "whites" in Santiago do Iguape indicates that 56.5% of all "white" households in that parish owned at least 1 slave.

b. Does not include slave-owning households where the head was absent, which numbered 6 in Santiago do Iguape and 11 in São Gonçalo dos Campos.

Source: See note 5.

In turn, within the free population of color, African-born blacks, who were all freed former slaves, were the least likely to own slaves. The two 1835 censuses list only 2 African-born slaveowners, who together owned less than 1 percent of all slaves belonging to free non-whites in the two parishes.[13]

Along the same lines, it is probably not surprising that the most prosperous slaveowners of color in the two parishes were freeborn pardos. For example, in Santiago do Iguape, the wealthiest non-white slaveholder was Francisco de Marinho e Aragão, a freeborn pardo sugarcane farmer who employed 16 slaves. Even wealthier than Francisco de Marinho e Aragão were three freeborn pardo tobacco growers in the neighboring parish of São Gonçalo dos Campos, namely, Antônio Ferreira de Brito, Luís Martins Souto, and José Coitinho de Oliveira. They owned 30, 43, and 48 slaves respectively; that is, between five and eight times more than the average tobacco grower in the same parish. Indeed, if wealth was measured by the number of slaves owned, then Antônio Ferreira de Brito, Luís Martins Souto, and José Coitinho de Oliveira ranked among the wealthiest 15 percent of all tobacco growers in Bahia at the time.

The hierarchies based on color and birthplace that show up clearly in the distribution of slave-holdings among non-whites, in turn, raise another question: Were those same hierarchies also replicated between non-white slaveowners and their slaves? In other words, did slaveowners of color seek to own slaves who were in some way different from themselves? The question is pertinent because research on colonial and nineteenth-century Brazil has firmly established that Brazilians of African ancestry or birth neither saw themselves nor were seen as a homogeneous group. Instead, amongst themselves, they often drew sharp distinctions based on color, birthplace, and, in the case of Africans, also on ethnicity. Perhaps the best example of those distinctions comes from a large, but unsuccessful revolt by urban slaves in Bahia in early 1835. The revolt involved almost exclusively African-born slaves and former slaves. Although the African rebels were black, they certainly did not identify with blacks born in Brazil. At least some of the African rebels claimed that their goal was to kill not only all the whites, but also all Brazilian-born blacks, and then keep the mulattos as slaves.[14] So, from the point of view of the African rebels, blacks born in Brazil, including slaves, were the enemies. Given that Afro-Brazilians often did draw such distinctions, one might ask whether the non-white slaveowners in the two Bahian parishes tried to own slaves who were different from themselves in terms of color or birthplace.

In examining the matter, I found no clear and consistent pattern in the censuses. Native-born black slaveowners owned native-born blacks; pardos owned pardo slaves; Africans owned other Africans; and cabras could be found amongst the slaves held by cabra slaveowners.

To be sure, pardos made up the largest single group of non-white slaveowners in the two parishes. Most pardo slaveowners owned only black slaves. Indeed, 87 percent of the slaves belonging to pardos were classified in the censuses as being black. But it would be unwise to press that bit of evidence too far. According to the 1835 censuses, blacks made up about 88 percent of the *total* slave population in the two parishes. So, that 87 percent of the slaves owned by pardos were black may have little to do with any selective preference for owning black slaves. Instead, it may simply reflect the fact that, according to the censuses, about 88 percent of the slave population consisted of blacks. If free pardos were going to own slaves, then—given the makeup of the local slave population—it was more than likely that those slaves would be black. For the very same reason, black slaveowners had little chance to own slaves who were not also black.

Moreover, non-white slaveowners would have faced real difficulties in trying to manipulate and control the composition of their slave-holdings. Where they acquired slaves through inheritance, they would have had no control over the color or birthplace of the slaves they inherited. Along the same lines, even if native-born non-white slaveowners may have perhaps preferred to own African slaves, the birth of a slave child to an African slave woman they owned would have instantly made them into the owners of a native-born slave. Thus, neither color nor birthplace—as recorded in the 1835 censuses— clearly and consistently distinguished non-white slaveowners from the slaves they owned.

The quantitative evidence from the 1835 censuses for the two Bahian parishes might be summarized in three fairly straightforward observations. First, non-white slaveowners were neither an anomaly nor a rare occurrence in the Bahian countryside. On the contrary, pardos, blacks, and cabras constituted a sizeable share of the slave-owning population in the two rural parishes. Second, the distribution of slave-holdings closely paralleled the racial and color hierarchies that characterized Brazilian society as a whole at the time. Whites owned far more slaves and were far more likely to own slaves than their free non-white neighbors. In turn, within the free population of color, the presumably lighter-skinned pardos were the most likely to own slaves; pardos also formed the wealthiest group of non-white slaveowners. Third, the information from the censuses does not suggest that non-white slaveholders consistently owned slaves who were different from themselves by either color or birthplace.

But the evidence on non-white slave-holding from the 1835 censuses has broader and, in some cases, contradictory implications for understanding slavery, race, and social structures in early-nineteenth-century Brazil. Evidence on non-white slave-holding reinforces the research during the past twenty years that has shown that slave-holding had deep roots within Brazilian society. Wealthy planters may have owned the majority of slaves in Brazil, but most Brazilian slaveowners were not wealthy planters; most owned only a few slaves. Precisely, slaveownership was widespread. Support for slavery as an institution came from ample segments of society—not only from wealthy planters, but also from small farmers, artisans, and petty traders who could claim ownership of no more than a handful of slaves. The wide base of support helps explain why slavery lasted so long in Brazil.

But what has been largely lacking until now is any recognition that, by the early-nineteenth century and perhaps before, direct support for slavery often crossed color lines. Most of the non-white slaveowners in the two Bahian parishes owned only 1 or 2 slaves. But those 1 or 2 slaves would have been their single most valuable possession. And, in face of any threat to slavery, the non-white slaveowners in Santiago do Iguape and São Gonçalo dos Campos had every reason to band together not only with their white slave-holding neighbors, but also with other pardo, black, and cabra slaveowners to defend slavery. That would be true whether they owned 10 or more slaves or just 1 or 2.

At the same time, because slaves were a measure of wealth, the evidence from the censuses points to the real possibility of upward social mobility open to the free population of color in early-nineteenth-century Brazil, notwithstanding prejudice and discrimination. The extent of that upward mobility should not be underestimated. Even where non-whites owned only 1 slave, they still outranked in wealth nearly 28 percent of all white householders in the two parishes.

Yet the extent of upward social mobility—despite prejudice based on race and color—should not be exaggerated. The disparities in the distribution of slave-holding make clear the very wide gap between whites and the free population of color, including pardos. Here it is also worth recalling that the majority of all non-white slaveowners in the two parishes were classified as "pardos."

Furthermore, insofar as prejudice based on color in early-nineteenth-century Brazil was a product of racial ideology linked to slavery, non-white slaveowners, through their ownership of slaves, were—perhaps unwillingly and unwittingly—helping to perpetuate that ideology.

The presence of so many non-white slaveowners in these two parishes also warns against reducing slavery to a mainly racial relationship, that is, a relationship defined or explained by race. Nearly a decade ago, Barbara Fields, a U.S. historian who works on the U.S. South, raised that very issue in discussing research on slavery in the United States. Although the views among U.S. historians may have changed in more recent years, Fields's remarks still bear repeating. "Probably most American historians," Fields noted, "think of slavery as primarily a system of race relations—as though the chief business of slavery were the production of white supremacy, rather than the production of cotton, sugar, rice, and tobacco."[15] That race neither defined nor explained slavery was equally clear to the African-born Mahommah Baquaqua, one of the very few Brazilian slaves who had something similar to an autobiography. Drawing on his own experiences both in Africa and Brazil, Baquaqua wrote: "Slaveholding is generated in power, and anyone having the means to buy his fellow creature can become a slaveowner, no matter what his color, creed, or country." Baquaqua added: "the colored man would as soon enslave his fellow man as the white man, if he had the power."[16]

Indeed, it should be more than obvious that the 278 black, pardo, and cabra slaveowners in the two Bahian parishes did not acquire and hold slaves with the goal of promoting white supremacy and hence their own racial subordination. Like their white neighbors, they owned slaves first and foremost because slaves were labor and hence a source of wealth.

But setting aside race as the defining element in slavery does not imply reviving older and now rightly discredited views that, despite slavery, racism failed to take root in Brazil or that Brazilian society was or is some sort of "racial democracy." Rather it means confronting the truly complex problem of analyzing the link between slavery and the construction of categories based on color and race in nineteenth-century Brazil.

Tackling that problem requires taking into account a point that historians of Brazil have long recognized, namely, that Brazilians in the colonial period and the nineteenth century could not take it for granted that darker skin and African ancestry automatically indicated slave status. Instead, they had to adjust their views of race and color to take into account a large and growing free population of color. But what has largely gone unrecognized and unexplored is the extent to which Brazilians also had to adjust those views to take into account non-white slaveowners. By the early-nineteenth century, Brazilians in Bahia and elsewhere could not equate slave-holding exclusively with "whiteness." Nor, inversely, could they assume that darker skin and African birth or ancestry automatically precluded the ownership of slaves.

Yet it is no easy task to analyze how, in making those adjustments, nineteenth-century Brazilians elaborated—from one day to the next—categories and identities based on race and color. The two 1835 censuses yield questions that illustrate the complexity of the problem, but those are for the most part questions that cannot be answered with census data.

For example, noticeably absent from the censuses is the term "Negro," which—like "preto"—literally means "black." The two words are synonyms when referring to the color of something. But, in colonial and nineteenth-century Brazil, "Negro" was employed almost exclusively in referring to slaves. In fact, "Negro" could be used to designate any slave, regardless of his or her color. By contrast, while "preto" indicated blackness, it did not automatically imply slave status. That raises the following question: Did black (preto) slaveowners in the two parishes perhaps see themselves as pretos while, at the same time, they regarded their black slaves as Negros? Or it could be that, while calling their slaves "Negros," black slaveowners preferred to avoid any explicit reference to their own color; they could resort to seeing themselves as *homens* and *mulheres de cor,* in other words, as men and women of color. In either case, the color scheme used in the censuses may mask a distinction that was meaningful and perhaps crucial both for black slaveowners and for their white and pardo neighbors. In that case, the color scheme used in the census would also mislead people into believing that racial ideology played no role in situations where black slaveowners owned other blacks as slaves.

Non-white slave-holding also forces people to confront questions about the definition of "whiteness" and about the practice of selective individual reclassification, a practice that had and has interesting parallels in the United States. That practice is, in any event, summed up in the well-known Brazilian saying: "*O dinheiro embranquece* (Money whitens)." Perhaps the best-known historical incident of selective individual reclassification comes from a case recounted by Henry Koster, an Englishman who lived for several years in northeastern Brazil in the early-nineteenth century. Koster became confused when he learned that a free mulatto had become a captain-major in the militia, because he knew that non-whites were legally barred from holding the rank of captain-major. Koster asked his Brazilian servant whether the captain-major was not in fact a mulatto. The servant answered: "'he was but is not now.'" Even more confused, Koster asked for further explanation. His servant responded with another question: "'Can a Capitam-mor [captain-major] be a mulatto?'" Koster then went on to note that, in Brazil, what he called even "a considerable tinge" could pass for white under some circumstances.[17]

The two 1835 censuses contain numerous examples of non-whites who would seem to be ideal candidates to be reclassified as "whites." To cite merely one example: José Coitinho de Oliveira, the freeborn pardo tobacco grower in São Gonçalo dos Campos, owned 48 slaves, making him one of the wealthiest tobacco growers in Bahia. If it could be accepted that José Coitinho de Oliveira was of mixed European and African descent, then the question would come up: How many slaves did he need to own—50, 75, 100?—before it could be said that, like Koster's captain-major, he used to be, but was no longer, a mulatto? How many slaves would it take before the census-takers would be willing to overlook his perhaps very distant African ancestry and reclassify him as "white"? In truth, José Coitinho de Oliveira and other better-off freeborn pardo slaveowners may have seen themselves as "white."

The example of José Coitinho de Oliveira suggests that there were limits to the practice of selective reclassification. But the census data do not allow one to locate those limits; nor do they determine whether there was a fixed set of specific criteria used in distinguishing whites from pardos and hence in defining "whiteness."[18]

Along the same lines, the apparently clear-cut distinction made in the censuses between "pardo" and "black" (or "preto") should be questioned. For example, where color is concerned, the censuses suggest, at first view, a sharp contrast between the slaves and the free non-whites living in the two parishes. On the one hand, over 80 percent of all slaves were listed as being black. That holds true even for those slaves born in Bahia. But, on the other hand, the census-takers classified as "pardo" fully 70 percent of the free non-white population. That contrast reflects the fact that pardos had better chances of winning their freedom.

Yet there is another possibility. It could be that some free pardos were classified as "pardos" not so much because they were of mixed European and African ancestry, but rather because they were free. Along the same lines, it could be that so many slaves were listed as "pretos" not so much because they lacked any mixed ancestry, but rather they were slaves. In other words, one needs to consider the possibility that freedom may have made free non-whites look lighter in the eyes of the census-takers. And, in the opposite direction, slave status may have darkened the slave population in the eyes of those same census-takers.

That possibility raises still another question. According to the 1835 censuses, the great majority of non-white slaveowners were pardos. But was that the case because free pardos had greater chances of overcoming, at least in part, racial discrimination and achieving upward social-economic mobility than their free black neighbors? Or could it be that so many non-white slaveowners were classified as "pardos" because they owned slaves?

If that was the case, even though the 1835 censuses-takers could not make slave-holding an exclusively "white" privilege, they could still create a link between ownership of slaves and lighter skin color and European ancestry. They could create that link by classifying non-white slaveowners as "pardos" whenever that classification was minimally plausible. And in that way, the designation as "pardo" would further distance non-white slaveowners not only from their African-born ancestors, but also the overwhelming majority of all slaves living in the two parishes.

All of these are, however, questions that cannot truly be answered with the information from the 1835 censuses. The problem does not lie so much in the methodology used in carrying out those censuses; rather it lies mainly in the very nature of census data. Censuses place individuals into fixed categories according to preconceived classificatory schemes. As the British historian Benedict Anderson has noted in a different context: "The fiction of the census is that every one is in it and that everyone occupies one and—only one—extremely clear place. No fractions."[19]

Thus, censuses capture for a given moment in time the efforts by the state and its agents to give each individual one specific and fractionless identity. But the fixed and static categories in censuses and other forms tell very little about the cultural dynamics that come into play in the way that, from one day to the next, people create identities for themselves and identify other people. That is true whether talking about identities based on race or color or some other criterion. Indeed, both in Brazil and in the United States, census categories, even in recent times, have failed to provide a clear, objective, and unambiguous guide to racial or color identities. On the contrary, census categories in both countries have at times become the focus for debate and for efforts to contest or redefine racial and color identities.

It is not that census data are useless; clearly they are useful. But one needs to recognize the limits of their usefulness. Censuses provide no more than a very blunt knife for dissecting identities based on race or color and the day-to-day dynamics of racial ideology.

And it is worth recalling that the classificatory scheme imposed by the 1990 U.S. census made it virtually impossible for Brazilians living in the United States to identify themselves as Brazilians in the census. Moreover, black *and* Brazilian, or white *and* Brazilian or, in the case of Brazilians of Japanese ancestry, Asian *and* Brazilian—according to the U.S. Census Bureau in 1990—simply did not and could not exist.[20]

NOTES

1. This paper summarizes some of the main research findings I have presented in an article available only in Portuguese: "As cores do escravismo: escravistas 'pretos,' 'pardos' e 'cabras' no Recôncavo baiano em 1835," *População e Família* (São Paulo) 2, no. 2 (July–December 1999): 7–62. The article not only presents my findings in greater detail, but also includes an extensive bibliography of works cited (more than 140 items). Because this paper has been written mainly as an oral presentation, I have, for the most part, provided references in the notes only for direct quotations. For further references, see "As cores."

2. At the same time, the Portuguese language makes it difficult to discuss non-white slaveowners. The most common expression for "slaveowner" is *senhor de escravos,* which, in the plural, becomes *senhores de escravos.* "Black slaveowners" would translate as *senhores de escravos pretos*. That expression grammatically parallels such entirely unambiguous expressions as *lavradores de fumo baianos* (Bahian tobacco farmers) or *senhores de escravos paulistas* (Paulista slaveowners). Nevertheless, most Portuguese speakers would, at first reading, assume that "pretos" (black) in "senhores de escravos pretos" modifies "escravos" and would hence understand the expression as meaning "owners of black slaves." Likewise, the expression *senhores de escravos brancos* (white slaveowners) would seem, at first view, to mean "owners of white slaves" and thus refer to a situation that, for all practical purposes, did not exist in colonial and nineteenth-century Brazil.

3. For source, see note 5 below. Here it should be pointed out that, unlike its U.S. counterpart, the 1824 Constitution of the Empire of Brazil did not require the central government to take regular population counts. Indeed, not until 1872 would the central government sponsor and successfully carry out a national census. In the half-century between independence and 1872, responsibility for collecting population statistics rested with provincial governments. In provinces, such as São Paulo, Minas Gerais, and Paraná—all in southeastern Brazil—where census-taking had been a regular feature of the previous colonial administration, provincial governments did take that responsibility. In the past thirty years, scholars have made ample use of the fairly large body of surviving household censuses carried out in those provinces between the late-eighteenth century and the 1820s and 1830s. But comparable censuses are extremely rare for northeastern Brazil.

Also note that no scholar to date has ever located the original enumerators' sheets from the 1872 national census. Apparently they were destroyed.

4. On the Recôncavo and the history of slave-based agriculture in the region, see Stuart B. Schwartz, *Sugar Plantations in the Formation of Brazilian Society: Bahia, 1550–1835* (New York:

Cambridge University Press, 1985); and B. J. Barickman, *A Bahian Counterpoint: Sugar, Tobacco, Cassava, and Slavery in the Recôncavo, 1780–1860* (Stanford: Stanford University Press, 1998).

5. "Relação do Numero de Fogos, e moradores do Districto da Freguezia de Sant-Iago Maior do Iguape, da Comarca da Villa da Cachoeira da Provincia da Bahia" (1835), Arquivo Público do Estado da Bahia (Salvador), Seção Histórica, maço 61575-1; "Relação do No de Fogos e moradores do Districto da Freguezia de São Gonçallo da Va da Cachoeira" [1835], Arquivo Público do Estado da Bahia, Seção Histórica, maço 5683. Unfortunately, some sheets are missing from the census of São Gonçalo dos Campos, and the entire last section (for the subdistrict of the Capela dos Humildes) is too fragile for use as are several sheets for the other subdistricts. Thus, the figure of 11,406 used here for the parish's total population derives from a direct count of the nominal lists for the 1,760 households on the sheets that could be examined. Also note that, in the independent Empire of Brazil, parishes served as both ecclesiastical and political-administrative units.

As stated in the text, the two censuses are the result of failed attempts to carry out a province-wide population count in Bahia. In early 1835, the provincial assembly passed a measure authorizing the count. Immediately thereafter, the provincial president (that is, governor) sent circular letters to all vicars and justices of the peace, ordering them to conduct censuses in their parishes. They were also ordered to send the censuses (both the household-by-household lists and a summary) to the provincial government by the end of 1835. The circular letters also contained threats to those vicars and justices of the peace who did not comply. But the threats seemed to have carried little weight. Over the next few years, vicars and justices of the peace in various parts of Bahia offered, in their correspondence with the provincial government, a wide range of excuses for not having carried out censuses in their parishes.

And, to date, the household lists from only four parishes have come to light: Santiago do Iguape, São Gonçalo dos Campos, São José do das Itapororocas (corresponding to modern Feira de Santana), and São Pedro Velho (in Salvador).

Also note that census-takers designated plantations *(engenhos)*, farms, and the like as "households" *(fogos)*.

6. The difference in crops was largely the result of different soil types.

7. See Carlos Hasenbalg and Nelson do Valle Silva, *Estrutura social, mobilidade e raça* (Rio de Janeiro: Instituto Universitário de Pesquisas do Rio de Janeiro; São Paulo: Vértice, 1988), p. 146.

8. Here, to avoid misunderstandings, it should be pointed out that pardos were not necessarily the direct offspring of one white and one black parent. They might also be and often were the children of two pardos.

9. For instance, not a single "cabra" appears in the household lists for one of the four subdistricts *(capelas)* of São Gonçalo dos Campos; the census of Santiago do Iguape includes only six "cabras."

10. The total population was 7,410 in Santiago do Iguape and 11,406 in São Gonçalo dos Campos. In Iguape, slaves accounted for 53.8 percent of the total population; in São Gonçalo dos Campos, they represented 34.4 percent of the total.

11. Whites accounted for only 29.9 percent of all free residents in São Gonçalo dos Campos and even a smaller share in Santiago do Iguape (17.2 percent).

12. In 1830, more than 3,500 free African Americans living in the South were slaveholders; collectively they owned almost 12,000 slaves. Loren Schweninger, *Black Property Owners in the South, 1790–1915* (Urbana: University of Illinois Press, 1990), p. 104. Also see Larry Koger, *Black Slaveowners: Free Black Slave Masters in South Carolina, 1790–1860* (Jefferson, N.C.: McFarland, 1985). On the Caribbean, see B. W. Higman, *Slave Populations of the British Caribbean, 1807–1834* (Baltimore: Johns Hopkins University Press, 1984); Carl Campbell, "The Rise of a Free Coloured Plantocracy in Trinidad," *Boletín de Estudios Latinoamericanos y del*

Caribe 29 (1980): 33–53; and John Garrigus, "Blue and Brown: Contraband Indigo and the Rise of a Free Colored Planter Class in French Saint-Domingue," *The Americas* 50, no. 2 (October 1993): 233–263.

13. The small number of African-born slaveowners in these two parishes should not be attributed to any *general* reluctance to purchase slaves among freed Africans. Although scant, evidence from other areas of Brazil indicates that, when they could afford to do so, freed former African slaves often did purchase slaves (including African-born slaves). For instance, in the urban parish of Santana do Sacramento in the city of Salvador, 68, or roughly one fifth (21 percent), of all freed Africans were slaveholders; collectively, they owned a total of 133 bondsmen. "Relação dos africanos libertos na Freguezia de Santa Anna" (1849), Arquivo Público do Estado da Bahia, maço 2988. Also see Maria Inês Côrtes de Oliveira, *O liberto: o seu mundo e os outros: Salvador, 1790/1890* (São Paulo, 1988), pp. 35–36; and Mary C. Karasch, *Slave Life in Rio de Janeiro, 1808–1850* (Princeton: Princeton University Press, 1987), p. 211.

At least, in part, the fact that both Santiago do Iguape and São Gonçalo dos Campos were rural districts helps explain the low proportion of slaveowners found among freed Africans in the two parishes. The rural context would have limited the opportunities of freed African slaves, since most of them would have been field hands; and the same rural context would have also restricted their opportunities after achieving manumission. Many of the freed African slaveowners in Santana do Sacramento in 1849, according to their declared occupations, gained their living in various types of petty trade (including trade in prepared foodstuffs), as artisans, and as sedan-chair carriers. From those activities, which, undoubtedly, many had already exercised as slaves, they apparently could earn a more or less regular cash income both before and after manumission. But, if, as it would seem, it would be possible not only to earn a living, but also to acquire the resources needed to purchase a slave by selling *mingau* in the streets of Salvador, the same would not have been true in rural areas. Likewise, in the cane and tobacco fields of Iguape and São Gonçalo dos Campos, there would have been little demand for sedan-chair carriers.

Also note that, according to the 1835 censuses, Africans comprised 53.6 percent of the total slave population in Iguape and 19.0 percent in São Gonçalo dos Campos.

14. On the 1835 rebellion (the revolt of the Malês), see João José Reis, *Slave Rebellion in Brazil: The Muslim Uprising of 1835 in Bahia,* trans. Arthur Brakel (Baltimore: Johns Hopkins University Press, 1993).

15. Barbara Jeanne Fields, "Slavery, Race, and Ideology in the United States of America," *New Left Review* 181 (May–June 1990): 99. See the parallel observation made by Brazilian historian Sílvia Hunold Lara: "a questão da dominação e exploração é bastante complexa para ser reduzida a uma questão racial." Lara adds: "a escravidão africana existiu para produzir a riqueza, não para produzir a subordinação racial." Sílvia Hunold Lara, "Trabalhadores escravos," *Trabalhadores* (Campinas, SP, 1988), pp. 13, 15.

16. Baquaqua was enslaved in Africa by Africans. Before being shipped to Brazil, he was owned by more than one African slaveowner. At one point in Brazil, a "man of color" attempted to purchase him as a slave. Mahommah G. Baquaqua, *A History of Mahommah G. Baquaqua, a Native of Zoogoo, in the Interior of Africa . . . Written and Revised from His Own Words,* by Samuel Moore, Esq. (Detroit, 1854), pp. 34–45, 47–48.

17. Henry Koster, *Travels in Brazil* (London: Longman, Hurst, Rees, Orme, and Brown, 1816), p. 391.

18. Here it is also necessary to recall that by no means did all "white" household heads in the two parishes own slaves.

19. Benedict Anderson, *Imagined Communities: Reflections on the Origin and Spread of Nationalism,* rev. ed. (London and New York: Verso, 1991), p. 106.

20. On Brazilians and the 1990 U.S. census, see, for example, Maxine Margolis, *Little Brazil: An Ethnography of Brazilian Immigrants in New York City* (Princeton: Princeton University

Press, 1993), pp. 252–257. According to the Census Bureau, Portuguese-speaking Brazilians were supposed to identify themselves as "Hispanics." If they chose not to do so, they could still identify themselves as belonging to "other" under the category for race. Although the 2000 census adopted a different format, the categories used in the 1990 census, or their near equivalents, remain in common use on forms used by the federal government and by various state governments. And, as far as I know, none of those forms (except perhaps in parts of New England) includes a category such as "non-Hispanic Latin American" or "Luso-Hispanic," which was also true in the case of the 2000 census; nor, as far as I know, are there any proposals to include a category of that sort.

Also note that recent scholarship has begun to dismantle the conventional and still common view that draws a sharp contrast between the United States and Brazil where racial and color classification are concerned. According to that view, whereas Brazilians use a complex scheme to classify individuals by color, North Americans have always relied on a simple "white-black" dichotomy. See, for example, Thomas Skidmore, "Bi-racial U.S.A. vs. Multi-racial Brazil: Is the Contrast Still Valid?" *Journal of Latin American Studies* 25, no. 2 (May 1993): 373–386; and Matthew Frye Jacobson, *Whiteness of a Different Color: European Immigrants and the Alchemy of Race* (Cambridge: Harvard University Press, 1998). It is not that there are no differences between Brazil and the United States in this regard (both in the past and in the present); rather the conventional view not only overlooks the historical record, but also vastly simplifies the complexities of racial/color classification in *both* countries. The very existence of categories such as "white, not of Hispanic origin," "black, not of Hispanic origin," "Hispanic," and "Asian or Pacific Islander" immediately reveals the faults in assuming that the U.S. classification scheme rests on a simple "white-black" dichotomy. And, of course, even as late 1920, the U.S. census included the category "mulatto."

5. Afro-Cuban Identity and the Black Press in Spanish Cuba, 1878–1898

Rafael E. Tarragó

The periodicals published by Afro-Cubans between 1878 and 1898 were instrumental in the formation of an Afro-Cuban identity, meaning a consciousness by Afro-Cubans of their civil rights as citizens in Cuban society, and of the actual limitations to those aspirations because of their racial phenotype on account of the racial prejudices of the white majority in Cuba. This Cuban black press of the nineteenth century acted as a means of communication among Afro-Cubans, served as an educational tool, and was used to express grievances and to influence political events in Cuba.

The first periodical published by Afro-Cubans was *El faro,* founded in Havana in 1841.[1] The repression following the discovery of the abolitionist conspiracy in Matanzas known as Conspiración de la Escalera in 1844 brought about its closing. In 1856, a literary publication edited by Afro-Cubans, titled *El Rocío,* was published in Havana.[2] After slavery was really abolished in Cuba by a decree of the Spanish crown in 1880, Afro-Cuban periodicals proliferated. According to the Afro-Cubanists Jorge Castellanos and Isabel Castellanos, the last twenty years of Spain's sovereignty in Cuba saw the publication of at least 108 periodicals edited by Afro-Cubans.[3]

Slaves and Free Blacks in Cuba before 1878

Patriarchal Slavery and Its Demise

Baron Alexander von Humboldt says in the Spanish edition of his essay on Cuba, published in 1826 and written after his visits to Cuba in 1800 and 1804, that in 1825 the African slave population of Cuba was smaller proportionally than in the English, Dutch, and French sugar islands of the Caribbean, and that in Cuba a large free black population had a place in society and some of its members had attained economic prosperity.[4] Jane L. Landers has argued that the exceptionally rich documentary evidence in African Americans in Florida demonstrates how, given the proper conditions, the enslaved could actually *work* the Spanish system, in which a slave's humanity and rights were acknowledged, and a manumission policy existed, which made possible a free black class that had a place in society.[5] Gwendolyn Hall and Kimberly S. Hanger have reached similar conclusions from their research on Spanish Louisiana.[6] The long-standing dispute in the seventeenth and eighteenth centuries between African slaves and their descendants in the area of El Cobre in eastern Cuba with the Spanish monarchy described by José Luciano Franco and María Elena Díaz, in two works diametrically opposed in philosophy, corroborates the fact that the Spanish monarchy granted slaves certain rights which, given the proper conditions, they would use in their interest.[7]

The fact that African slavery was not a driving force in the Cuban economy, combined with the provisions in Spanish slave legislation in the Laws of the Indies, seems to have fostered the growth of a considerably large free black population in Cuba by the middle of the eighteenth century.[8] Many of these free blacks became prosperous artisans and traders. Some became educated and were able to obtain waivers to the estatutes of purity of blood that forbade blacks and Jews from entering the University of Havana.[9] During the last quarter of the eighteenth century, two battalions of mulattos and one of free blacks (euphemistically called *pardos* and *morenos* respectively) were formed in Cuba. The blacks and mulattos in these battalions were granted the *fuero de guerra militar,* which permitted militiamen to present their legal causes before military tribunals, and in a hierarchical colonial society conveyed special distinction and prestige.[10]

Franklin W. Knight has argued, in his study *Slave Society in Cuba,* that the *patriarchal* African slavery system existing in Spanish America until the end of the eighteenth century resulted less from the benevolence of Spanish legislation or the doctrine and intervention of the Roman Catholic Church than it did from the realities of the situation.[11] The first half of the nineteenth century in Cuba saw a gradual increase of restrictions on blacks, from the proscription of preaching Christianity to plantation slaves to governmental restrictions to interracial marriages.[12] This happened as Cuba—at the request of the Cuban elite—became a wealthy sugar-producing colony, whose economy required a massive slave-labor force, and slaves acquired high economic value. In 1844 an abolitionist conspiracy of free blacks and slaves was discovered, and its brutal repression almost destroyed the middle classes among the free blacks in Cuba.[13]

Impact on Blacks of the First War of Independence in Cuba, 1868–1878

The first Cuban War of Independence began October 10, 1868, one month after a military coup had overthrown Queen Isabel II (r. 1833–1868) in Spain, and a liberal government sat in Madrid. One of the first acts of the leader of the insurrection, Carlos Manuel de Céspedes, was the liberation of his slaves. But the men who wanted Cuba free from Spain were not keen about the immediate liberation of all the slaves on the island. In order to gain the support of slaves and free blacks, the insurgents declared the qualified freedom of slaves in the territory under their control. Then the liberal government in Madrid passed a law (drafted by the statesman Segismundo Moret) declaring free in Cuba all children born after 1868 and all slaves over the age of sixty, and promising some form of emancipation of the rest after the end of the insurrection.

The challenge of the Moret Law was taken up by the civil government established by the Cuban insurrectionists in eastern Cuba, and after 1870 slavery practically disappeared in that area.[14] The peace treaty signed by the Cuban insurrectionists and General Arsenio Martínez Campos, a representative of the Spanish government in 1878, freed those slaves who had fought on either side. In 1879 the remaining slaves in eastern Cuba unexpectedly challenged their masters, refusing to work unless they were granted freedom "like those freed by the peace treaty." Eastern planters backed down, promising freedom in four years and wages during the interim.[15]

Free blacks in Cuba were dramatically affected by the first Cuban War of Independence. In eastern Cuba, free blacks who joined the insurgents rose through the ranks and became officers. The decision did not go unchallenged, but it stood.[16] In the areas controlled by the government, free blacks of substance were wooed by the authorities.

Blacks in Spanish Cuba after 1878

There had been a movement for the abolition of slavery in Spain before the war of 1868 in Cuba, and one of its leaders was Rafael María de Labra, a Cuban resident in Madrid.[17] The best study of the Spanish abolitionist movement and its influence in bringing about the complete abolition of slavery in Cuba is Arthur F. Corwin's *Spain and the Abolition of Slavery in Cuba, 1817–1886*.[18] The Cuban revolution of 1868 did not end slavery in Cuba, because slavery existed in Cuba until 1886, eight years after the end of the insurrection.

Several Cuban statesmen and publicists advocated the end of slavery in the first half of the nineteenth century—Father Félix Varela (1797–1879), Francisco Arango y Parreño (1767–1837), and José Antonio Saco (1797–1879) were the most prominent—but, except for Father Varela, their projects favored the gradual abolition of slavery. After the conspiracy of 1844, slavery was not discussed publicly in Cuba. One example of the sensitivity of island authorities on the subject is that the government censored Cuban distribution of the romantic novel *Sab,* by Gertrudis Gómez de Avellaneda, because it was implicitly critical of slavery.[19] It was only after the insurrection of 1868 and its limited and tentative abolitionist efforts that the Spanish government began to pass and implement abolitionist laws in Cuba. Although the insurrectionists did not bring an end to slavery in Cuba, they created the conditions that facilitated that happy event. Eduardo Torres Cuevas and Eusebio Reyes analyze thoroughly this interrelation of events and ideas in *Esclavitud y sociedad: Notas y documentos para la historia de la esclavitud negra en Cuba*.[20]

Facing the actual dissolution of slavery in Cuba, and under pressure from abolitionists in Spain, the Spanish government passed a decree abolishing slavery in Cuba in 1880, albeit providing an eight-year period of apprenticeship. In 1878, Cuba had obtained representation in the parliament in Madrid

(Cortes), and the political parties formed in Cuba by reactionaries and reform-
ists took positions in regard to slavery. In 1886 the deputies of the *Partido
Liberal Autonomista* (the Cuban home rule party), Rafael María de Labra,
Rafael Montoro, and Miguel Figueroa, influenced the government into pro-
mulgating the complete abolition of slavery in Cuba.[21]

In addition to the abolition of slavery, the Spanish government passed
several antidiscriminatory laws in Cuba between 1878 and 1898 to tear down
the segregationist establishment that it had fostered in the previous three hundred years. Even before the official end of slavery in 1886, desegregationist
laws were passed, like the April 18, 1879, law allowing black children to go
to the same schools as white children, and abolishing legal impediments to the
admission of blacks and mulattos in secondary schools and at Havana University. In January 1881, all laws interfering with interracial marriages were
abolished. In March 1881, the practice of keeping separate books of entries for
blacks and whites in birth, marriage, and death registries was ended. In 1882,
a law was passed allowing blacks and mulattos to go to parks, gardens, res-
taurants, and other public places where they had been excluded. In November
1887, the governor general issued a decree allowing blacks to use first-class
compartments in trains.[22] These laws did not bring an end to racial prejudice
and inequality in Cuba, but a situation that made a visitor critical of Spain
in 1898 to say, "Spanish civilization has left one enduring monument in the
Antilles; it has not denied opportunity to the black man."[23]

Afro-Cubans themselves were instrumental in the demise of slavery, not
only by obvious gestures like the refusal of slaves in eastern Cuba to work in
1879, but by learning to use the legal system to hasten their own emancipation. By 1885, only 53,381 apprentices *(patrocinados)* remained in Cuba, thus
the complete abolition decreed in 1886 merely confirmed an existing state of
affairs. Rebecca J. Scott's *Slave Emancipation in Cuba: The Transition to Free
Labor, 1860–1898* is a thorough analysis of the involvement of blacks in Cuba
in their own liberation.[24] Afro-Cubans were also instrumental in the demise of
the segregationist legal system. Jorge Castellanos and Isabel Castellanos analyze the participation of Afro-Cubans in bringing about legal equality during
the last twenty years of Spanish Cuba in the second volume of their *Cultura
afrocubana*.[25] The induction of two prominent Afro-Cubans, the publicists don
Juan Gualberto Gómez (1891) and don Martín Morúa Delgado (1894), into
the prestigious Sociedad Económica of Havana (equivalent to the American
Academy of Science in the United States) was telling of how much the position
of blacks and mulattos changed in the last twenty years of Spanish sovereignty
in Cuba.

Afro-Cubans and Political Movements

The political system established in Cuba in 1878 did not forbid free blacks
and mulattos to vote, but the high-income restrictions in the electoral laws

for the island marginalized them the most, because only a small minority of blacks and mulattos met them. When the Spanish parliament granted universal male suffrage in Spain in 1890, it denied its extension to Cuba and Puerto Rico partly because many deputies were wary of non-white participation in the political system.[26]

Governmental authorities in Cuba did not promote the political participation of non-whites, but they cultivated conservative blacks and mulattos like José Bernabeu and Rodolfo de Lagardere. These men and other prosperous non-whites in Cuba organized *casinos españoles de la raza de color,* which promoted loyalty to Spain and advocated the abolition of legal racial segregation. The militia battalions of blacks and mulattos, created in the eighteenth century and abolished in 1844, had been reestablished in 1854 and continued attracting loyalist non-whites in Cuba after 1878, even during the Cuban War of Independence of 1895, when a guard of thirty Afro-Cubans formed the personal escort of Governor General Valeriano Weyler.[27]

After 1891 the Cuban home rule party began to demand universal male suffrage in Cuba. Some leaders of that party advocated the political participation of Afro-Cubans with values like theirs. Rafael Montoro proposed the education of freedmen as early as 1882, and in 1892, F. A. Conte praised the political aptitude of Afro-Cubans in a controversial tract.[28] In 1894, the Afro-Cuban publicist don Martín Morúa Delgado joined the Cuban home rule party, and promoted this party as the party that Afro-Cubans had to join if they wanted to attain the full rights of citizens. Even after the breaking of the War of Independence of 1895, don Martín continued supporting the Cuban home rule party under Spain until the instauration of repression by Governor General Weyler in 1896, when he fled to the United States.[29]

In an influential tract published in Nice in 1897, home rule party leader Eliseo Giberga dedicated a section to Afro-Cubans, concluding that "Blacks are Cubans, they are in Cuba, and nothing can be accomplished in Cuba without them."[30] When the Spanish crown granted home rule to Cuba in the fall of 1897, it also extended universal male suffrage to the island.[31] The Cuban autonomous government lasted only one year, because the end of Spanish sovereignty in Cuba brought about by the U.S. military intervention in 1898 made it irrelevant. There were elections in Cuba where universal male suffrage was exercised during that year. Although the disruptions of war rendered these late electoral rights largely moot, the establishment of integrated electoral lists in itself established precedents for the future. Indeed, in 1900, when the U.S. governor in Cuba passed a restrictive electoral law for the election of a constitutional assembly in Cuba, the separatist general Dr. Eusebio Hernández protested, calling the American governor's law inferior to that granted by the Queen of Spain. In 1901, in an article published by the American Academy of Political and Social Sciences, U.S. Senator Orville H. Platt marveled that in

Cuba it was not questioned that "a colored man was as much entitled to be a voter as a white man."[32]

Most Afro-Cubans did not openly join any of the colonial political parties, and the attitude of many of their leaders and organizations suggests that they favored Cuban independence. An Afro-Cuban leader who was open about his separatist sympathies was don Juan Gualberto Gómez, editor of the newspaper *La fraternidad*. In 1890, he published an article in *La fraternidad* justifying his separatist views, "Por qué somos separatistas." Because of this article, he was condemned to exile for treason by a Havana jury. Through the legal assistance of the home rule party leader Rafael María de Labra, don Juan Gualberto was able to appeal to the Supreme Court at Madrid, and the Spanish Supreme Court ruled in his favor because, according to the Constitution (extended to Cuba in 1881), it was legal to express one's political opinions provided one did not conspire or rebel. After that court decision of November 1891, freedom of the press was firmly established in Spanish Cuba.[33] After the Cuban separatist leader José Martí founded the Cuban Revolutionary Party in the United States in 1892, he contacted don Juan Gualberto Gómez and made him the representative of that party in Cuba. Afro-Cubans responded to Martí's gestures, and were convinced of his sincerity by his closeness to don Juan Gualberto. When the Cuban War of Independence organized by Martí broke in 1895, most Afro-Cubans supported it mainly because don Juan Gualberto Gómez was Martí's deputy, and because the Afro-Cuban general Antonio Maceo was included in its leadership. After the death of Martí in May 1895 and that of Maceo in November 1896, the leadership of the revolution fell to men who were not committed to racial equality in Cuba, but this did not transpire at the time.[34]

After the urging of don Juan Gualberto Gómez, a coordinated body of Afro-Cuban societies was formed, the Directorio Central de la Raza de Color. Together, the societies united in the Directorio petitioned the government to make changes in segregationist laws and to implement existing desegregationist laws. Their efforts brought about changes in the penal code of 1879, whose article #16 stated that any black committing a crime involving a white man under any aggravated circumstance faced execution, and the abrogation of the words "pardo" and "moreno" from personal identification cards. Also, they protested against the inadequacy of the public school system in Cuba and the continuation of school segregation. The Liberal Governor General Emilio Calleja (1893–1895) had a good working relationship with the Directorio, and showed his commitment to end social distinctions based on race by granting Afro-Cubans the right to place the titles Don and Doña before their names, a radical empowering action in the context of Cuban society at that time. More surprising was the grudging respect for Afro-Cubans shown by the Conservative Governor General Camilo Polavieja (1890–1892) when he wrote to Madrid in 1891: "It is only logical that the free negro should have equal rights and powers like the white."[35] Nevertheless, under the influence of don Juan

Gualberto Gómez, the Directorio ended up becoming a covert vehicle of separatist agitation.

The Cuban Black Press and the Afro-Cuban Identity between 1878 and 1898

The Publications of the Afro-Cuban Mutual Aid Societies

Pedro Deschamps Chapeaux's *El negro en el periodismo cubano en el siglo XIX,* published in Havana in 1963, has the most complete listing of the periodicals edited by Afro-Cubans in the nineteenth century. According to him, many of the mutual aid societies of Afro-Cubans founded between 1878 and 1898 in Cuba published periodicals. These periodicals informed society members about its activities, published educational articles, and provided literary gifted members with the opportunity to be published. In Cienfuegos, central Cuba, the society La Hijas del Progreso published *La familia* (1884); in Matanzas, the society La Armonía published *La armonía* (1879–1880), and the society La Unión published *El pueblo* (1880); in Puerto Príncipe (present-day Camagüey), the society La Nueva Aurora published *La nueva aurora* (1882–1890, 1894); in Havana, the Casino Español de la Raza de Color published *El ciudadano* (1879), and the society La Igualdad published *El africano* (1885–1887).

Cultural Publications

Many of the Cuban black periodicals were cultural publications. That was the case with *Minerva,* a biweekly magazine for Afro-Cuban women, published between 1888 and 1890 in Havana. *Minerva* published poems and songs, and tackled social issues such as the value and preservation of the institution of the family. In one of its articles, the writer states that without the presence of the family all social organization was impossible.[36] The importance of education was a ubiquitous theme in all the periodicals that Afro-Cubans published in Spanish Cuba. In 1880, many articles published in *El pueblo* contended that it was a duty of Afro-Cubans to acquire formal education and to develop a work ethic.[37]

In 1878, there were 712 schools in Cuba. Of those schools, 418 were public ones that had a total of 18,278 students, and the rest were private schools that had a total of 9,502 students. In 1880, the Madrid government established in Cuba a public school system that was going to be administered and paid at the provincial level. In 1887, 32.4 percent of Cubans were black or mulatto, and 67.6 percent were white, but only 11 percent of all Afro-Cubans could read and write while 33 percent of all Cuban whites could. By 1895, 13.9 percent of all Afro-Cuban children and 16.6 percent of all white children were attending school, and the literate Cuban population had increased to 43.2 percent of the total population.[38] It can be argued that the agitation by Afro-Cubans demanding public education, urged in the Afro-Cuban press, influenced the provincial government officials responsible for schools. There is a correlation between the increase in the literate Afro-Cuban population and its interest in becoming educated, and the proliferation of publications addressed to and edited by Afro-Cubans.

Political Publications

Some of the periodicals edited by Afro-Cubans between 1878 and 1898 were partial to a political position. Several periodicals were associated with the loyalist Casinos Españoles de la Raza de Color, such as the Havana papers *La unión* (1878), *El ciudadano* (1879), *La lealtad* (1880), *El hijo del pueblo* (1879–1881), *La España* (1882–1884, 1887), and *La América* (1890). After the Spanish Supreme Court decision of November 1891, confirming the right to political expression in the Cuban press, quite a few periodicals favored Cuban independence from Spain, such as *La fraternidad* (1890–1892) and *La igualdad* (1892–1895). The biweekly *La nueva era* (1892–1896), edited by don Martín Morúa Delgado, supported Cuban home rule under the Spanish crown.

Most Afro-Cuban newspapers did not support a particular political option, but took sides on certain issues, and they practiced political activism in matters concerning the civil rights of Afro-Cubans. The Cuban black press consistently denounced cases of opposition to school integration; in 1886 *El emisario* of Sagua la Grande published several articles protesting against the harassment of black children by whites in the public schools of that town.[39] In 1887, a society in Trinidad received permission to publish a periodical, *La antorcha,* to advocate for the freedmen in that city.[40]

Conclusion

By 1898, Afro-Cubans cherished African traditions and culture, but their identification with Cuba as their fatherland, and their desire not to be second-class citizens on the island were their common characteristics. In the Afro-Cuban press of the last twenty years of Spanish sovereignty on the island, recurring themes were their rights as citizens, the importance of Afro-Cuban solidarity, and education as a means for the socioeconomic self-improvement of Afro-Cubans. This press contributed to the formation of individuals aware of their common interests as Cubans of African ancestry, but who saw themselves foremost as citizens with civil rights in Cuba.

The low literacy level of the Afro-Cuban population in the last quarter of the nineteenth century (11 percent) does not mean that the Afro-Cuban periodicals did not have an impact on the Afro-Cuban masses, because in early modern times people read to each other. Furthermore, in Cuba, workers' associations developed in the 1860s the tradition of hiring literate persons to read to them while they worked. By discussing the issues related to the common experiences of Afro-Cubans, and by informing them about their civil rights as citizens in Cuba, the Afro-Cuban press fostered the formation of the group self-identification mentioned above, which could be described as an Afro-Cuban identity.

SELECT BIBLIOGRAPHY

Archival Sources

I have been able to ascertain that the following Cuban libraries have issues of Afro-Cuban periodicals of the last twenty years of Spanish Cuba. Unless otherwise indicated, the periodicals listed were published in the city of the home library.

Havana: Biblioteca de la Sociedad Económica
La España (#85, August 1885)
La fraternidad (#1, April 1879; 1888 incomplete)
La igualdad (1892–1893 incomplete)
La nueva era (1893–1895 incomplete)
La unión (1886 incomplete)
Minerva (1888–1890)

Havana: Biblioteca Nacional José Martí. Manuscripts Division
El pueblo (1880; published in Matanzas)
La fraternidad (1888–1890)
La igualdad (1894)
La unión (1890)

Villa Clara: Biblioteca Provincial José Martí
El hogar (1888)
El trabajo (1888–1891)

Secondary Sources

Not all the following essays analyze specifically the Afro-Cuban press of the nineteenth century, but all of them contain useful information.

Castellanos, Jorge, and Isabel Castellanos. *Cultura afrocubana,* 5 vols. Miami: Ediciones Universal, 1988–1994.

Deschamps Chapeaux, Pedro. *El negro en el periodismo cubano en el siglo XIX.* Havana: Ediciones R., 1963.

Hevia Lanier, Oilda. *El Directorio Central de las sociedades negras de Cuba, 1886–1894.* Havana: Editorial de Ciencias Sociales, 1996.

Howard, Philip A. *Changing History: Afro-Cuban Cabildos and Societies of Color in the Nineteenth Century.* Baton Rouge: Louisiana State University Press, 1998.

Montejo Arrechea, Carmen V. "Minerva, A Magazine for Women (and Men) of Color," In *Between Race and Empire,* edited by Lisa Brock and Digna Castañeda Fuentes. Philadelphia: Temple University Press, 1998. Pp. 33–49.

———. *Sociedades de instrucción y recreo de pardos y morenos que existieron en Cuba colonial.* Veracruz: Instituto Veracruzano de Cultura, 1993.

NOTES

1. Pedro Deschamps Chapeaux, *El negro en el periodismo cubano en el siglo XIX* (Havana: Ediciones R., 1963), p. 50.

2. Ibid., p. 101.

3. Jorge Castellanos and Isabel Castellanos, *Cultura afrocubana* (Miami: Ediciones Universal, 1990), 2:254.

4. Alexander von Humboldt, *Ensayo político sobre la Isla de Cuba* (Havana: Publicaciones del Archivo Nacional de Cuba, 1960), pp. 159–193.

5. Jane L. Landers, "Traditions of African American Freedom and Community in Spanish Colonial Florida," in *The African American Heritage of Florida,* ed. David R. Colburn and Jane L. Landers (Gainesville: University Press of Florida, 1955), p. 18.

6. See Gwendolyn Hall, *Africans in Colonial Louisiana: The Development of Afro-Creole Culture in the Eighteenth Century* (Baton Rouge: Louisiana State University Press, 1992); and Kimberly S. Hanger, "Origins of New Orleans' Free Creoles of Color," in *Creoles of Color of the Gulf South,* ed. James H. Dormon (Knoxville: University of Tennessee Press, 1996), pp. 1–27.

7. See María Elena Díaz, *The Virgin, the King, and the Royal Slaves of El Cobre: Negotiating Freedom in Colonial Cuba, 1670–1780* (Stanford: Stanford University Press, 2000); and José Luciano Franco, *Las minas de Santiago del Prado y la rebelión de los cobreros, 1530–1800* (Havana: Editorial de Ciencias Sociales, 1975).

8. See Laird W. Bergad, Fe Iglesias García, and María del Carmen Barcía, *The Cuban Slave Market, 1790–1880* (Cambridge: Cambridge University Press, 1995).

9. "Expediente sobre un memorial de Andrés Flores, comandante del batallón de infantería de milicias de pardos libres, solicitando que no se ponga embarazo alguno a sus hijos para estudiar filosofía y teología y demás actos literarios" of January 18, 1760, in *Colección de documentos para la historia de la formación social de Hispanoamérica, 1493–1810,* ed. Richard Konetzke (Madrid: Consejo Superior de Investigaciones Científicas, 1952–1962), 3:287–292.

10. Alan J. Kuethe, *Cuba 1753–1815: Crown, Military, and Society* (Knoxville: University of Tennessee Press, 1986), pp. 41–44.

11. Franklin W. Knight, *Slave Society in Cuba during the Nineteenth Century* (Madison: University of Wisconsin Press, 1970).

12. Rafael E. Tarragó, "All Humankind Is One: Archbishop Claret and Racism in Nineteenth-Century Cuba," in *Religion and Latin America in the Twenty-First Century: Libraries Reacting to Social Change,* ed. Mark L. Grover. Papers of SALALM XLII, Rockville, Maryland, May 17–21, 1997 (Austin, Tex.: SALALM, 1999), p. 49; see Verena Stolcke, *Marriage, Class, and Colour in Nineteenth-Century Cuba* (Cambridge: Cambridge University Press, 1974).

13. See Robert L. Paquette, *Sugar is Made with Blood: The Conspiracy of La Escalera and the Conflict between Empires over Slavery in Cuba* (Middleton, Conn.: Wesleyan University Press, 1988).

14. Knight, *Slave Society in Cuba,* pp. 154–178.

15. Rebecca Scott, "Explaining Abolition: Contradiction, Adaptation, and Challenge in Cuban Slave Society, 1860–1886," in *Between Slavery and Free Labor: The Spanish-Speaking Caribbean in the Nineteenth Century,* ed. Manuel Moreno Fraginals et al. (Baltimore: Johns Hopkins University Press, 1985), p. 28.

16. See Philip Foner, *Antonio Maceo* (New York: Monthly Review Press, 1977).

17. See Elena Hernán Sandoica, "Rafael María de Labra y Cadrana (1841–1919): una biografía política," *Revista de Indias* 54, no. 200 (1994): 107–136.

18. See Arthur F. Corwin, *Spain and the Abolition of Slavery in Cuba, 1817–1886* (Austin: University of Texas Press, 1967).

19. José Servera, "Introducción," in *Sab,* by Gertrudis Gómez de Avellaneda (Madrid: Cátedra, 1997), pp. 47–48.

20. See Eduardo Torres Cuevas and Eusebio Reyes, *Esclavitud y sociedad: Notas y documentos para la historia de la esclavitud negra en Cuba* (Havana: Editorial de Ciencias Sociales, 1986).

21. Ibid., pp. 247–269.

22. Manuel Moreno Fraginals, *Cuba/España, España/Cuba, Historia común* (Barcelona: Cátedra, Grijalbo Mondadori, 1995), pp. 262–263; Castellanos and Castellanos, *Cultura afrocubana,* 2:257–261.

23. Charles M. Pepper, *To-Morrow in Cuba* (New York: Harper and Brother, 1899), p. 156.

24. See Rebecca J. Scott, *Slave Emancipation in Cuba: The Transition to Free Labor, 1860–1898* (Princeton: Princeton University Press, 1986).

25. Castellanos and Castellanos, *Cultura afrocubana,* 2:257–261.

26. Spain. Congreso de Diputados. *Diario de las Sesiones 1889–90,* no. 133, session of April 9, 1890, pp. 4051–4054.

27. Kuethe, *Cuba 1753–1815,* p. 172; Aline Helg, *Our Rightful Share: The Afro-Cuban Struggle for Equality, 1886–1912* (Chapel Hill: University of North Carolina Press, 1995), pp. 84–85.

28. Rafael Montoro, "Discurso pronunciado en la Junta Magna del Partido Liberal de Cuba celebrada el día 1° de abril de 1882," in *Discursos y escritos,* by Rafael E. Tarragó, ed. Rafael Montoro (Miami: Editorial Cubana, 2000), pp. 6–10; F. A. Conte, *Las aspiraciones del partido Liberal de Cuba* (Havana: Imprenta de A. Alvarez y Compañía, 1892), pp. 197–198.

29. Martín Morúa Delgado, "Factores sociales," in *Obras completas de Martín Morúa Delgado* (Havana: Publicaciones de la Comisión Nacional del Centenario de don Martín Morúa Delgado, 1957), 3:234.

30. Eliseo Giberga, "Apuntes sobre la cuestión de Cuba por un autonomista," in *Obras,* by Eliseo Giberga (Havana: Imprenta y Paperlería de Rambla, Bouza y Ca., 1931), 3:113–117.

31. See Cuba. *Constitución de las Islas de Cuba y Puerto Rico y Leyes Complementarias del Regimen Autonómico* (Havana: Imprenta del Gobierno y Capitanía General por S. M., 1897).

32. *Diario de la Marina,* Edición de la mañana (Havana), August 4, 1900, p. 2; Hon. Orville H. Platt, "Our Relations to the People of Cuba and Porto Rico," *Annals of the American Academy of Political and Social Science* 18 (July–December 1901): 153.

33. See Rafael María de Labra, *La raza de color en Cuba* (Madrid: Establecimiento Tipográfico de Fortanet, 1894).

34. See Ada Ferrer, *Insurgent Cuba: Race, Nation, and Revolution, 1868–1898* (Chapel Hill: University of North Carolina Press, 1999).

35. See Philip A. Howard, *Changing History: Afro-Cuban Cabildos and Societies of Color in the Nineteenth Century* (Baton Rouge: Louisiana State University Press, 1998); Oilda Hevia Lanier, *El Directorio Central de las sociedades negras de Cuba, 1886–1894* (Havana: Editorial de Ciencias Sociales, 1996); and Carmen V. Montejo Arrechea, *Sociedades de instrucción y recreo de pardos y morenos que existieron en Cuba colonial* (Veracruz: Instituto Veracruzano de Cultura, 1993).

36. See Carmen V. Montejo Arrechea, "Minerva, A Magazine for Women (and Men) of Color," in *Between Race and Empire,* ed. Lisa Brock and Digna Castañeda Fuentes (Philadelphia: Temple University Press, 1998), pp. 33–49.

37. Howard, *Changing History,* p. 136.

38. Jorge L. Domínguez, *Cuba: Order and Revolution* (Cambridge: Belknap Press of Harvard University, 1978), p. 24.

39. Castellanos and Castellanos, *Cultura afrocubana,* 2:255.

40. Howard, *Changing History,* p. 184.

6. Identidad afroperuana y exclusión social en el Perú

Teresa Aguilar Velarde

La exposición que haré es una síntesis de investigaciones no sólo externas y académicas, sino también es producto de una investigación permanente interna y profunda sobre mi propia realidad personal vivencial. Considero que los términos identidad y cultura están íntimamente ligados al problema de la exclusión social, de ahí que en la primera parte de mi exposición voy a tratar de definir estos dos conceptos para poder comprender, a partir de ello, el tema que presentaré sobre la realidad e identidad afroperuana y la exclusión social en el Perú. Para ello voy a tomar las definiciones que Adolfo Colombres (argentino, doctor en Derecho y Antropología) plantea.

Identidad

Identidad es aquello con lo cual nos identificamos en el sentido de pertenencia, "hay una identidad personal o individual y otra social o colectiva, es decir de grupo de pertenencia.

La identidad personal es el conjunto de elementos, rasgos y circunstancias que distinguen a una persona de otra en dos niveles: (a) Los datos de su procedencia, edad, hijo de tal . . . , es decir rasgos superficiales, (b) Los datos que dan un juicio de valor y que dan cuenta de la personalidad del individuo.

La identidad social es el conjunto de características que permiten a una sociedad, comunidad o grupo de personas distinguirse de otros, y a los individuos reconocerse o ser reconocidos como miembros del mismo. Esta también se da en dos niveles: (a) Los datos exteriores que permiten nombrar o reconocer a una persona como miembro de un grupo y otro más profundo: (b) Que hace a las características especiales del comportamiento del mismo, y que entrañan juicios de valor.

También cabe distinguir entre la identidad activa y la pasiva. La activa se refiere a la idea que un individuo tiene de sí mismo y a su sentimiento de pertenencia a un grupo social determinado. La identidad pasiva toma el punto de mira de los otros, por lo que importa aquí como es visto". Por ejemplo, "el caso de un indígena o indio, éste puede no sentirse ya indio, renegando de su cultura, pero es visto como indio por los mestizos. Y viceversa, hay quienes reafirman una identidad étnica tras haber completado el proceso de mestizaje cultural, cuando ya los otros han dejado de verlos como indios o se muestran dispuestos a olvidar esta circunstancia. Los desajustes entre un caso y otro conflictúan la vida del individuo, situación que necesita ser trabajada por la psicología social. En el caso del individuo negro, éste será siempre visto como negro haya renegado o no de su cultura y esto conflictuará también su situación, sobre todo en el caso de que haya renegado de ella".

"También hay que hablar de la identidad de status social. Que un individuo no quiera identificarse con el status al que de hecho pertenece (identidad activa o subjetiva), en reconocimiento a una identidad cultural, no quiere decir que se desvincule totalmente de esa identidad, pues los otros lo verán como un miembro, aunque renegado, de la misma (identidad pasiva u objetiva), la que seguirá de un modo u otro determinando su vida real, más allá de las veleidades de su conciencia.

Otro tanto ocurrirá con los que sobredimensionan su identidad de clase o status hasta borrar su identidad étnica o nacional, lo que es como renegar de su propia cultura en nombre de un universalismo abstracto que no llega a conformar una verdadera cultura" (Colombres I: 64–65).

La cultura

"La cultura es algo específicamente humano, un contenido mental que se adquiere por herencia o creación dentro del marco referencial de un grupo determinado. Comprende el conocimiento, la moral, la ley, la costumbre y otras facultades y hábitos adquiridos por el hombre en cuanto miembro de la sociedad—comprende toda clase de comportamiento aprendido—será algo así como el alma de un pueblo, una suma de mito y ciencia que define su identidad específica, que da un sentido a cada hecho y cohesiona a los individuos, motivando a un nivel inconsciente su conducta.

La cultura comprende todos los conocimientos, creencias, costumbres, usos y hábitos propios de una sociedad determinada. Es decir, todo nuestro comportamiento es cultural. También forman parte de la cultura las técnicas que usamos para hacer las cosas: una vivienda, una silla, etc. Comprende la religión, la moral, el orden jurídico, el pensamiento, la lengua, las artes (literatura, teatro, música y danza, pintura, grabado, dibujo, cerámica y alfarería, tejidos, fotografía, video y cine).

Otra dimensión también muy importante son los conocimientos científicos, los aspectos materiales y los espirituales. Toda cultura posee una visión del mundo, en ese sentido la cultura se nos presenta como una totalidad que norma la vida de un grupo humano, pero que está compuesta por una multitud de partes o elementos interrelacionados, que son manifiestos y también cubiertos" (Colombres I: 14).

Ausencia de identidad

Quisiera incluir aquí un término necesario para poder enfatizar el problema de la ausencia de identidad y la exclusión social. Se trata del colonialismo, término utilizado para nombrar una situación histórica ocurrida hace cinco siglos que fue la invasión y dominio físico (territorial), cultural y mental de Occidente sobre América y África y que prevalece hasta hoy bajo la forma de dominio cultural y mental, y cuyo resultado es la ausencia de identidad de los individuos y grupos sociales pertenecientes a estas zonas geográficas.

La ausencia de identidad cultural provocada por el colonialismo, la explotación y la miseria ha producido en los individuos frustraciones, angustias, inadaptaciones y disociaciones que deben convertirse en materia de trabajo de la psicología social. A ésta disciplina le corresponde hacer importantes aportes a una teoría y práctica de la liberación, de la descolonización.

La ausencia de identidad cultural provocada por el colonialismo ha desvinculado al hombre de su pasado, del proceso que había dado hasta entonces el contenido de su identidad. Como bien dice Enrique Iglesias (Presidente del Banco Interamericano de Desarrollo): "Las colectividades que olvidan su historia, son como las personas que pierden la memoria, pierden también su identidad, no saben quiénes son, de dónde vienen, ni para dónde van" (566).

Colombres indica que hoy en día las culturas invadidas por el colonialismo tienen factores de identidad que no tienen un mismo origen, pero que se pueden reunir en cuatro grandes tipos:

1. Elementos de origen precolombino que no sufrieron mayores modificaciones aún.

2. Elementos de origen precolonialista que sufrieron modificaciones en la interacción con la cultura dominante.

3. Elementos introducidos por la cultura dominante.

4. Elementos tomados en préstamo de otras culturas (I: 69).

A menudo una misma persona usa los diferentes patrones de identidad o identificación conforme el medio en que le toca actuar.

La ausencia de identidad con la cultura originaria fuerza a las personas y grupos sociales a conductas imitativas y de encubrimiento como una forma de reducir la discriminación y exclusión social. El colonialismo ha enquistado en las poblaciones sometidas una suerte de subestima que genera desprecio respecto a nuestras culturas originarias, llámense africana o amerindias, y por ende desprecio de unos a otros. Tal como expresa Max Hernández, psicoanalista peruano: "Yo no me siento mejor que usted sino que creo que usted es peor que yo" (6). En este sentido Hernández propone la apertura del diálogo abierto entre todos sobre esta situación. Julio Ortega también toca este tema cuando expresa que "el Perú es un país en el cual un hombre no puede hablar libremente a otro. Interferida por los prejuicios raciales y sociales, la comunicación se torna jerárquica, sospechosa, recusatoria" (7). Se trata de un racismo y exclusión muy sútil.

Los africanos en la historia del Perú

La población africana llegó al Perú con la conquista española y adoptó con el devenir de los años la identidad criolla (devenida del proceso de independencia de los actuales estado-naciones), olvidando y enterrando su pasado africano, quedando así atrapada en una suerte de sociedad que la relega a papeles sociales de segunda y tercera. Categoría que no le permite logros significativos ante la cultura dominante y que, por otro lado, la aleja del otro gran sector humano victimado por el colonialismo: la población autóctona devenida en indígena. Es más, en muchos casos de la historia la población negra en el Perú ha sido por obligación, o por coerción, el medio a través del cual se subyugó al indígena, naciendo de ahí un odio racial y cultural, y un desprecio de unos a otros.

La población negra en la ciudad asumió la identidad de su amo criollo pero no llega a ser igual que él. Existe un refrán absolutamente racista y excluyente, que aunque hoy en día poco se escucha, su contenido ha quedado grabado en la mentalidad de quienes lo crearon y de quienes lo recibieron (la población afroperuana) y que ilustra de una manera muy precisa la relación amo y criollo: "Aunque el mono se vista de seda, mono se queda".

Identidad afroperuana o afroindia

En la actualidad encontramos una corriente de afroperuanos que empezamos a ver como factores de identidad no sólo el África como continente originario, sino también América con su población autóctona e indígena como parte de nuestra historia y cultura local y como parte de nuestra realidad biológica. Cómo diría Juan Mariátegui (doctor en Derecho y Ciencias Políticas y profesor de la Universidad de Argelia): "La sociedad es poco sensible al tema y debe ser más motivada, primero se debe estudiar África en su contexto y problemática para luego adentrarnos en la relación cultural con el Perú" (5).

La mujer negra

Producto de la discriminación racial y social, las mujeres negras solemos tener baja autoestima y un concepto subvaluado y distorsionado de nuestra realidad biológica, específicamente sexual. Aquí tres testimonios que pueden ayudarnos a distinguir estos problemas.

- *Susana Baca (cantante y cultora de la música afroperuana):* "No es fácil tener negra la piel en Lima. Y era más difícil en los tiempos en que Susana Baca era niña. Además, pobre. Cuando estudiaba la primaria en un colegio público llegó una profesora a enseñar ballet clásico. Preguntó quienes tenían talento para la danza. Maestros y alumnas señalaron a Susana Baca. Susanita baila lindo, lo hace en todas las actuaciones, y no se chupa, dijeron. Hasta que llegó el momento de la selección. Tú no, tú si, tú no. Susana Baca no estaba entre las elegidas.

Miró a su alrededor y descubrió que las desterradas eran todas como ella: cholas y negras con el rostro prieto del color local.

Falté dos días al colegio. Me quedaba jugando por ahí, caminando, sola. No lloraba, pero por dentro me moría de la pena. Me miraba al espejo—tendría unos diez años, no más—y me daba cólera ser negra" (14).

- Mónica Carrillo (miembro de la revista *Voces Negras*): "Me han dicho que las negras son buenas para curar los riñones. . . . A las chicas de tu 'color' no les queda el pantalón rojo, se les ve muy escandalosas (comentario de una vendedora de ropa).

  Creemos importante rescatar 'lo erótico como poder', como dice la escritora Audre Lordre. Es necesario convencerse de que lo erótico entendido como un recurso profundamente femenino y espiritual significa la afirmación de una energía creativa que permite compartir el goce físico, emocional, espiritual o intelectual, es decir, es el disfrute de la vida misma. . . . La noción de la sexualidad de la mujer negra ha sido vulgarizada, corrompida y satanizada a lo largo de los años por la sociedad, los medios de comunicación e incluso confundida por las propias mujeres que no han descubierto su real significado" (5).

- *Elsa Velásquez Zamudio (abogada y educadora):* "Me recibí de maestra en 1943 y de abogada en 1946. En ese sentido soy la primera mujer negra, de color oscuro, en alcanzar tal situación. El lograrlo no ha sido fácil, tanto por el hecho de ser mujer, como por ser negra. La mujer negra tiene con respecto al hombre negro, la desventaja agravada de ser mujer y negra. En la época en que yo estudié, el ser mujer, universitaria o profesional era un caso insólito.

  En el Perú, existe un racismo de hecho, que por el caso de ser de hecho se vuelve oficial. Es un racismo presente en las actitudes, en los comportamientos y en las valoraciones de muchas de las autoridades estatales. El pueblo copia e imita este racismo.

  Pienso que no puede existir una democracia sólida cuando los ciudadanos son discriminados por el color de su piel, sus ideas o cualquier otro motivo. Creo, además, que la pobreza y el desempleo son hoy los mecanismos a partir de los cuales se priva a los negros y la mujer de iguales oportunidades, se perpetúa el racismo contra nosotros. Superar el racismo implica, entonces, una gran dosis de humanidad y realismo. En ese sentido, creo que la labor de los medios de comunicación e información es realmente vital para superarlo" (53).

El problema de la educación

La educación ha jugado y juega hasta hoy un rol muy importante. La educación es uno de los vehículos a través del cual se produce el proceso de aculturación, de pérdida de la identidad y de exclusión social. Es una educación que no reconoce la existencia de población negra, su historia y devenir en su verdadera magnitud.

Las propuestas educativas por bien intencionadas que sean, no resuelven la forma de aplicar una educación con reconocimiento y respecto a la diversidad y pluralidad cultural que permita una revaloración de la misma. Es una educación que aún da como resultado la "integración" a un modelo de sociedad con patrones establecidos y no superados mentalmente de dominio y exclusión.

Por falta de acceso a la educación y por ser esta negadora de nuestra historia, existen en el Perú muy pocas historias de negros contadas por negros, nuestras propias experiencias que sirvan de referente y ello se debe a la desidentidad en lo africano e identidad forzada y como mecanismo de supervivencia en lo criollo. Se debe a la escasa existencia de intelectuales afroperuanos que hablemos y escribamos a nombre propio del problema.

La integración cultural latinoamericana

La ansiada integración cultural latinoamericana no podrá realmente efectuarse si no se logra recuperar la memoria histórica e identidad de las culturas que conforman Latinoamérica, fundamentalmente las de raíces indígenas (andinas y amazónicas) y la de raíz africana en América. Como bien señala Enrique Iglesias (Presidente del BID), "el progreso sin identidad es canto de sirena que no lleva a buen puerto . . . , debemos apoyar nuestro desarrollo económico y político en nuestra cultura, estimarla en lo que vale, quererla y convertirla en aliada principal de nuestro devenir histórico". "Es preciso asumir la necesidad de conformar un 'agenda social' de la integración, que destaque la prioridad que merece el tema cultural y la recuperación de la memoria histórica" (566).

Hacia la promoción cultural

Desde esta perspectiva Colombres plantea "sólo la cultura puede dar al progreso una dirección, una razón de ser" (II: 13), entendiéndose que se habla de la cultura en un sentido antropológico, y no sólo del arte. La práctica de la promoción cultural para la recuperación de la identidad y la lucha contra la exclusión social, debe darse a través de cinco niveles fundamentales:

- Rescate
- Sistematización
- Difusión
- Desarrollo
- Defensa de la cultura.

Rol de los profesionales que manejamos información (bibliotecólogos, documentalistas y archivistas)

Para desarrollar la promoción cultural que nos lleve a la recuperación de la memoria histórica y a combatir la exclusión social, se necesita del concurso de todos los que hemos tomado conciencia del problema. En el caso de los manejadores de información necesitamos su cooperación para reconstruir nuestra cultura, nuestra historia y ponernos de pie, y en igualdad de condiciones ofrecer al mundo nuestra alternativa cultural como posibilidad vivencial, que no es otra cosa que una propuesta de vida más humana y, cuando no, permitir que vivamos en libertad y respeto de la diversidad y pluralidad.

Con el apoyo de la investigación, recopilación de materiales e información obtenida debemos (como señala Juan Mariátegui) "impulsar la creación de cátedras del tema así como se han formado cátedras de estudios orientales", pues "los medios de comunicación transmiten una imagen negativa, deformada, no venden la cultura sólo la pobreza" (5). Debemos impulsar la creación de bibliotecas y centros de información y cultura afroindianos en las ciudades y zonas rurales y, fomentar el cambio en los contenidos y formas educativas.

Conclusión

La población afroperuana no disfruta correspondencia o correlato alguno en nuestra sociedad, que no sea la invisibilidad o, en su defecto, el reconocimiento de nuestra existencia sólo como ciudadanos de segunda y tercera categoría. Algunos intelectuales nos "reconocen" como población que pertenecemos a una "subcultura", es decir, somos subestimados. La gran mayoría de afroperuanos viven en condiciones de mucha pobreza sin posibilidad de salir de ella. Los últimos aportes de intelectuales oficiales hablan de nuestra pertenencia a un "lejano origen africano", pretendiendo quitarnos de esta manera nuestro derecho a reencontrarnos con nuestra cultura originaria africana para superar la baja autoestima y recobrar nuestra memoria histórica y nuestra personalidad cultural. Somos muy pocos aún los que hemos tenido y tenemos acceso a la educación, y a espacios desde donde podemos de alguna forma pacífica luchar contra esta injusticia histórica-social, luchar por recobrar y defender legítimamente nuestra identidad y personalidad cultural. Las organizaciones de afroperuanos en la forma de ONGs, sufren todavía la discriminación y subestimación (de la capacidad intelectual, de organización y conducción de la misma) por parte de instituciones que apoyan el desarrollo, y no logran, por falta de medios, cumplir con sus objetivos de educación de líderes, de alfabetización e investigación de nuestra realidad histórica y actual, de recuperación de nuestra identidad y en general, de ingreso con una personalidad cultural propia, a una sociedad que hasta la actualidad nos excluye.

BIBLIOGRAFIA

Baca, Susana. "Jaque de reina". *El Comercio* (9 de enero de 2001): 14.

Carrillo, Mónica. "Dicen que estoy brillante . . . ". *Voces Negras* (Asociación Negra de Defensa y Promoción de los Derechos Humanos) 1: 1: 5.

Colombres, Adolfo. *Manual del promotor cultural.* 3a. ed. Buenos Aires: Ediciones Colihue, 1997.

Hernández, Max. "Los peruanos tenemos muy baja autoestima". *El Dominical/Diario El Comercio* (15 de octubre de 2000): 6–7.

Iglesias, Enrique. *Cambio y crecimiento en América Latina 1988–1998: ideas y acciones.* Washington, D.C.: Banco Interamericano de Desarrollo, 1999.

Mariátegui, Juan. "Existe una gran necesidad de cátedras sobre estudios africanos". *Voces Negras* (Asociación Negra de Defensa y Promoción de los Derechos Humanos) 1/1 (2001?): 5.

Ortega, Julio. "Leer hoy *Los Ríos Profundos*". *El Dominical/Diario El Comercio* (19 de noviembre de 2000): 6–7.

Velarde, Federico. "La sociedad civil en el Perú: estudios y propuestas". Documento interno de consultoría para el BID, Lima, 2000.

Velásquez Zamudio, Elsa. "Desigualdad dentro de la desigualdad". *IDEELE* 81 (noviembre 1995): 53.

Identity, Gender, and Sexuality

7. *Actos prohibidos:* Documenting Sexuality in Colonial Mexico from Documents in the Latin American Library, Tulane University

Guillermo Náñez-Falcón

Spanish colonial documents provide a rich font for the study of sexuality. In a society in which church and state exerted control over almost every aspect of peoples' lives and proscriptions existed against many types of behavior; civil, criminal, and ecclesiastical judicial records contain countless cases in which individuals appeared before authorities for one alleged transgression or another. Colonial America was a highly legalistic world. Spanish officials and church authorities, often Inquisition courts, thoroughly investigated each case and transcribed evidence uncovered in meticulous detail. Files for each case included related documents that spanned the entire period of the litigation. These files, or *legajos,* often comprised dozens of stamped-paper pages of text. Scholars are uncovering in these materials an extensive documentary resource for the study of gender relations and sexual behavior in Spanish colonies.

In the Latin American Library at Tulane University, there are several thousand legajos from colonial Mexico that cover the period from the mid-1500s to the early independence period. The library purchased the manuscripts in the early 1930s from dealers and collectors in Mexico. The collection does not constitute a real "archive" in the sense that the documents do not have an organic unity. Rather it is an artificial, "created" collection of disparate, though historically valuable, documents from all parts of Mexico. The purpose of this paper is to examine a corpus of cases that relate to commission of acts prohibited by law or that in other ways document the sexual mores of colonial Mexico. The documents themselves touch upon varied themes that historians have investigated, such as status, power, prestige, and church-state relations, but this paper only focuses on the issue of sexuality. All the documents that I cite are in the Viceregal and Ecclesiastical Mexican Collection (VEMC). There are similar documents in other colonial collections at Tulane, with many in the Greenleaf Mexican Inquisition transcriptions. Manuscript collections at Duke, Yale, the Benson, the Bancroft, and other repositories also have extensive collections of colonial Latin American documents.

A frequent theme in the documentation is that of the seduced and abandoned woman, and ecclesiastical courts sometimes interceded on the woman's behalf. In Saltillo in 1729, Nicolasa del Castillo appeared before the *Cura Vicario y Juez Eclesiástico* Joseph de la Garza to request the apprehension of Antonio de los Cobos, a mestizo.[1] The deponent swore that Cobos betrayed her with a promise of marriage. She became pregnant, and then he abandoned her. The judge questioned Cobos, who declared that he owed Nicolasa nothing and did not want to marry her. Testimony showed that Cobos had pursued Nicolasa "day and night"; consequently, the judge ordered him to marry her.

Girls in Saltillo seemed to have had trouble with their boyfriends in 1729. María de Villalobos appeared before ecclesiastical authorities demanding that Antonio de Villalón, a Spaniard, be incarcerated.[2] He had seduced her with a promise to marry and then refused to do so. Before the authorities, Villalón declared that he merely entered the girl's house to ask for grapes and a little *aguardiente*. He refused to marry the girl "aunque lo aorcasa su merced." The Juez Eclesiástico ordered Villalón to be put in the public jail and the girl in a secure home while authorities investigated the case. In a subsequent deposition Villalón asked to be set free and blamed "la conocida pasión del denunsiante." He asked witnesses to declare whether they had seen him commit "algunas demonstraciones pecaminosas" or other actions to have warranted the charges. The judges further examined María, who then admitted that Villalón seduced her without promising to marry her. When she discovered that she was pregnant, Villalón said that he would marry her if she had a son and that he, and no other man, was the father. As a pledge, he gave her a gift of some ribbons. The judges finally ordered Villalón to be released under guarantee of two bondsmen. In a closing statement, María swore that Villalón had not promised to marry her.

Church authorities in 1727 issued an order to Cathalina de Nieves, alias "la China," and her parents to leave Saltillo within six days and to settle at least thirty leagues away from the city under threat of being excommunicated and jailed.[3] The reason for the banishment was that "se experimentan grabes ynquietudes entre algunos casados vecinos de dha villa" and the aforesaid Cathalina. It was charged that her parents had made no effort to stop her scandalous behavior. Cathalina's father, Juan de Arellano y Nieves, came to his daughter's defense with a sworn statement "sobre haversele ymputado y falsamente calumniado." Doña Lucía de Treviño, a rich woman and wife of Martín de la Peña, was the author of the charges against Cathalina. The Peñas had a house across the street from that of the Nieves family. Cathalina's father presented a number of witnesses who swore that Sra. Treviño was a very jealous woman and that her suspicious hostility was the motivation for her false accusations.

The case lasted a year, but finally testimonies convinced officials that Cathalina was innocent. The *Promotor Fiscal* rescinded the order "para que pueda libremente restituirse a la villa de Saltillo su Patria en compañía de sus padres." The taint on Cathalina's and the family's reputation persisted, however. The order gave the Nieves family permission to continue living in their house across the street from the Peñas, on condition: "se les apresiba cuiden a su hija para que viba onestamente y sin dar la menor nota, ni escandalo porque de lo contrario se prosedera contra ellos por todo rigor de derecho."

Church and state control over society created a situation in which false accusations provided a person an opportunity to get even with a rival or enemy. In a similar case, in Mexico City in 1763, doña María de Salas, *doncella española,* daughter of Francisco Martín de Salas, Alcalde Mayor of Acayucán, appeared before government authorities to demand that her father's black slave, María de la Trinidad, be brought before them to answer certain questions under oath.[4] The first question was whether or not her mistress was a virgin. Trinidad stated that her mistress was indeed a virgin. The slave explained that her master had locked her up in a room from which she had escaped through a window. She had gone to the rectory of the church and, upon knocking, was admitted inside. She had later become intimate with Lieutenant General Antonio Guerrero in the army barracks. He had promised freedom to her, if she were to tell people that her mistress was having relations with the priest Patricio de Herrera. Church authorities removed Trinidad from the barracks and, after she attested that she had spoken falsely, ecclesiastical officials ordered her to a convent. The documents do not provide motives for the lieutenant's prompting Trinidad to impugn the reputation of her mistress. If ecclesiastical authorities also questioned Guerrero, his testimony is not in the file.

Religious officials could also be guilty of making false charges of sexual misconduct for reasons of their own. In 1795 in Mérida, Yucatán, Bishop Fray Luis de Piña y Masa paid a pastoral visit to doña María Antonio del Castillo y Aguirre, Condesa viuda de Miraflores, during which he exhorted her to cease her scandalous relationship with the *Teniente Auditor de Guerra* don Fernando Gutiérrez de Piñeres.[5]

> [L]e amoasté corrigiese su conducta en la familiar correspondencia con el Licenciado don Fernando Gutiérrez de Piñeres, y obiase el continuo escandalo y mal exemplo con que toda esta [ciudad] está expuesta â la voracidad de la carne . . . [y] repito por segunda, y ultima vez, se separe en lo absoluto, de la comunicacion y asistencia del nominado Licenciado don Fernando.

The highborn widow, unintimidated by the bishop's warning, responded defiantly to defend herself. She was a widow and had a son old enough to marry. In her household lived eighteen or twenty persons and, if anyone acted scandalously she would put them out on the street. The gentleman had been in the house for *tertulias* at which were present a number of other respectable persons, including several important churchmen, whom she named in the document. The case escalated, and at one point the lieutenant invoked the *Recurso de Fuerza.* The Governor General Arturo O'Neill became involved on the side of the lieutenant. Testimony finally revealed that the bishop may have been resentful of the charges Gutiérrez made against the bishop's nephew in the murder of Governor Lucas de Gálvez.

The testimony of witnesses about the widow's conduct of her private affairs is revealing of behavior of elites and of what constituted "scandalous" behavior. The bishop called witnesses and asked each of them the same questions, which he worded to elicit the incriminating responses he wanted. Answers ranged from "hán continuado en la amistad con mayor disipacion" to the more explicit "lo han visto pasar lo mas del día, y en la noche en la casa de dicha señora bebiendo, y cenando allí en traje familiar, y domestico, de chupita y chinelas . . . les han visto algunas veces juntos como marido y muger paseandose en calesa, de noche," and riding through the Plaza Mayor on Sundays to attend mass together. The widow's servants even washed, ironed, and sewed the lieutenant's clothes. The widow, a colonial Florence Nightingale, attended to and nursed the lieutenant during an illness, entering his bedroom alone, unaccompanied by servants. The bishop may have had reason to be suspicious, but laymen bested the church in this case.

Priests also faced accusations of illicit behavior and concubinage. In 1789, Manuel de Flon, the intendant of Puebla, denounced the *Cura y Juez Eclesiástico de la Doctrina* Francisco Garrido before the archbishop of Mexico, accusing Garrido of being habitually drunk and living in concubinage with doña María Magdalena Fresnero, who it was alleged had borne him two children.[6] Civil and ecclesiastical authorities carried out separate investigations, gathering testimony from witnesses as to the conduct of the priest. Twenty witnesses appeared before the intendant. The testimony, often hearsay, varied from "es cierto y de publico notorio, que se halla amancebado y que tiene los dos hijos, como tambien su ebriedad" to "Doña Magdalena vibe en el curato, como tambien un niño . . . , que nada consta de que esten amanbecados." As to the drunkenness, witnesses had heard speak of this, and some declared that he drank occasionally but was not a drunkard: "lo ha visto tomar sus tragitos, pero que no lo ha visto tirado de remate borracho." A number of fellow priests testified on Garrido's behalf. They praised his high moral life "[de] ser un sugeto de total arreglo, muy caritativo, y exacto al cumplimeniento de su obligacion. Y siendo cierto, que el buen exemplo, y perfeccion de vida es el argumento mas fuerte (especialmente para los filigreses) para fundar el honor y fama de un sugeto de las expresadas excelencias." Both the archbishop and the viceroy, the Conde de Revillagigedo, absolved Garrido and restored him to his parish. The archbishop admonished him, however, "apercivi seriamente que se abstenga de toda comunicacion con la muger que se cita, y del uso de todo licor."

A priest, in the confessional, exerted great power over his faithful parishioners, over women in particular. There are numerous cases of abuse of this power. In 1783, the Office of the Inquisition published an edict addressed to all priests, prelates, and confessors in New Spain, Guatemala, Nicaragua, and

the Philippines that reiterated what had been decreed in earlier pronounce-
ments issued in 1668, 1679, and 1713.[7] Confessional booths were to have a
dividing partition to prevent accidental touching of the feet, and the openings
of the grid of the lattice window were to be so small that fingers could not be
inserted from one side to the other. Confessional booths were not to be situated
in dark or solitary places. Confessors were mandated not to greet a penitent in a
familiar manner or to have any personal conversations with one before or after
confession. These casual contacts, the decree stated, are "portillos, que abren
la malicia, y el demonio para las ilusiones del corazon, y para que se hagan tal
vez citas, ofertas, ô expresiones, que efectuadas aunque en diferentes sitios, y
tiempos, no dexan duda de que tuvieron principio en el Confesionario, y que
las dictó en èl un espíritu reprobado y maldito." Priests were not to hear confessions of women after sunset or at night, except by special dispensation.

In the mid-seventeenth century, in Manila, several women reported
having been spoken to and touched improperly in the confessional by Fray
Plácido de Ángulo, a member of the Dominican order.[8] The women ranged
in age from about fourteen to thirty. The Inquisition received testimony as
early as 1647 that Fray Plácido had been committing transgressions against his
female parishioners. His approach was strikingly similar in each instance. The
widow Andrea de Guillestigui related that Fray Plácido had sent a boy to her
house to call her to the Church of Santo Domingo. When she arrived, he was in
the confessional, and she "se sento de rodiallas, no con animo de confessarse,
sino para saber loqel Pe. Queria, y estando en esta forma, el Pe. Sentado en
el Confessonario, y ella de rodillas, y Pe. La persuadio, a que tubiessen mala
amistad." Sometime later, he again propositioned her: "Y en virtud de esto, fue
dho Pe a casa de esta declarte a persuadirla, que ofendiesse a Dios con el."

In 1652, de Ángulo was called before the Inquisition in Manila "por aver
hablado en el confesonario con mugeres palabras obcenas." He was age thirty-
seven, he said, a native of Córdova, and had lived in the Philippines for twenty-
seven years. During his first years he was a missionary among the *Indios,*
working at their conversion. His behavior, which he attributed to his youth (he
was in his early twenties at the time), had caused him problems, and he had
been summoned by the Holy Office. He had reformed "Como en mis primeros
años de ministro, y venido a esta tierra, me avia valido del lugar santo del confesonario, para hablar y dexar me hablasen algunas mujeres, materias de livi-
andad y prohibidas." He was defensive in placing blame for his transgressions
and blamed some of his problems on the commissioner of the Inquisition, Fray
Francisco de Paula, who de Ángulo said was "uno de los hombres mas o pues-
tos a mi sangre condicion y trato de quantos e tratado en mi vida y con quien
desde que entre enestas yslas hasta oy assido notoria nra poca sin bolicacion."
The commissioner issued an edict of excommunication and ordered the priest
be sent to the Inquisition in Mexico City to be tried.

De Ángulo remained defensive and defiant before the judges of the Holy Office in Mexico. In the court of the Inquisition, an officer read the charges in great detail and with formal legality. The judge then ordered that the priest be tortured until he admitted to the charges against him and confessed to other sins that he may have committed. The file, unfortunately, is incomplete and ends in mid-sentence, so the outcome of the case of Fray Plácido de Ángulo is unknown. Given the gravity of his violations, he could expect no leniency.

As late as 1819, the Inquisition was still hearing cases of solicitation by priests in the confessional. In February of that year, in Durango, officers of the *Santo Oficio* questioned Juana María Noriega, age thirty, "doncella de calidad Española," about the behavior of her confessor, *Presbitero Secular* Juan Guevara.[9] In confessing to another priest, she had related what had occurred on several occasions with Guevara, and the priest said that he could not absolve her until she went before the Holy Office. She related to the Inquisitors that Guevara had made insinuating remarks and sexual overtures to her during confession. He had asked her if she thought of marrying and, when she responded no, "le propuso que si queria irse á su casa quando la pusiera aqui, ó donde se proporsionara, y que hiciera cuenta que el era su Padre, su marido, y su madre, que si le daria gusto en todo, que si alguna ocacion le pegaba habria de ir contenta haciendole algun cariño, abrazandolo." Innocent, or concupiscent, Juana María acceded, as long as what they did was not offensive in the eyes of God. He had a ready answer, "Que todo eso no era malo; que los Santos dormian juntos, y no tenian hijos; que la noche que quiciera ir a su cama diciendole Padresito, ya vengo á acompañar á VM." Where could they go? He lived in the bishop's house, and they could go there.

Juana María gave more details. The officers of the Inquisition asked her what particular words Guevara used. She replied that "á la pila del agua bendita le dixo dame la mano, y que habiendosela dado la tubo agarrada diciendo algunas palabras que ella no entendio." Under further interrogation, she was more specific. Questioned about similar behavior of Guevara with other women, she answered that she had heard Dominga Villanueva say that Guevara had also made overtures to her. The document is only the testimony of Juana María Noriega, given during several sessions. There is no record of the questioning of the priest by the Inquisition, or of the sentence that the court of the Holy Office passed on him. The commissioner of the Inquisition who had conducted the inquiry appended a defense of Guevara's character, which was contrary to that given by the woman. He had known the accused since Guevara was a boy, the commissioner said, and had heard his confession many times over the years, "y no he advertido en sus conversasiones libertinaje, ni desarreglo alguno."

The power of the confessional and of the clerical habit gave a priest an opportunity to act out his fantasies or obsessions with the women who came to him for absolution. One of the most unusual documents in the Latin American Library archive is the file on a Franciscan friar in Puebla, Fray Juan

Francisco del Valle.[10] In 1779, he came before the Santo Oficio to be tried for a "notoria transgresion de las Bulas Pontíficas expedidas contra solicitantes." The offenses that resulted in the charges, multiple testimonies documented, were that he had administered corporeal punishment as absolution on the bare flesh of young female penitents who came to his confessional. An odd element in this case is that the friar's actions had gone unreported and unchecked for fifteen years before the Inquisition began its investigation.

The court asked the friar if he knew why he was being held in the *cárceles secretas*. He replied that it was over his relationship with female penitents "en el hecho de mandarles en el mismo acto del sacramto antes, y despues en el confesionario, y qe se diciplinasen de mano agena en las asentaderas à carnes descubiertas, y à algunas por mano del confesante . . . todo con el fin de deleytarse, y satisfazer a la pasion lividinosa qe le dominava." While committing these sins, he told the court, he had been plagued by an epidemic of fleas but, since entering the secret jails of the Inquisition, the fleas miraculously disappeared.

He began the practice of administering physical punishment to female penitents in Puebla in 1763, when he was in his mid-twenties, at the Franciscan church with a doncella española Ángela Francisca Patiño, whose confessions he heard until 1776. He persuaded her "que se havia de dejar azotar de mano del Confesante en la parte posterior, y a carnes descubiertas." He could not recall how many times he had heard the lady's confession in this manner. Between August 1777 and May 1778, he visited the lady at her house and there carried out his punishment "a luz clara."

Fray Juan Francisco's confession continued. He gave the names of other penitents, and certain patterns emerged. The women were all doncellas españolas; the acts took place in the church, sometimes in the confessional, behind the altar, or in an alcove; relationships that he developed with the penitents lasted for several years, although in a few cases girls stopped going to him for confession, "pr temor de pecar contra la castidad" through his punishment of them; and with each whipping he uttered words about the vileness of the part of the body that he was striking, and he made the women repeat the words. As his obsession intensified, he would instruct two sisters or cousins to flagellate themselves at home, speaking the words he taught them, and then to return to his confessional to relate to him what they had done. In about 1777, he began to hear the confessions of nuns in the convents of Santa Clara, San Juan, and Santa Isabel. It was about this time that he moved to Toluca, where he continued his practices. The Inquisition, not satisfied to have on record only the statement of the accused, gathered graphic testimony from many of the women who had been involved with him, and their words are transcribed in the file.

One can feel the fury and indignation of Dr. Antonio Bergora y Jordán, the chief prosecutor of the Inquisition, as he addressed Fray Juan Francisco. The priest had solicited the daughters of God before and after confession "para saciar sus torpes apetitos, traeindo capa de sus libiandedes à tan purissimo sacramto . . . conviertiendoles . . . en veneno, en el vazo del Demonio pa perderlas con notoria transgresion del las Bulas Pontíficas expedidas contra solicitantes." For these "abominable acts," the judge branded him a heretic and an apostate.

The transcript of the actual trial is not part of the file, but the chief prosecutor dictated how the Inquisition was to proceed. Self-confession was not reason for leniency. If the case against him was not proven to the satisfaction of the tribunal, "pido qe este reo sea puesto a question de tormento en el qe esté, y persevere y se repita en su persona todas las veces, qe necesario fuere hasta tanto, qe diga, y confiese enteramente la verdad." Under the prescribed torture, the accused had to demonstrate that he was truly penitent, to seek God's forgiveness for all the offenses that he had committed, and to accept with resignation whatever punishment was imposed on him.

Our final case concerns the commission of the *pecado nefando* by an oblate, Beato Juan de la Asumpción, about age thirty, and a fifteen-year-old *mulatillo blanco,* Francisco Servando, in Tecpán in 1725.[11] Indian villagers discovered the lay brother and the boy in a chapel that was under construction at the Calvario in the act of committing sodomy. The villagers tied up the two, whipped the mulatto boy, and took the two to the house of the *Alcalde.*

The following day, five villagers of Tecpán testified before a judge in their native language through an interpreter. Their accounts were full of explicit details, which the notary transcribed faithfully. They had discovered the oblate on his hands and knees on the ground, his habit over his head, and his underwear at his feet. The mulatto "was playing the part of a man with a woman." They were "like two dogs," one of the villagers commented. Before the judge, the Beato admitted having partaken of the act, but insisted that it was the only time in his life that he had done this. He was asked if he knew the gravity of the crime of which he was accused and of others that he may have committed. He replied that he did not know. Did he not know "con que a los putos los queman?" He refused to answer. The young mulatto stated that the oblate had been following him around for several days and had brought him to the Calvario with deceit and the offer of a real. After entering the chapel under construction, the older man pressed him against the wall and initiated intimacies, which the young man described. The Alcalde then ordered soldiers to escort the two to the Royal Prison in Mexico City, where they were to be tried on criminal charges.

In Mexico City, Judge Francisco de Barbadillo Bitonea ordered the accused placed in separate cells in the dungeon of the Royal Prison. They were not allowed to communicate with each other or with anyone else, and they were guarded by soldiers day and night. The judge ordered several *Maestros cirujanos* to examine both of the accused for evidence that they had committed the *delito nefando*. The doctors reported that there was not sufficient evidence four days after the alleged act. The accused then came separately before the *Real Sala del Crimen* for questioning by the judges.

The oblate, now called Juan de Castro, his given name, was recalcitrant through several sessions of questions. He did not know why he was taken prisoner, he insisted. Did he not admit "que havia hecho dha picardia?" "Que picardia?" he asked obstinately. The questioning that followed was a long courtroom drama, with the accused maintaining silence, feigning a loss of memory, or in the end making distorted admissions under repeated questioning on the same matter. Asked in numerous ways what had happened, he finally whispered, "[me] metio un poco el miembro . . . pero que fue mui poco." He insisted that the mulatto was the instigator. "How can a young boy like Servando force a grown man like you to commit such a crime?" He was silent. The court told him that his silence was proof of his guilt and ordered that his first statement, made in Tecpán, be read into the record. The questioning of the young man was also thorough. His replies were full of prevarications, and what he answered was inconsistent from his statement in Tecpán, but the court pressed for the truth. Unfortunately, there is not enough time to cover this part of the investigation in greater detail.

At this point, the case becomes complicated by the Beato's invocation of the ecclesiastical *fuero*. As an oblate, he said, he lived in the convent of the Charitable Order of San Hipólito. Although he had not taken vows, he wore the habit and tonsure of the order. The court, however, had testimony that the accused had come to the convent of his own volition, and only four months before. The Prior General of the order wrote to the court to demand the release of "Juan de la Asumpción" to be judged in an ecclesiastical court. The fiscal ruled that "Juan de Castro" was a self-accused and convicted criminal and rejected the jurisdiction of ecclesiastical fuero in this case. The documentation of the criminal trial and sentence are not part of the file.

Conclusion

The documents that I have presented here can have many different interpretations. Scholars, such as Asunción Lavrin, have used this type of material for their studies. There are also questions among historians of what the written testimony means, and its veracity.

For this venue, I do not want to dissect the documents, but rather to conclude with a proposal to the members of SALALM. A number of institutions in the United States have collections of valuable colonial materials. The provenance of these documents is often unknown. Since, in some instances, the legajos are incomplete, are only a part of a larger file that has been separated, I have often speculated whether the companion sections may be in some other North American library. I propose to the curators of Latin American collections and SALALM libraries to begin to study the possibility of constructing a central database of colonial documentary collections in this country. The database can include references to place of origin, the names of the principal participants, and the general subject covered. The availability on microfilm of the Yale collection, for instance, gives impetus to the filming of similar collections and of creating a database that will provide researchers access to documents in other repositories.

NOTES

1. Viceregal and Ecclesiastical Mexican Collection (VEMC), Legajo 59, Expediente 37.

2. VEMC, Legajo 59, Expediente 18.

3. VEMC, Legajo 41, Expediente 35.

4. VEMC, Legajo 74, Expediente 44.

5. VEMC, Legajo 50, Expedientes 1, 2.

6. VEMC, Legajo 15, Expediente 3; Legajo 28, Expediente 16.

7. VEMC, Legajo 74, Expediente 8.

8. VEMC, Legajo 33, Expediente 1.

9. VEMC, Legajo 41, Expediente 50.

10. VEMC, Legajo 8, Expediente 48.

11. VEMC, Legajo 57, Expediente 30.

8. Sexuality and Gender in Colonial and Nineteenth-Century Mexico: New Uses and Interpretations of Photographs in the Tulane Collection

Paul Bary

In November 2001, Professor Robert Irwin hosted a conference at Tulane on sexuality and gender issues arising from the scandal of the "Famous 41" *maricones,* who were arrested by Mexico City police during a November 17, 1901, raid on a party attended by men, many of whom were dressed as women. The scandal incited an explosion of the nascent discourse of homosexuality at a time when modernist poets, naturalist novelists, positivist social scientists, scandal sheet illustrators, and journalists and their readers had become fascinated with issues of sexuality. In this paper I will use the scandal of the Famous 41 as a jumping-off point to discuss some broader historical issues of sexuality and gender in Mexico.

To accompany the conference, Professor Irwin created an exhibit of some fifty photographic representations of gender and sexuality in Latin America, including the twelve images I will discuss. Irwin's virtual exhibit is entitled "Galería de fotos: género y sexualidad en América Latina," and is located at http://www.tulane.edu/~rirwin/picturegallery/index.html. In gathering materials for the exhibit, Irwin received the generous assistance of the Benson Latin American Collection at the University of Texas, which lent newspapers and broadsides, including a José Guadalupe Posada broadside with a banner headline that evokes the scandal surrounding the public discovery of large-scale homosexuality in Mexican society: "Los 41 Maricones Encontrados en un baile de la Calle de la Paz . . . Aquí están los Maricones Muy Chulos y Coquetones." The image of that broadside was used on the conference's "Call for Papers."

All of the photographs cited are housed in the Photographic Archive of the Latin American Library at Tulane University. Six images are from the Pedro Guerra Collection and show people in social and occupational settings in Mérida and elsewhere in Yucatán. Four images are from the Cruces y Campa Collection of cartes-de-visites and show Mexican men, women, and children in a diversity of occupations. These four images were taken by Antíoco Cruces and Luis Campa, who were well-known Mexican photographers in the late-nineteenth century. The image of the priest is from the CIRMA Collection of

Juan Yas and José D. Noriega Photographs of Guatemalans in social settings, and was taken by these two early Guatemalan photographers between 1880 and 1940. Lastly, the photograph of the woman bullfighter is from the "Album of Mexico," by C. Lambert. The captions that were assigned to the twelve images are listed in the appendix.

Each image reveals characteristics of the personality and sexuality of each person, as well as the nature of any relationship, sexual or otherwise, there might be between or among the people portrayed in them. These photographs have been looked at many times by researchers seeking images to include in their book projects, but seldom if ever was sexuality the main interest of these scholars, until Professor Irwin looked at the photographs.

The literature on sexuality and gender in colonial and nineteenth-century Mexico is both voluminous and diverse, but the following historical background is largely based on the work of Asunción Lavrin in her chapter "Sexuality in Colonial Mexico: A Church Dilemma." At the end of the paper, I will point out recent developments related to academic publishing on sexuality and gender in Mexico.

Sexuality and Gender in Mexico

The early Spanish priests in Mexico were scandalized by the simultaneous use of the public vapor baths, or *temazcalli,* by nude Indian men and women. The priests tried to prohibit the custom, calling it sinful. Indeed, the sixteenth-century Codex Tudela suggests that there was no lack of promiscuous sexual behavior in the baths, specifically in this description:

> Many men and women were used to entering this public vapor bath, where men enjoyed the illicit company of women, as did women with men, and men with men; and there were homosexual men in Mexico who dressed in women's clothes and did women's work such as weaving and sewing, and some gentlemen kept one or two of them for their vices. (Alcina Franch 2000, 134; my translation)

The conquest of Mexico was certainly a sexual as well as a political and religious conquest, and the mestizo ethnicity of most modern Mexicans is the result of forced or consensual sex between Spanish men and Mexican women. This process of *mestizaje* began soon after initial contact between the races, and lasted beyond the colonial period. As time passed, immigrants of other national and racial identities, including a large force of African laborers, were incorporated into the mix, bringing an increased diversity of expectations about sexual behavior and gender roles.

The subtitle of Irwin's conference, "Sexuality and Social Control in Latin America," recalls the efforts of religious and political authorities to regulate sexual behavior. The Catholic Church was the most important social institution involved in these efforts throughout the colonial period and the nineteenth century, but the church failed to stamp out premarital, extramarital, or other "unorthodox" forms of sexuality, however its officials may have tried. But the pervasively repressive morality of New Spain is conveyed in this description of church efforts to control sexual behavior:

> In mid-colonial New Spain problems of a sexual nature were routinely dealt with by the religious authorities. . . . Among young couples, premarital sexual relations after a betrothal vow seemed to have been a common occurrence; cases of consensual unions were brought frequently to the attention of the ecclesiastical judges; illegitimacy and bigamy were not uncommon. Such instances of religiously unorthodox sexuality raise questions on the degree of acceptance by the common folk of the behavioral models set by the church as a codifier of sexual behavior, and on its role as witness and judge of the many irregularies committed by the faithful. The manner in which the church interacted with those who either challenged or broke its moral norms is a key element in understanding its effectiveness as a mechanism of social control. (Lavrin 1989, 47–48)

Regarding lust and its moral consequences in seventeenth-century Mexico, there were seven categories of sexually forbidden behavior, all of which were conducive to mortal sin. The categories were (1) fornication, or sex outside marriage; (2) adultery, or sex with at least one married partner; (3) incest, or sex between partners with blood ties; (4) rape, or forced sex *(estupro);* (5) abduction, or the forced seizure of a woman *(rapto);* (6) sins against nature (masturbation, sodomy, or bestiality), which were all sins involving sex for purposes other than procreation; and (7) sacrilege, where one or both partners broke a vow of chastity. Thus, a person could incur several sins in a single act, as in the case of a married man who by raping a woman also commits adultery (Lavrin 1989, 50–51).

One of the main ways in which illicit sexual relationships became public knowledge was the requirement that couples had to declare any impediments standing in the way of their marriage. This requirement led to the revelation of sins because the couple had to confess any premarital sex with each other or with blood or spiritual kin. All such relations were sinful and required dispensation by the church, which voided any marriage contracted without dispensation. Investigation of the couple's proposed marriage could be instigated by a third party alleging that the bride or groom had been betrothed, had been romantically involved, or had engaged in sex with another person (Lavrin 1989, 55).

A woman was expected to resist all male advances during courtship if she wished to preserve her reputation, honor, and virginity. Easy submission to the man's desire was typically seen as a sign of lacking moral fiber. While seducing a woman did not tarnish a man's reputation, courtship presented him with the chance to prove his honor by making it clear that marriage, rather than sex, was his objective.

In the early 1720s, the courtship of Juan de Cárdenas and doña Josefa Monasterios, a member of a wealthy family in San Luis Potosí, had all the elements of passion, guilt, and honor to become a textbook case of colonial sexual mores, as described below:

> Don Juan, a *peninsular* in the service of the alcalde of the town, did not hesitate to court Josefa after they made acquaintance while he walked on her street. He used letters to communicate with her until he succeeded in obtaining a midnight date in her own home. . . . The stories tell of kissing, embracing, and exchanging of love words in a brief courtship. Within a short time the man attempted to engage in sex with the willing but frightened woman, who feared the physical and moral pain of losing her virginity. . . . Several other meetings took place during which don Juan apparently failed to consummate his desire and was only able to have seminal emissions *extra vas,* prohibited by the church. Josefa was willing and able to continue seeing the suitor under pretense of visiting a relative, and their meetings continued until, as he claimed, don Juan became tired of failing to have sex with doña Josefa. It is unclear whether or not he deflowered her, but she felt she had lost her honor and confessed to a priest. Soon enough her powerful brother-in-law established a legal suit against don Juan, demanding the repair of the family's honor. (Lavrin 1989, 60)

The explicitness of the descriptions of the meetings between don Juan and doña Josefa reveals the lack of privacy in which personal relationships were conducted. While his right to seek satisfaction for his sexual drive remained unquestioned, hers was never acknowledged by the authorities, who were interested only in the legal and social consequences that her sexual relations could have for her and her family (Lavrin 1989, 61).

Most women who brought lawsuits for breach of promise initially demanded marriage, but some women were willing to settle for a dowry, which would help them to find a husband. Of course, the dowry also represented payment for the woman's lost virginity, but the woman's social position usually determined the amount of money she received. Doña Josefa was awarded one thousand pesos, while a more humble *mulata* woman was awarded one hundred pesos in damages incurred from her affair with a white man (Lavrin 1989, 63).

The initiation of a sexual relationship typically depended on the exchange of a verbal promise of marriage, which legally and religiously bound the couple to marry, even if no witnesses were present. An astute woman tried to have a witness present in case the man later tried to break his word, but the promise apparently gave many women enough assurance of the man's intentions or sufficient confidence in its legal and religious implications to engage in sexual relations. If the promise was not carried out, a question of honor was raised. The woman in particular was seen as having lost face, stained her family's name, and lost her chances to marry someone else. But the fulfillment of the marriage vow was the key for both partners to regain personal honor, as well as social and religious grace (Lavrin 1989, 61).

Premarital sex in a society so encumbered by religious and social controls may be interpreted as a form of escaping those controls. The apparent ease with which women acceded to sexual relations after an exchange of gifts or a promise of marriage suggests a desire to transcend the constraints imposed on them by family, religion, and law. In any case, once the union was consummated, the couple had a card in their favor, because the situation called for an ecclesiastical review of their cases and removed the final decision from parental or family influence (Lavrin 1989, 62).

As for sex within marriage, which was the only form of sexuality endorsed by the church, the confessional of Friar Clemente Ledesma, published in 1695, examined six potential objectives of the conjugal union: (1) the propagation of the species, (2) the satisfaction of the duty to preserve the faith upon which marriage was built, (3) the respect of the marriage sacrament, (4) the preservation of the body's health, (5) the prevention of concupiscence or immoderate sexual desire, and (6) the pleasure of the sexual act.

Ledesma affirmed that procreation for the preservation of the human species was the main purpose of marriage and that any action taken to impede it was sinful. While the remaining four objectives were acceptable, the sixth was not. This denial required all couples to assess the importance of procreation versus pleasure. Since the church said that enjoyment of sex could take place only within marriage, how much pleasure could a couple take in the sexual act? Physical expressions of love were permissible where they stimulated mutual love, but limitations did exist. Pleasure for pleasure's sake, excessive enjoyment of the "delectations," or delights of the flesh, and situations leading to "pollution" outside the sexual act were condemned as indecent and alien to Christian modesty and leading to mortal sin. Thus, the church attempted to control the sexuality of all persons, by limiting the permissible forms of sexual behavior, and by ensuring that sex was not enjoyed for its own sake (Lavrin 1989, 73).

In the nineteenth century, the family served as the ideological transmitter of Mexico's patriarchal culture, maintaining the established division of sex roles. Women were the victims of discrimination in families, schools, and in the language of publications such as religious pamphlets and romance novels. The messages conveyed in these publications played an important role in the construction of gender identities. The *porfiriato* supported the family as a sacred institution in much the same way as the Catholic Church had supported the family since the early colonial period. The only difference was that the liberal state regulated the family through civil matrimony (Barceló 1997, 75).

With this background of orthodox religious and family values in Mexico, the turn of the twentieth century saw a growing public awareness of unorthodox sexuality. This public awareness in no way implied public acceptance, however. The party of the Famous 41 in Mexico City in 1901 is a prime example. The degree of public disgust with the Famous 41 is reflected in the following commentary published one week after the party in the Mexico City newspaper called *El Hijo del Ahuizote:*

> The unprecedented scandal reported in this week's newspapers saw a dance attended by many men and not a single woman. The women's places were taken by a few individuals dressed up as women with elegant gowns, false hair and breasts, embroidered shoes, shining earrings, rouged cheeks, and romantic eye-makeup applied in disgusting and degrading imitation. . . . The police arrested forty-two of these men, who have been sentenced to military service in Yucatán. This sentence is comparable to the two-edged sword, which upon wounding the guilty also wounds the innocent, at once sending that aristocracy of Sodom to face the danger of yellow fever, but forcing the innocent Army to accept men(?) who are marked with the most dirty and repugnant of deprivations. (*El Hijo del Ahuizote* 1901, 915; my translation)

Regarding gender roles at the start of the twentieth century, both the Mexican church and society in general still gave strong support to the dominant macho man and the submissive woman who stayed by the hearth, but these models were not universally accepted. Women's roles in society had been changing for several decades:

> In spite of the rigidity of late-nineteenth-century Mexican society, some women diverged from the accepted model of femininity. . . . During the *porfiriato,* the numbers of women teachers grew, and so to a lesser extent did the numbers of women lawyers, doctors and dentists. . . . By the end of the *porfiriato,* middle-class women began to get jobs in government and business offices. . . . In 1887, Matilde Montoya received the first medical degree granted to a woman in Mexico; and in 1898, María Sandoval de Zarco became the first woman to receive her law degree. (Barceló 1997, 100–101)

As the twentieth century progressed, there was an increased questioning of traditional gender roles, as well as a greater awareness of unorthodox forms of sexuality in Mexican society. But the explosion of interest in Latin American sexuality and gender as subjects of academic research did not occur until the 1990s. As Amy Kaminsky wrote in an issue of *Latin American Research Review,* among Latin Americanists, "queer theory and criticism have bloomed like spring in far northern climates—late but with great intensity" (Kaminsky 2001, 209). For instance, as of May 2001, the Tulane library catalogue included ten books about homosexuality in Mexico. But none of those books was published before 1985, and seven of them were published since 1994, reflecting an explosion of research on the topic during the last decade.

Another sign of this publishing explosion is the recent special issue of *Revista Iberoamericana,* which was entirely devoted to the subject of eroticism in recent Latin American fiction. In his issue introduction, Daniel Balderston wrote:

> Ten years ago, the title of this issue would have evoked images of the erotic writing of Octavio Paz and Georges Bataille: celebratory, somewhat abstract, inevitably heterosexual and misogynistic. But the articles that follow suggest new approaches to the nexus between Eros and textuality. . . . The preparation of this issue, and the book *(Sexualidad y nación)* that accompanies it, allowed me to identify several tendencies in current criticism. In response to the call for papers for this special issue, scholars sent in a deluge of proposals. . . . It is reason to celebrate that Latin American literary criticism has now been definitively opened to the ideas of Queer Theory, to the point that heterosexuality is examined, not simply accepted as stable or settled. (*Revista Iberoamericana* 1999, 263; my translation)

At any rate, the party, raid, punishment, and public scandal of the Famous 41 signified a growing public awareness, although not much acceptance, of unorthodox forms of sexuality in turn-of-the-century Mexico. The Catholic Church and society at large held very conservative views on sexuality and gender roles, but the events surrounding the Famous 41 were an indication that unorthodox views were percolating below the surface, waiting for the chance to enter the public discussion.

APPENDIX

Images from the Latin American Library's Photographic Archive shown during the presentation of this paper at SALALM:

Imágenes de hombres

El dandy, ca. 1900 (Guerra Collection)

Los luchadores, ca. 1900 (Guerra Collection)

El sacerdote, ca. 1907 (CIRMA Collection of Juan Yas y José D. Noriega Photographs)

Los soldados, ca. 1900 (Guerra Collection)

Imágenes de mujeres

La pensativa, ca. 1900 (Guerra Collection)

La planchadora, ca. 1860 (Cruces y Campa Collection)

La ramera, ca. 1900 (Guerra Collection)

La torera, ca. 1908 (Lambert, "Album of Mexico")

Imágenes de parejas

Los cuates, ca. 1860 (Cruces y Campa Collection)

El triángulo amoroso, ca. 1860 (Cruces y Campa Collection)

Espacios homosociales

El equipo de béisbol, ca. 1900 (Guerra Collection)

La orquesta, ca. 1860 (Cruces y Campa Collection)

BIBLIOGRAPHY

Books

Alcina Franch, José. 2000. *Temazcalli: higiene, terapéutica, obstreticia y ritual en el nuevo mundo.* Sevilla: Escuela de Estudios Hispano-Americanos, Consejo Superior de Investigaciones Científicas.

Balderston, Daniel, and Donna J. Guy, comps. 1997. *Sex and Sexuality in Latin America.* New York: New York University Press.

Debroise, Olivier. 1994. *Fuga mexicana: un recorrido por la fotografía en México.* México, D.F.: Consejo Nacional para la Cultura y las Artes.

Foster, David William, and Roberto Reis, eds. 1996. *Bodies and Biases: Sexualities in Hispanic Cultures and Literatures.* Minneapolis: University of Minnesota Press.

Molloy, Sylvia, and Robert McKee Irwin. 1998. *Hispanisms and Homosexualities.* Durham: Duke University Press.

Prieto, René. 2000. *Body of Writing: Figuring Desire in Spanish American Literature.* Durham: Duke University Press.

Schaefer, Claudia. 1996. *Danger Zones: Homosexuality, National Identity, and Mexican Culture.* Tucson: University of Arizona Press.

Smith, Paul Julian. 1989. *The Body Hispanic: Gender and Sexuality in Spanish and Spanish American Literature.* New York: Oxford University Press.

Book Chapters

Barceló, Raquel. 1997. "Hegemonía y conflicto en la ideología porfiriana sobre el papel de la mujer y la familia." In *Familias y mujeres en México: del modelo a la diversidad,* compiled by Soledad González Montes and Julia Tuñón. México, D.F.: El Colegio de México, Programa Interdisciplinario de Estudios de la Mujer.

Gonzalbo Aizpuru, Pilar. 1997. "Religiosidad femenina y vida familiar en la Nueva España." In *Familias y mujeres en México: del modelo a la diversidad,* compiled by Soledad González Montes and Julia Tuñón. México, D.F.: El Colegio de México, Programa Interdisciplinario de Estudios de la Mujer.

Lavrin, Asunción. 1989. "Sexuality in Colonial Mexico: A Church Dilemma." In *Sexuality and Marriage in Colonial Latin America,* edited by Asunción Lavrin. Lincoln: University of Nebraska Press.

Articles

Irwin, Robert McKee. 1998. "*El periquillo sarniento* y sus cuates: el 'éxtasis misterioso' del ambiente homosocial en el siglo diecinueve." *Literatura Mexicana* 9 (1), 23–44.

Kaminsky, Amy. 2001. "The Queering of Latin American Literary Studies." *Latin American Research Review* 36 (2), 209–219.

Revista Iberoamericana 65, no. 187 (April–June 1999). Issue entitled "Erotismo y escritura." Includes twelve articles related to eroticism in Latin American literature.

"Salidas de tono. La aristocracia de Sodoma al servicio nacional." 1901. *El Hijo del Ahuizote* 17 (786), 915–918.

9. Estereotipos gay en la literatura y el cine (Argentina)

Ricardo Rodríguez Pereyra

En las últimas tres décadas, se han extendido los trabajos de investigación sobre temas referidos a los estudios de género sexual, como producto de una creciente comprensión de la distancia que existe entre los aspectos biológicos y culturales del sexo. Algunos antropólogos comprobaron la inexistencia de un comportamiento universal femenino y masculino en las distintas culturas, si bien todas atribuyen actitudes y personalidades diferenciales a varones y mujeres. Existe una creencia universal que atribuye bases biológicas de la masculinidad y la femineidad, pero no las características que se atribuyen a uno y otro sexo ni al estilo de relaciones que se establecen entre ellos. Anne Oakley da cuenta de casos de varones y niñas que nacieron sin pene y sin útero pero que desarrollaron una identidad masculina y femenina, porque crecieron en un medio familiar que los formó de acuerdo a las pautas sociales y culturales que corresponden a los criterios "normales" de masculinidad y femineidad. Las características de personalidad que históricamente se han atribuido a las hembras y a los machos en cada cultura están relacionadas con las funciones que cada uno de ellos tiene en la reproducción humana aunque no son atribuibles totalmente a dicha función. La domesticidad, vinculada con el rol afectivo de protección y contención, es una prerrogativa femenina y la división social del trabajo entre los sexos, su rol en las crianza de los hijos y su lugar en la producción y en la organización política tienen que ver en casi todas las culturas con una cierta división entre el mundo público y el mundo privado. Esto implica modalidades de relaciones interpersonales y vínculos de poder. Diversas teorías dan cuenta de los orígenes de la subordinación entre los sexos, por ejemplo en raíces griegas que relegaban a los siervos, a los niños y a las mujeres al mundo de la casa, de los servicios personales y de los afectos.

Otras teorías creen en la existencia de poderes y mundos paralelos, concomitantes con el afuera y el adentro de la vida cotidiana. Las teorías de la subordinación establecen diferencias de jerarquía entre el mundo femenino de la domesticidad y la vida pública de la política y de la racionalidad en la que los hombres priman, por su capacidad de liderazgo y de agresividad desarrollada en el comienzo de la socialización.[1]

Como veremos más adelante, al analizar lo que llamaré *estereotipo primario gay,* a través de sus representaciones en el cine, el teatro y la literatura, y también en la televisión argentina, es obvio que se tiende a asimilar al varón homosexual con la mujer. A partir de esta forma de estereotipo, se trataría de acomodar todas las categorías de subordinación femenina al varón homosexual, otorgándole un rango de inferioridad en cuanto al liderazgo y el poder físico y la virilidad, aunque ejemplos de homosexuales célebres como el malogrado actor Rock Hudson, no confirmen la regla de hombre homosexual igual mujer igual afeminado. Esta asimilación con la mujer no sólo proviene de la mirada heterosexual sino que la podemos encontrar en autores gay, tal es el caso del siguiente ejemplo tomado de una novela de Hermes Villordo:

> El me confundía con una mujer; nuestras relaciones tenían no sé qué de parecido con las del hombre y la mujer. Hasta creo que se divertía cambiándome el sexo en el diminutivo de mi nombre.[2]

Algunos personajes de las novelas de Villordo tienen actitudes femeninas tales como ponerse ruleros y vestir batones de entrecasa.

En varios países, distintas universidades han abierto departamentos de estudios sobre "Queer Theory" a partir de 1991. En Argentina, por la misma fecha, la Corte Suprema de Justicia de la Nación había confirmado el fallo de la Cámara de Apelaciones que confirmó la resolución de la Dirección de Personas Jurídicas que denegó la personería jurídica a la Comunidad Homosexual Argentina (CHA). En enero de 1992 luego de un cambio de autoridades se dio trámite favorable a la CHA. Al mismo tiempo, en Canadá, el Ministerio de Inmigración le otorgó el status de refugiado político al estudiante de la Universidad de Córdoba, Jorge Alberto Einaudi, quien había demostrado que por su orientación homosexual, era miembro de un grupo social perseguido en la Argentina. En julio de 1993, el Consejo Económico y Social (ECOSOC) de las Naciones Unidas, responsable de la observancia de los derechos humanos, otorgó a la Asociación Internacional de Lesbianas y Homosexuales (ILGA) su inclusión en la lista con el voto favorable de la Argentina. El caso de la personería jurídica a la CHA promovió un encendido debate en los medios de comunicación pero los otros dos casos pasaron inadvertidos. En ninguno de los casos se oyeron los puntos de vista de los científicos argentinos. "Fuera de la Argentina, la investigación sobre las causas y el significado de la homosexualidad se ha desarrollado de forma muy importante en los últimos años".[3] Los científicos argentinos no investigan sobre el tema, ni en la UBA ni el CONICET, tampoco en la Asociación Psicoanalítica Argentina. Jaime Stubrin, miembro didacta de la APA, señala que no tuvo inscriptos en los seminarios que ofreció la asociación. "Subraya que hay que señalar el tema en una sociedad enferma de homofobia, en especial 'los homosexuales y los psicoanalistas'". La APA no admite candidatos homosexuales.[4] Durante varios siglos la homosexualidad ha estado unida al delito y en algunos casos el castigo era la muerte.

En el siglo XX, en 1973, la American Psychiatric Association retiró la homosexualidad de su "Manual de Diagnósticos y Estadísticas de Desórdenes Psiquiátricos" (*Diagnostic and Statistical Manual of Psychiatric Disorders,*

DSM III) y en 1990 reiteró su posición con la oposición a la exclusión o rechazo de los homosexuales por las fuerzas armadas. Barrios Medina,[5] sostiene que el proceso de despatologización había comenzado en 1957 con la psicóloga Evelyn Hooker quien administró tests proyectivos a individuos heterosexuales y homosexuales cuyo resultados fueron evaluados por colegas que desconocían esa orientación sexual y que no pudieron discriminar ninguna patología entre los testeados.

El propósito de mi investigación es analizar la existencia de distintos tipos de varones homosexuales y sus formas de representación, en tanto que están presentes a través de la imagen, en una sociedad altamente influida por los medios de comunicación de masas. Asimismo intentaré analizar el enfoque del estereotipo gay en la cinematografía argentina, la literatura, el teatro y la tele-visión desde una perspectiva de los estudios culturales, partiendo de la base de que toda investigación que ayude a comprender los fenómenos sociales es de gran importancia para el avance de la sociedad.

Me interesa investigar la existencia de un imaginario "gay" dentro y fuera del grupo de pertenencia determinado por la orientación sexual. En la revisión que efectué de la literatura de ficción argentina, no encontré el término "gay". En realidad es relativamente nuevo y se ha popularizado en el lenguaje colo-quial hace dos décadas. En cuanto al término *homosexual* no es muy antiguo, recién aparece a mediados del siglo XIX en Alemania, con los primeros estu-dios sobre el tema a nivel científico. A los fines de mi investigación usaré el término "gay" para designar a varones homosexuales, tomando como ejemplo la afirmación de Giddens,[6] quien sostiene que la popularización de esta palabra como término auto descriptivo, es ejemplo de un proceso reflexivo donde un fenómeno social puede verse apropiado y transformado por medio de un com-promiso colectivo. Merton señala que existe una polarización de la sociedad entre "los de adentro" y "los de afuera", como consecuencia del florecimiento de movimientos basados en la clase, la raza, el sexo, la orientación sexual y la religión. Esos movimientos expresaban la afirmación pública del orgullo por cierto status y la solidaridad con colectividades que durante largo tiempo han sido socialmente degradadas, estigmatizadas o acosadas de otras maneras en el sistema social.[7] Esta afirmación, sostiene Barrios Medina, "es aplicable a los movimientos que afirman el derecho a la identidad y la diferencia de la orient-ación social".[8] El historiador John Boswell plantea que la historiografía de las minorías y el desarraigo histórico es "uno de los estigmas de la colectividad de lesbianas y gays quienes a diferencia de otras minorías perseguidas como los judíos, son despojadas del sentimiento de comunidad en el presente, y con el pasado, que resulta de la rememoración histórica".[9]

Este trabajo forma parte de una investigación que analiza la representa-ción del sujeto gay en el plano de las diferentes modalidades de producción artística en la Argentina. Las preguntas básicas que intentan orientar esta tesis se refiere a los estereotipos gay y masculinos en general, tratando de rastrear los orígenes históricos de la homosexualidad en el país. Las fuentes para el estudio de los estereotipos abarcan películas, novelas, obras de teatro y programas de televisión del período 1950–2000. También se han consultado ensayos académicos, se realizaron entrevistas personales y estudios de casos. Como pretendo darle a mi investigación un grado de objetividad aceptable, y evitar el encasillamiento en un escenario planteado a partir de una variante sexual, he elegido autores gay y heterosexuales en el caso de la literatura y no califico las orientaciones de éstos, excepto que las mismas sean de dominio público a partir de la decisión del interesado.

Fuentes para la investigación

Uno de los primeros obstáculos que debí enfrentar fue la inexistencia de bibliografía, lo cual por un lado constituye una ventaja en lo que hace a la originalidad del tema y por otro una desventaja por la falta de referentes académicos con los cuales ir armando mi propuesta. En general, existen poco trabajos sobre el tema de la homosexualidad en la Argentina. Mientras que en varias universidades de Europa y de Estados Unidos existen departamentos que se dedican al tema, en Argentina, los investigadores de distintas áreas de las ciencias no parecen estar interesados en esta materia. Si bien han aparecido estudios culturales y de género, en especial sobre mujeres, no existen estudios de "teoría queer". A lo sumo pueden encontrarse algunos temas sobre la homosexualidad en publicaciones de psicología, y en menor proporción en revistas de algunas cátedras o facultades de humanidades.

Otra dificultad es la falta de organización de las fuentes bibliográficas. En Argentina no se realiza la compilación de la bibliografía nacional y el depósito legal se cumple en forma realmente deficiente. El acceso a los documentos es difícil para los investigadores en general y se complica en un tema de esta índole, porque además de la falta de catálogos centralizados y de bibliografías especializadas en la materia, hay que enfrentarse contra los prejuicios y el escozor que llegan a provocar la solicitud de títulos que pueden ser considerados incluso pornográficos. En Buenos Aires no existen, o al menos no pude localizar librerías que se dediquen a literatura sexológica, mucho menos puede pensarse en la existencia de librerías dedicados a la cultura gay, como pueden ser las que se encuentran en San Francisco, Madrid, Barcelona, y en otras ciudades del mundo. Según uno de mis entrevistados para este trabajo, se pueden encontrar algunos libros en especies de tiendas clandestinas que funcionan en domicilios privados y que muchas veces se dedican también a la venta de videos pornográficos, lencería erótica y otros artículos comúnmente comercializados en los "pornoshop".

Estereotipos

El sentido que pretendo darle a la palabra "estereotipo" es la que se entiende usualmente como un equivalente a "personaje". En general suele equivaler a "criatura, clisé, prejuicio, etc." El término también implica referencia, simplificación, reiteración o fijación de comportamientos y actitudes, así como opiniones. Walter Lippman, ya en 1922, introdujo el significado científico para referirse a ciertos mecanismos cognitivos de simplificación de la realidad. Esta simplificación, impuesta por razones de economía del esfuerzo, comportan el peligro de la distorsión. En el marco de las ciencias sociales se ha tratado de diferenciar conceptualmente términos tales como "actitud", "imagen", "prejuicio" y "estereotipo". Gerhard Kleining (1959) hacía equivaler la "imagen" al complejo anímico legítimo de la persona; el "estereotipo" designaría un falseamiento de la realidad, en tanto que el "prejuicio" se limitaría a un falseamiento negativo de la misma. Reinhold Bergler (1966) sitúa el concepto de estereotipo a un nivel genérico del que los prejuicios, por ejemplo, sería una especificación.[10]

En una persona, el estereotipo estaría compuesto de una serie de elementos materiales e inmateriales, desde la psicología interna del personaje, hasta las características de su voz, la manera de hablar, impostar, susurrar, gritar, o hablar en un tono "normal". Otros elementos están relacionados con la manera de manejar el propio físico, es decir, la forma de caminar, de sentarse, los ademanes al hablar, la manera de mirar y por supuesto la vestimenta. Este amplio conjunto integrado por tan diversos elementos, se entroncan con las fantasías propias de los individuos pasibles de ser considerados estereotipos, y la del mundo que los percibe como tales, donde los integrantes aportan su propio conocimiento del saber popular adquirido a través de la educación formal o informal, el medio cultural y social donde el individuo se desarrolla. Ligado a esto están las representaciones surgidas de la literatura, el cine, el teatro, y desde mitad del siglo XX en adelante, de la televisión.

Estereotipo primario gay

Como uno de los primeros resultados de mi investigación podría concluir que existe lo que definiré "estereotipo primario gay". Para ordenar el planteamiento del mismo lo dividiré en cinco clases o subgrupos: *Loca/Mariquita, Asumido, Tapado /Onda nada que ver, Intelectual /Fino y Chongo.* La imagen del varón homosexual a veces es una mezcla de estas categorías o subgrupos. Cuando se analiza el discurso de la gente en general, hay una suerte de preconcepto frente al varón homosexual que tiende a encasillarlo en el estereotipo de mariquita. En la sociedad rioplatense, en el escenario urbano, se pueden observar distintas modalidades para calificar a este tipo de sujeto: "maricón", "del otro cuadro", "comilón", "muñeca quebrada" y "tira plumas", entre otras con mayor grado de estigma, humor o desprecio.

Desde el discurso legal, médico, o simplemente coloquial (en cuanto a lo ciudadano o popular), otro calificativo que parece predominar es el de *activo y pasivo,* directamente relacionado con el rol que cumple el gay en una relación sexual dada, circunstancial o dentro del marco de una pareja estable, denominando *activo* al sujeto que penetra, y *pasivo* al penetrado. En algunos casos se puede dar que el sujeto que penetra no sea considerado homosexual puesto que se le atribuye la condición femenina al varón penetrado.

Ya señalé las dificultades que encontré al iniciar mi investigación; no existen demasiados trabajos en Argentina relacionados a la homosexualidad. No encontré trabajos de autores argentinos relacionados con el tema que me ocupa. No debo dejar de citar para el caso del teatro, el cine y la literatura latinoamericana los trabajos de William David Foster. Para un enfoque general del tema de la homosexualidad en la Argentina no pueden desconocerse las obras de Carlos Jáuregui, Zelmar Acevedo y Jorge Salessi. A nivel literario son imprescindibles (además tienen el mérito de ser escasas en la producción literaria argentina) las obras de Hermes Villordo, Manuel Puig y Manuel Mújica Láinez. En mi exhaustiva búsqueda bibliográfica encontré muy pocos autores que hayan escrito sobre esta temática a lo largo del siglo XX. Las primeras son obras científicas, que incluyen el tema dentro de la psiquiatría y la criminología como en caso de Vieytes y Ramos Mejía. Tardíamente, en la década del 80 aparecen los libros de Acevedo y Jáuregui, las novelas de Villordo, y *Plaza de los lirios* de José María Borghello. No quiero olvidar que en la década anterior habían aparecido las novelas de Carlos Arcidiácono *Ay de mí, Jonathan* y la de Héctor Lastra, *La boca de la ballena*. Aunque se trata del tema del lesbianismo—que no voy a abordar en esta investigación—no quiero dejar de mencionar para el caso de las mujeres, a Ilse Fukova y Claudina Marek, quienes escribieron en conjunto *Amor de mujeres*[11] constituyendo uno de los primeros casos de reconocimiento público de una sexualidad diferente. Estas mujeres dieron un grado de visibilidad importante al tema de la homosexualidad en el país. Supieron aprovechar el juego sensacionalista de los medios de comunicación para confesar la relación amorosa que las unía y dar batalla por la aceptación y visibilidad del lesbianismo y de los gays en Argentina.

He recibido una ayuda inestimable de anónimos varones homosexuales conectados por correo electrónico que generosamente abrieron su intimidad para contarme cómo se veían a sí mismos, qué estereotipos creían observar en las pantallas y en la literatura. Esta suerte de encuestas, sumadas a las entrevistas personales con personas de distinta orientación sexual (hetero y homo) me permitieron ir armando varios estudios de casos, que me resultarían útiles a la hora de contrastarlos con la ficción a través de los distintos vehículos tomados. Además de la bibliografía tradicional (libros, artículos y "papers"), también recurrí a diversas bases de datos en texto completo y a innumerables páginas de internet dedicados al área de homosexualidad, teoría queer, y cine, algunas provenientes de universidades norteamericanas.

Varones homosexuales en la pantalla de plata

Las obras teatrales, cinematográficas y literarias; aún la televisión, como productos surgidos y consumidos por la cultura popular, son el reflejo de un tiempo y de un espacio geográfico y social determinado. En el caso de las películas "retratan su tiempo en una doble dirección: describen la vida social y política de los pueblos, registrada en el acontecer contemporáneo, y advierten asimismo sobre las apetencias y referencias del receptor medio, el hombre de la calle, que llena o deja vacíos a los cines".[12]

Cuando se rastrea en la historia de nuestro cine en busca de personajes gay se observan pocos casos. A lo sumo en alguna comedia de la década del '50 podemos encontrar la viñeta de unos segundos de duración dedicada a algunos coreógrafos, como en una escena de la película *La casa grande* (1953), dirigida por Leo Fleider, cuyo protagonista principal es Luis Sandrini, el popular actor argentino; y en *La edad del amor* (1954) de la no menos famosa Lolita Torres, dirigida por Julio Saraceni. En ambos casos se trata del *estereotipo primario de mariquita,* como hemos visto, un hombre muy afeminado, cercano a la caricatura de una mujer y que se corresponde con la creencia de que los homosexuales estaban mayoritariamente relacionados con profesiones como bailarines, modistos y peluqueros de damas, en una visión de la homosexualidad que parece llegar hasta nuestros días. Eran apariciones breves que mostraban al gay, generalmente en situaciones cómicas, con arranques de histeria, diálogos afeminados con voz chillona y ademanes aspaventosos. En el imaginario social habría una tendencia a sospechar de que quienes cultivan una sexualidad diferente son los hombres de modales menos masculinos que el resto común del género. Se podría citar a *Vidalita* (1949) como testimonio de un tema instalado en la sociedad aunque no se hablara demasiado. Allí es una mujer disfrazada de hombre la que sacude la heterosexualidad de un joven soldado que comienza a sentir sentimientos perturbadores por el simpático paisanito. Si tomamos al filme despojado de su estética histórica, puede advertirse lo osado del tema planteado: travestismo, sentimientos homosexuales de un varón "normal" por otro, aunque se tratara de un gauchito afeminado.

Los varones homosexuales aparecieron pocas veces en la pantalla argentina y cuando lo hicieron, la mayoría de las veces fue envueltos en situaciones de comedia, fácilmente digeribles para el público. En general se los veía como personajes patéticos, mezcla de payasos y caricatura femenina, a los cuales seguirían los personajes de las películas de Armando Bo, interpretados por el actor Adelco Lanza, quien encarnó a innumerables mucamos, todos iguales, muy amanerados, que atendía a las visitas masculinas que recibían las heroínas interpretadas por la actriz Isabel Sarli.

A comienzos de los '60, *Extraña ternura* (1963, Daniel Tinayre, sobre novela de Guy des Cars) tocó de una manera sutil la extraña relación de un tío por su sobrino, en un producto brumoso, vehículo tardío de la *nouvelle vague* europea.

Habrían de pasar varios años, para que en la década del '70 se tocara el tema de la homosexualidad, como en el caso de *La tregua* (1974) y *Piedra libre* (1976), prohibida por la censura del gobierno militar debido a la actriz Marilina Ross y a una situación de lesbianismo sugerida en el film. Más tarde, la pantalla argentina de determinada clase de películas de baja calidad, se colmaría de escenas lésbicas en las cárceles de mujeres, por ejemplo en *Atrapadas* (1984) y *Correccional de mujeres*. En la década del '80 surgieron escasos filmes con historias de amor entre hombres. En forma paralela la televisión comenzó a incluir personajes gay, ridiculizados en su mayoría en distintos programas cómicos, y también a tono con la televisión de Estados Unidos, empezaron a aparecer personajes secundarios en los teleteatros. También aparecieron caricaturas de varones homosexuales en las películas de Jorge Porcel y Alberto Olmedo, quien representó su propia versión de *Tootsie*. Los cómicos interpetaron una serie de personajes gay o travestidos, siempre justificados en el argumento por la persecución de provocadoras mujeres, cuyos roles eran jugados por "vedettes" surgidas en su mayoría de la televisión.

Una experiencia de mayor seriedad fue la que reunió a la actriz Susana Giménez y a Alberto Olmedo en la película *Mi novia él* . . . (1975), dirigida por Enrique Cahen Salaverry. El film, quizás inspirado en *Victor-Victoria,* cuenta la historia de una chica que para abrirse paso en el mundo del espectáculo se hace pasar por un travesti del cual se enamora Alberto Olmedo. Refleja la pintura de las actitudes del mundo circundante frente a este tipo de parejas, aunque finalmente llega el *happy end* cuando todos se enteran de que en realidad el travesti es una verdadera mujer. La película, cuya título original era *Mi novia el travesti,* tuvo que enfrentar problemas con la censura de la época que obligó a sacar la palabra "travesti" del título. En definitiva con el pronombre masculino "él" seguido de puntos suspensivos el título dejaba abierta la ambigüedad de una manera más desconcertante.

En 1990, la obra teatral *Anclado en Madrid,* con Hugo Grosso y Roberto Carnaghi se atrevió a mostrar una relación de estas características con inteligencia y buen gusto. El proceso militar que había permitido la exhibición de películas como la norteamericana *Tootsie* (1982) prohibió en cambio *La jaula de las locas* (1977). Esta película muestra una pareja masculina conviviendo como un matrimonio convencional y regenteando un local bailable de la Riviera francesa, cuyo nombre da título a la película. Más tarde fue representada en el teatro por Tato Bores, y Carlos Perciavalle. *La jaula de las locas* había conocido una versión teatral no musical a fines de los años sesenta con Osvaldo Miranda, otro mítico galán del cine y el teatro argentino.

Las sociedades en general son más permisivas con sus artistas y toleran comportamientos y elecciones sexuales que no son fácilmente aceptados en la gente común. Quizás por esta razón "desde la comedia se trataron algunos temas urticantes para el cine argentino e imposibles de tocar con naturalidad en tiempos de censura: la homosexualidad masculina y femenina".[13]

La tregua (1974)

Parece un título emblemático, la ruptura de un largo silencio. Por primera vez el cine argentino mostraba un personaje homosexual surgido del seno de una familia de clase media. Oscar Martínez, el actor que representa al gay, puede ser el chico de la puerta de al lado. Este permiso que se concedió el cine argentino en el período del recién estrenado retorno al gobierno del general Domingo Perón, al que sucedería su viuda Isabelita (María Estela Martínez), inaugurando en América Latina, un brusco cambio de género en el cargo de jefe de estado y abriendo la puerta en el caso argentino a una de las dictaduras más crueles del siglo XX.

En *La tregua* aparece por primera vez con un planteo serio la figura del varón homosexual, presentado bajo distintos estereotipos. El joven de apariencia común a la mayoría, torturado por asumir y ocultar una sexualidad diferente. El gay asumido (interpretado por Sergio Renán), de cuarenta años, cínico y de vuelta, algo afeminado, que enfrenta al padre del muchacho (Héctor Alterio) con un mundo desconocido. El tercer estereotipo está dado por el personaje del obsesivo oficinista interpretado por Antonio Gasalla, un hombrecito histérico, afeminado y patético.

El personaje de Oscar Martínez está vinculado desde la imagen al mundo de los libros. Cuando está juntando sus pertenencias para irse de la casa, se le cae de las manos una pila de libros; esta escena se conecta con la imposibilidad de manejar la carga cultural que lo condiciona y lo culpabiliza a la hora de decidir una elección de vida diferente a partir del eje del conflicto al que lo enfrenta su sexualidad. Se vincula con el estereotipo del "intelectual". En cambio, el personaje de Renán es presentado como un hombre vestido en forma excéntrica, quizás como la descripción de los personajes de la novela de Arcidiácono *Ay de mi Jonathan*. La impresión que recibe el padre del joven es la de un ser cínico, desagradable y amanerado. Es quizás la visión del futuro que él imagina para su hijo como consecuencia directa del ejercicio de una sexualidad contraria a lo establecido.

Es interesante observar el universo masculino de estos tres hombres (los dos hermanos y el padre) que viven con la hermana (Marilina Ross), la única mujer de esa familia que ha perdido a la madre años atrás. La historia no se centra en absoluto en el problema del hijo menor del protagonista. Plantea diversos temas, la felicidad y los distintos caminos que pueden conducir a la misma, la diferencia de edades entre la pareja (heterosexual), la soledad y también la homosexualidad. Si tenemos en cuenta que la película se basa en una novela que transcurre en el Montevideo de fines de la década del cincuenta, es comprensible, la reacción del padre ante la noticia de la homosexualidad de su hijo, a pesar de que él mismo vive una historia de transgresión, aceptada dentro de los canones sociales contemporáneos, siempre que no sea la mujer mayor que su pareja. Una tregua es la que encuentra el personaje de Héctor Alterio en su aburrida y rutinaria soledad de viudo a punto de jubilarse cuando entra a la oficina una nueva empleada, "Avellaneda", interpetada por la actriz Ana María Picchio. Es una tregua también para descubrir los verdaderos lazos que lo unen a sus hijos y a los hermanos entre sí. De todas formas, quizás por los quince años que separan a la novela de la película—la primera edición salió publicada en 1960—el tono marcadamente homofóbico que Mario Benedetti, su autor, imprimió a la obra, queda notoriamente desdibujado.

Adiós Roberto y Otra historia de amor

Como comenta Diana Paladino,[14] a los tradicionales conflictos románticos, la comedia de mediados de los 80 suma el tema de la pareja homosexual. Un tema, que más allá del núcleo amoroso, "es un disparador para desenmascarar hipocresías, intolerancias y prejuicios en nuestra sociedad". En *Adiós Roberto* (1985, Enrique Dawi), el film confronta dos modelos sociales diferentes, Roberto (Carlos Andrés Calvo), es un muchacho de barrio y Marcelo (Víctor Laplace), es el intelectual refinado. Más que por la atracción física, Roberto parece seducido por el mundo que Marcelo representa, con él descubre una sensibilidad y un lenguaje distintos. El conflicto no está planteado en relación con la pareja, sino que se centra en la lucha de Roberto consigo mismo. Los padres, el cura y el amigo del barrio se le aparecen en sus fantasías una y otra vez para recriminarle por no cumplir con el supuesto mandato social.

Foster sostiene que esta película "se caracteriza por la insistencia en la utilización del espacio público para presentar varios niveles, reales e imaginarios de identificación gay . . . esta película todavía no tiene igual en su tratamiento de las dimensiones sicológicas de la homofobia internalizada y del autodesprecio".[15] Concuerdo con Foster sobre el marcado tono homofóbico de la película, que si bien es bastante pobre en su realización cinematográfica, tiene el mérito de haber puesto el tema de la homosexualidad para consumo masivo. *Otra historia de amor* (1986, Américo Ortiz de Zárate) se sitúa en las antípodas; presenta un aspecto positivo de una relación entre dos hombres, pese a los inconvenientes derivados de la misma, ya que se trata del romance entre un joven empleado y su jefe, un hasta entonces exitoso ejecutivo padre de familia, que descubre su homosexualidad, cuando ingresa a trabajar un nuevo oficinista. La importancia de la película es quizás, que se aparta del estereotipo trágico del homosexual. Vuelvo a citar a Foster:

> el título de Ortiz de Zárate sugiere la narración de otra historia de amor. Ha sido ampliamente documentado que hasta el surgimiento del movimiento revisionista de liberación gay, la forma dominante de la representación homosexual en la cultura occidental había sido la modalidad trágica con sus matices melodramáticos . . . concuerda con este discurso en su rechazo a la representación de la homosexualidad como una forma trágica de existencia. Es verdad que Y y Z confrontan muchos problemas en su relación, pero la pregunta es ¿En qué relación no hay problemas?[16]

Contrariamente a lo que habría de esperarse, el cine no volvería a abordar un tema de historia de amor entre dos hombres; por supuesto hubo personajes gay en varias películas: *Nunca estuve en Viena, Señora de nadie, Abierto de 18 a 24* y *Dios los cría*. En el año 2000 se filmó *Apariencias* (Alberto Lecchi) pero la historia es sobre un joven que se finge gay, porque como anuncia su subtítulo "¿que no harías por el amor de una mujer?" La película muestra los clisés más o menos convencionales para retratar el estereotipo gay, a partir de movimientos afeminados, aflautamiento de la voz y caídas de ojos consideradas propias de los homosexuales. Por el lado del entorno familiar del personaje del chico que se finge gay, está presente una alta dósis de homofobia, representada sobre todo a partir de la actitud de la madre que moteja a su hijo con los epítetos más soeces usados en el Río de la Plata para un homosexual. De todas formas es un producto comercial, en un tono de comedia liviana, muy cercana a los formatos televisivos, que no plantea el tema de la diferencia con profundidad, y siempre a partir del humor para tranquilizar a la audiencia heterosexual, seguidora de Adrián Suar, un actor y exitoso productor de televisión y de la actriz Andrea del Boca, niña prodigio en los setenta; heroína de las telenovelas que viene interpretando desde hace tres décadas.

Otro título reciente es *Plata quemada,* sobre una novela de Ricardo Piglia. La historia está basada en un hecho real acontecido en Buenos Aires, en 1965, cuando una banda de ladrones asaltó un camión de caudales y escapó al Uruguay. Dos de los integrantes de la banda, son la pareja principal de la historia, los amantes llamados "Los mellizos". El estereotipo mostrado es el de dos hombres rudos, enamorados uno del otro, alejados de la simplicación de roles activo-pasivo, pero marginales.

Los gay en la ficción literaria

En cuanto a los orígenes literarios de la homosexualidad, algunos autores establecen que el cuento fundacional de la literatura argentina *El matadero* de Esteban Echeverría (1805–1851), escrito en 1840 tiene características homo-eróticas. Quizás vean el sometimiento e intento de violación contra un joven unitario por un grupo de mazorqueros como un cuento específicamente gay, en lugar de una historia de rivalidades políticas. La villanía de los mazorqueros está descripta con un "pecado" de características oprobiosas, la sodomía. Una historia similar es referida en el poema *La resfalosa* (música con la que los mazorqueros tocaban a degüello) de Hilario Ascasubi (1807–1875). También Eugenio Cambaceres (1843–1890), en su novela *En la sangre* describe al inmigrante como un ser vil y corrupto, incluyendo la homosexualidad entre sus defectos. Otro autor, Roberto Arlt (1900–1942), expresa sentimientos homofóbicos en su primera obra *El juguete rabioso* (1926). En esa novela "describe a un joven homosexual con todas las características que le atribuía la sociedad de entonces, es decir, corrupto, de clase acomodada, poco afecto a la higiene y admitiendo francamente su pretendida condición de enfermo mental".[17]

Gracias a su traslado al cine, *El beso de la mujer araña* (1976), se hizo popular esta obra de Manuel Puig (1932–1991), un conocido autor homosexual que escribió obras tales como *La traición de Rita Hayworth* (1968), donde narra la educación sentimental de un chico de provincia. Son numerosos los estudios sobre la obra de este autor, que tuvo problemas con la censura en la década del sesenta y que más tarde triunfaría en el exilio. El estereotipo de Puig es el de un hombre atrapado en el cuerpo de una mujer, tal como gustaba definirse a sí mismo.

En el campo de la literatura, además, no debemos olvidar la breve "primavera alfonsinista" que daría lugar a un florecimiento del arte y de las libertades personales, aunque todavía subsistían edictos policiales que daban el poder a cualquier agente del orden para hacer bajar a un hombre del tren, en pleno verano, por vestir pantalones cortos. Pero si se compara con el oscuro período del Proceso de Reorganización Nacional, como se denominó a si misma la dictadura militar, la situación era notoriamente mejor. Sería falso, no apuntar también, que la represión de la homosexualidad había estado presente a lo largo de todo el siglo XX.

Además del muy conocido Manuel Puig, no puedo dejar de mencionar al poeta y periodista, Oscar Hermes Villordo (1928–1994), quien a principios de los ochenta se atrevió a hablar en sus novelas del amor que no se podía nombrar. Ya en la década del 70 había escrito *Consultorio sentimental,* obra que no puede incluirse dentro de su producción literaria gay. Las novelas del período democráctico, *La brasa en la mano* (1983), *La otra mejilla* (1986) y *El ahijado* (1990), constituyen una trilogía que refleja la vida y las costumbres de los varones homosexuales porteños de la década del cincuenta en adelante.

La voz de Villordo, es la voz de un poeta ciudadano, sus descripciones no son amaneradas, y a veces son francamente transgresoras por el lenguaje empleado para narrar los encuentros sexuales de sus protagonistas. Aún así, en este estilo, que puede ser aceptado o rechazado por los lectores (sería interesante realizar un estudio sobre quiénes son los lectores de autores como Villordo, si pertenecen a un gueto gay, o si es frecuentado por heterosexuales y qué conceptos merece por parte de unos y otros, su literatura), sus novelas arrojan luz sobre los amores entre hombres que en el imaginario de la cultura popular están instalados por medio de estereotipos vinculados a la marginalidad, la prostitución, la delincuencia y el afeminamiento.

Más cercana en el tiempo, la novela *Crónicas de la noche* (1998), del irlandés Colm Toibín, tiene la particularidad de dejar de "considerar al gay como un ser sólo marginal, le aporta tal vez más humanidad y lo utiliza como centro para poder contar la historia de un país, la Argentina, en tiempos de la represión y los primeros años de la recuperación democrática".[18]

Una visión patriarcal de la sexualidad, una mirada heterosexual nos daría una idea binaria (estoy pensando en los trabajos de Foster), dentro de todas las posibilidades del heterosexismo compulsivo (sigo pensando en Foster). No obstante, en los últimos tiempos, parece existir una fuerte fantasía homosexual de los varones trasladadas a sus parejas femeninas: el deseo de un *menage a trois* incorporando una tercera figura femenina en el juego sexual; la inclusión de escenas de lesbianismo en casi todas las películas pornográficas dirigidas a un mercado *straight*. A pesar de eso, parecería existir una barrera desde la mirada heterosexual, que impide pensar o comprender las amplias posibilidades de la conducta sexual entre dos hombres, que no pasa únicamente por la penetración anal. En este sentido, si bien la literatura de Hermes Villordo, contribuiría al fortalecimiento del mito del gay promiscuo creado desde el exterior de la cultura homosexual, sobre seres lindantes con la marginalidad, hambrientos de sexo, inmersos dentro de una preocupación falocéntrica (que encara a una sexualidad basada en la genitalidad, con un eje que pasaría por la bragueta); también estaría clarificando sobre los verdaderos parámetros de una práctica sexual diferenciada.

Conclusiones

En la etapa en que estoy en mi investigación, podría afirmar que el tema (inexplorado a nivel argentino) del estereotipo gay, está instalado en el imaginario popular, en una suerte de doble escenario con barreras lábiles e imprecisas, construidas a partir de la escasa visibilidad de la mayoría de los homosexuales en la Argentina. Este doble escenario está determinado, desde un lugar interior, propio del grupo de pertenencia de la gente gay (en el cual incluiría también a las lesbianas que no forman parte de esta investigación). Desde afuera, encuentro el lugar referido al "saber popular", donde sitúo el peso de la tradición histórica ligada a la delincuencia y al sanitarismo: el homosexual como enfermo y como delincuente, en ambos casos un hombre disminuido; la "memoria social" construida por acumulación de historias trasmitidas entre generaciones, referidas a historias propias, de familiares, amigos y conocidos. Estas serían las barreras imprecisas, contenidas en la historia de la vida cotidiana, si es que podemos aceptar esta denominación histórica, a las cuales deberíamos agregar como en un juego de espejos y cajas chinas, el mundo de la ficción. Aquí entraría la literatura, en todas sus manifestaciones, pero en especial en la novelística, las obras de teatro, el cine y en las últimas décadas del siglo pasado, la televisión.

Del análisis de la producción literaria, del cine, el teatro y la televisión, y de este enfoque con el estereotipo primario gay, el maricón, el hombre-mujer, podríamos concluir que la característica más anclada en el imaginario popular, es la del homosexual trágico, el hombre torturado, infeliz e incapaz de auto realizarse, como si todas las facetas de la vida y la personalidad estuvieran atravesadas por el eje de la orientación sexual. Esta visión olvida la totalidad del individuo. Habría que esperar si en el futuro, un mayor desarrollo y comprensión del tema de la homosexualidad posibilita una literatura gay con estereotipos más optimistas y felices.

NOTAS

1. Torcuato Di Tella, comp., *Diccionario de ciencias sociales y políticas* (Buenos Aires: Puntosur, 1989), pp. 540–541.

2. Oscar Hermes Villordo, *La brasa en la mano* (Buenos Aires: Bruguera, 1983), p. 8.

3. Ariel Barrios Medina, "Los científicos argentinos ante la homosexualidad", *Revista Quirón* 25, no. 2 (junio 1994): 72.

4. Ibid.

5. Ibid.

6. Anthony Giddens, *La transformación de la intimidad: sexualidad, amor y erotismo en las sociedades modernas* (Madrid: Cátedra, 1995), p. 23.

7. Merton, citado por Ariel Barrios Medina, en *Revista Quirón* 27, no. 3 (Sept. 1996): 99.

8. Ariel Barrios Medina, "Los científicos argentinos", p. 99.

9. Ibid., pp. 100–101.

10. Salustiano Del Campo, *Diccionario de ciencias sociales* (Madrid: Instituto de Estudios Políticos, 1975), 1:826.

11. Ilse Fuskova y Claudina Marek (en diálogo con Silvia Schmid), *Amor de mujeres. El lesbianismo en la Argentina, hoy* (Buenos Aires: Planeta, 1994).

12. Claudio España, comp., *Cine argentino en democracia* (Buenos Aires: Fondo Nacional de las Artes, 1984), p. 11.

13. Ibid.

14. Diana Paladino, "La comedia", en Claudio España, comp., *Cine argentino en democracia* (Buenos Aires: Fondo Nacional de las Artes, 1994), p. 143.

15. David William Foster, *Producción cultural e identidades homoeróticas* (San José: Editorial de la Universidad de Costa Rica, 2000), p. 194.

16. Foster, *Producción cultural,* p. 186.

17. Zelmar Acevedo, *Homosexualidad: hacia la destrucción de los mitos* (Buenos Aires: Ediciones del Ser, 1985), p. 117.

18. Carlos Pacheco, "Provocadoras historias nocturnas", *La Maga* (marzo 2, 2001), http://www.lamaga.com.

10. Gender Relations: Domestic Violence in Trinidad and Tobago

Elmelinda Lara

Introduction

Domestic violence is a worldwide scourge and is now recognized internationally as a crime. This issue is a concern to the United Nations, which has placed it on the United Nations' agenda. Also a manual for practitioners entitled *Strategies for Confronting Domestic Violence: A Resource Manual 1993* has been produced.

The focus of this paper is domestic violence in Trinidad and Tobago as it relates to women. While it is recognized that men also experience domestic violence, a lot of evidence and data point to men as the perpetrators of domestic violence. Studies that highlight similarities in patterns of domestic violence owing to historical reasons will be presented. Other areas that will be highlighted are reasons for and consequences of domestic violence, strategies for dealing with domestic violence, and a review of documentary sources on domestic violence.

The term domestic violence is used in a number of ways. It "is used narrowly to cover incidents of physical attack, when it may take the form of physical and sexual violations, such as punching, choking, stabbing, throwing boiling water or acid and setting fire, the result of which can range from bruising to killing." Or it can "include psychological or mental torture, which can consist of repeated verbal abuse, harassment, confinement, and deprivation of physical and personal resources."[1] Some people use the term "to describe violence against women in the family only" while others use it as a general label to cover any violation where the victim and perpetrator have some form of personal relationship or where they have had such a relationship in the past. "Trinidad and Tobago's Domestic Violence Act. No. 27 of 1999 defines domestic violence in terms of physical, sexual, emotional, psychological or financial abuse committed by a person against a spouse or any other person who is a member of the household or dependent."[2]

Domestic violence is not unique to Trinidad and Tobago or the Caribbean; it is happening throughout the world. It has been traced throughout history, and "evidence does suggest the existence of 'male' violence against women in all societies and across time."[3] But due to a variety of reasons women are no longer prepared to accept domestic violence, and in several countries steps are being taken to eradicate it. Violence against women and children in Caribbean societies cuts across all social and economic classes, color, creed, and race. Violence against women ranges from physical, psychological, and emotional abuse. It includes rape, wife beating, assault, incest, and sexual harassment. Subtle but equally severe are withdrawal of financial or economic support, emotional battering, mental abuse, and withdrawal of sex. However, the most common form of domestic violence in Caribbean societies is wife beating.

Some Reasons for Domestic Violence

According to Counts, Brown, and Campbell, "violence may vary considerably across cultures, depending on belief systems, forms of organization, and patterns of residence, and traditional patterns articulate with new forms, destabilizing the one and creating uncertain outcomes in the other. Immigration, colonization, and migration all serve to create social change, and violence and women's autonomy are often transformed, for better and for worse."[4] This observation when applied to Trinidad and Tobago was consistent with the United Nations' observation that domestic violence was experienced by persons from "all parts of the country, from all educational levels, from all races and from all religions."[5]

Historical Factors

Several factors that have contributed to domestic violence in Trinidad and Tobago include historical, religious, educational, socioeconomic, and cultural factors. Historically, Caribbean societies have experienced the violent and destructive forces of slavery, indentureship, and colonization. Consequently, the resulting family structures and the interpersonal relationships in these families are linked to conflicts leading to incidents of domestic violence, especially against women and children. These family structures in the Caribbean are diverse and encompass nuclear, extended, and single-parent families, as well as a host of other variants.

Religious Beliefs

Belief in the ideology of male dominance, male superiority, and male authority has also been linked to domestic violence. Some men believe in their right to use violence to control women and to reassert their authority if they perceive a threat. The belief in male superiority is usually supported by citing religious doctrine. In a multiethnic, multireligious society like Trinidad and Tobago, the situation is further complicated by adherence to different religious practices and the belief in the supremacy of these religious teachings above the law of the land in some instances.

Various viewpoints on the role of religion in domestic violence have been articulated. Priests and pastors have been blamed for the killing of women and other forms of violence against them, because instead of offering resources and alternatives, they have advised women to return to violent homes and to be "better wives"—violent homes where they are murdered and maimed by their male partners. Women often feel compelled to stay in abusive relationships by scripture mandating them to submit to their husbands or to turn the other cheek. Quite often women are encouraged to pray to relieve their suffering from abuse or pray with the hope that the abuse will end. Many women are also discouraged from revealing abuse to not bring shame to their families. Lack of spirituality was even considered to be the root of the abuse, since the emphasis on material wealth by married couples created emotional stress and eventually violence.

Yet another view is that there is a link between domestic violence and common-law unions, those living outside the confines of state or church sanctioned marriages. A 1990 Central Statistical Report estimated that 40,000 couples in Trinidad and Tobago live in common-law unions. An analysis of calls received by the Domestic Violence Unit of the Ministry of Community Development, Culture and Women's Affairs for 1998 revealed that 70 percent of the calls were from clients in union, common-law relationships. The unit is set up to assist victims and perpetrators of domestic violence.

The instability of these unions, with frequent changing of partners, breed insecurity, resentment, and hostility as well as violence and dire consequences especially for women. Admittedly the high incidence of deaths related to domestic violence has occurred and still continues in common-law relationships.

It was observed that those in common-law unions do not always have the financial or educational resources as their married counterparts and are not always able to cope with the challenges such living arrangements may pose. While married couples seem more stable and are able to conceal conflict better than common-law couples, marriage itself is no immunity against the scourge of domestic violence.

The extent to which religious doctrine has been used to legitimize male violence against women is well supported by Eva Lundgren in her study on religion-based abuse.[6] While there is no corresponding in-depth study of the Trinidad and Tobago situation, evidence exists that points to the role religion plays in domestic violence.

Educational and Socioeconomic Factors

Notwithstanding historical and religious factors, educational and socioeconomic factors have combined to produce a new set of dynamics that lead to domestic violence. These factors seem to be more dominant in issues relating to domestic violence. Some of the issues identified by men and women, which issues feature domestic violence, point to power relations; unemployment; infidelity; the socialization process; the changing role of women in society; and society's tolerance of violence, cultural norms, alcohol, and drug abuse.

Studies have shown that education has played a major role in the liberation and advancement of women in Trinidad and Tobago. While many of the gains benefited the family and the development of society, women have been victims of a violent backlash resulting from these improvements. Education is both beneficial and detrimental to women in Trinidad and Tobago.

Freedom, independence, and the changing role of women—brought about by greater access to information, education, and occupational opportunities— are perceived by men as threats to their power and authority over women. In these circumstances men resort to violence to maintain their control over women and to reassert their once-accepted male authority. Underlying the violence is the assumption of women's subordination to men, the battle for control in the relationship, and the assumption that men and women have certain fixed roles.

One sociologist commented that men are not coping with the new environment, particularly when their ideology is in conflict with reality. The belief taught by the church and various other religious organizations that the man is supposed to be the head of the home is not consistent with reality. Men are displaying an intensity of anger and reacting violently due to changing roles in society. Added to this, there is the view that women are now challenging biblical doctrine and the Bible's teachings about wives being submissive to their husbands. This challenging biblical doctrine is producing violent reactions from men.

Interestingly, the interpretation of domestic violence brought about by increased educational opportunities highlights tensions in gender relations in the society. On one side of the divide there is the view that domestic violence was brought about by "new levels of assertiveness of women which brought with it inordinate degree of arrogance and insensitivity that is tantamount to extreme psychological violence."[7] However, this view cannot apply to the vast majority of women but rather to women of the middle class, the professional type, the college and university graduates, and the female intelligentsia. The irony is that while this grouping is most likely to establish economic independence, project new demands on behalf of women, and are more vocal in asserting women's rights and championing the cause of women; it is the women who are least positioned to be assertive, who are not always financially independent, and who are not in stable unions who seem to be more vulnerable to violence often with deadly consequences.

Even so, professional and educated women are subjected to domestic violence as a consequence of their status. To the extent that men feel threatened by upwardly mobile women and women with greater earning capacity, men have been known to use violence to prevent or attempt to prevent wives, partners, and girlfriends from pursuing higher education or seeking improved job opportunities.

Men also feel threatened by being in direct competition with women for jobs that were once the preserve of men. As a matter of fact, men articulated the view that women were taking away their jobs and this accounted for increased unemployment among them. Needless to say, unemployment of males has often been cited as one of the many reasons for an increase in domestic violence. The problem is further aggravated by the inability to meet the demands of family and social obligations, and by male dependency on an employed female. In this situation feelings of inferiority, resulting tensions, and conflict culminate in violence.

A lack of proper communication skills by some men also accounts for violence against women. Anecdotal evidence points to men's inability to retort to women's sharp tongues. Frustration at not being able to effectively communicate their feelings or to propose meaningful solutions to problems results in a "lashing out" at women. Here can be seen the victim attitude of men who believe that women invite violence due to verbal abuse.

Women's response to the male view is that men are unable to engage in dialogue and to accept differences of opinion without resorting to violence, and are unable to resolve conflict without "killing" everybody. Women are of the view that men cannot cope with emotional stress, which manifests itself in the form of abuse.

Cultural Norms and Values

Culture in some ways sanctions domestic violence. Evidence is overwhelming in calypsoes, which celebrate the beating of women and the sexual exploits of men. An old calypso recommends, "Knock them down, saga boy, knock them down; they love yuh long, they love yuh strong." It is not unusual for lines like these to be used in advertisements to promote cultural events.

Double standards in cultures promote and accept male infidelity, which in local parlance is termed "horning," yet frown on this behavior from women. Death at the hands of a jealous spouse or lover occurs in response to horning or the suspicion of horning.

There is also the view that the way women socialized their sons can lead to violence against women. Mothers, grandmothers, and aunts are often blamed for having two separate codes of behavior for young men and women, that is, girls, not boys, must be responsible.

The accepted practice of corporal punishment for children as a form of discipline in homes and until recently in schools has been thought to contribute to violence against women. It teaches children that violence is acceptable as a legitimate means of resolving conflict. It has been confirmed that boys are beaten more regularly and severely than girls. Studies have shown that violence repeats itself whereby children who come from abusive homes become abusers themselves, and women who come from such environments accept abuse from men.

In addition, manhood and masculinity are equated with control, power, and violence, which is captured in the phrase so often heard in Trinidad and Tobago: "Yuh must show she who is man." According to Dobash and Dobash, "The perpetration of and participation in violent encounters are equated with masculinity, regardless of the outcome."[8]

Domestic violence is seen as a symptom of the violent society in which people live. Some people believe that "men are emotionally weaker than women" and that stress is man's worst enemy; that is, "that if the woman was to leave or horn him today or tomorrow, his world crumbles."[9] Infidelity or the perception of infidelity is often at the heart of many violent encounters and murders. Moreover, the absence of good male role models in a society where men are violent, coupled with alcohol and drug abuse, absentee fathers, and the single-parent (mother) as the head of most families are predisposing factors for domestic violence.

The following insightful comments underline popularly held beliefs and approaches to dealing with domestic violence. While on the surface these appear ludicrous and comical, they signal a seriousness that should these be breached, the outcome is violent explosion:

"If ah can't have, nobody will have her!"

"Look, woman, ah can't take this constant horning with yuh. Ah go kill you if yuh ent stop it!"

"The magistrate too fast to tell meh to keep 100 yards from my wife."

"Girl, if yuh man doh beat yuh, he ent really love yuh."

"Oh gosh! ah ent feeling for sex tonight."

"She ent giving meh enough bed life."

"If yuh only open yuh mouth in meh house, ah go give yuh one good cuff to yuh face. Ah do want no back chat from yuh."

The social advancement of women met with increasing incidence of violence is gleaned from newspaper reports and anecdotal experiences, yet these cases do not reflect the true picture. Len Ishmael, director of ECLAC, said: "It is not possible to get an accurate picture of its incidence in all its manifestation in the Caribbean, nor its variations, because of under-reporting and inadequate compilation of statistical data."[10]

Domestic Violence and Ethnicity

Trinidad and Tobago is a heterogeneous society and in any discussion of domestic violence consideration must be given to ethnicity. It has often been asserted that while "domestic violence transcends all races and classes, it is a fact that women within the East Indian community have been and continue to be victims of all forms of abuse and domestic violence as a common practice."[11] For this ethnic grouping, there is a direct correlation between alcoholism and domestic violence, since alcoholism is a serious problem among the East Indian population.

Domestic violence has been linked to a sense of powerlessness, insecurity, impotence (from alcoholism), infidelity, or a part of learned behavior. The practice of men developing extramarital relationships and the discontinuance of financial support towards wife and children create conflict in the home, giving rise to violence.

Remarriage by men and the expectation of harmony among the wives sometimes lead to violence against the first wife in order to force her to leave the house. Religious leaders in the East Indian community are known to encourage women to be loyal and obedient to their husbands regardless of marital problems. Some older parents also think that it is a shame for abused daughters and children to return to their home. There is much confusion and ambivalence between religious teachings and the laws of Trinidad and Tobago within the East Indian community. While domestic violence is such a common practice among East Indians, women in this community are now treating it as a problem and seeking assistance to deal with it.

Evidence from Guyana as documented in the study *Marital Violence Within East Indian Households in Guyana: A Cultural Explanation,* by Basmat Shiw Parsad, suggests high rates of domestic violence within both Indo- and Afro-Guyanese households and high rates of husband-to-wife violence within East Indian households.

Patterns of violence within East Indian households are attributed to societal and ethnic values concerning violence. Within this ethnic grouping, male dominance and the unquestionable male authority is rooted in religion. Social pressures are also exerted on men to "act in charge," to "show her who is the boss," and to "put the woman in her place."

In spite of current trends that point to increasing labor force participation among Indo-Guyanese women and stronger economic resources, there is still a tolerance of violence from husbands. The suggestion is that "female deference to male authority and power may have an overriding impact on the power derived from economic resources."

Another study of domestic violence in East Indian families in Suriname indicated the occurrence of physical and verbal violence with increasing frequency when the men are intoxicated. Domestic violence was also related to the subordinate position of women and economic dependence.

In Trinidad and Tobago there is the perception as reported by Campbell that Indo-Trinidadian women experienced a greater prevalence of domestic violence.[12] A radio poll in 1999 also supported this view.[13]

Consequences of Domestic Violence

The effects of domestic violence are felt throughout the society. Reports of murders resulting from domestic violence assault the senses with alarming frequency. Several children become orphans or are killed as a result of domestic violence. Statistics for the last decade reveal 36 children, 124 women, and

10 men were killed as a result of domestic violence. It is also believed that one woman was beaten every twenty-three minutes in Trinidad and Tobago.

Statistics for Trinidad and Tobago reveal that murder has reached "alarming proportions" in cases of violence against women. "In 1997, of the 12 persons who were murdered as a result of domestic violence, 83% were women while for 1998, of the 23 persons killed, 61% were women. As of November 1999, 14 women were killed with the month of September being the worst with six reported deaths."[14] During September 1999, which was described as "one of the worst" for domestic violence acts in Trinidad and Tobago, 6 women were killed by enraged spouses. Added to that, the shootings, stabbings, and beatings continued despite interventions by the authorities.

Assaults vary in frequency but follow a pattern, as a consequence of bouts of drinking and drug use. Injuries range from bruises, lacerations, swellings, fractures, and miscarriages. Women are killed at the hands of abusive husbands despite going to the police and exhausting every legal remedy to protect themselves. Apart from the social impact of domestic violence, the issue must also be examined in the context of health. Depression, death, suicide, physical injuries, and psychological problems are some of the health problems.

Additionally there are economic costs associated with domestic violence. Legal costs associated with providing relief sometimes exact a higher price from the victim, who might pay with her life for seeking legal redress. In instances where the perpetrator is removed from the situation, the victim still feels entrapped and emotionally disturbed. Court cases are time-consuming and costly, requiring time off from a job and in some instances transportation fees, legal fees, and loss of earnings. Loss of household belongings, medical costs, legal costs, and transportation costs are some of the domestic violence costs borne by women.

Why Women Endure

- Economic dependence, not in a position to support self and children

- Fear instilled by the man that if she leaves he would kill her

- Lack of support and no alternative

- Lack of education and training to get a job and be self-sufficient

- Unaware of legal rights

- Religious reasons.

Strategies for Dealing with Domestic Violence

Research data presented by Bissessar,[15] indicated that one in four women in Trinidad and Tobago experienced some form of domestic violence and over one quarter of the men on death row have been charged for killing their wives, girlfriends, or common-law spouses. In more recent times, there has been an increase in the brutality of domestic violence and an increase in the number of murders resulting from domestic violence.

In light of the emerging trend, the government of Trinidad and Tobago has prepared a comprehensive plan for tackling the problem. Strategies adopted include being a signatory to a number of international conventions relating to the rights of women; adopting international standards and initiatives; providing legislative reform, including nongovernmental and community-based organizations in plans to deal with the issue; and providing and strengthening support services for victims of domestic violence.

Legislation dealing with domestic violence in Trinidad and Tobago was introduced in 1991, due to mounting pressure from international agencies and nongovernmental organizations such as the Coalition Against Domestic Violence, Caribbean Association for Feminist Research and Action (CAFRA), the University of the West Indies, and various women's groups.

The Domestic Violence Act of 1991 proclaimed domestic violence to be a crime in keeping with the United Nations' recognition of violence against women as a human rights issue and a crime under international law. The act was intended to provide protection from abuse. Reports and data from the Magistrate's Courts revealed that soon after passage of the legislation, cases of domestic violence and applications for protection orders swamped the courts. There was also an increase in the savagery and brutality of domestic violence and murders resulting from domestic violence conflict. Police felt that arresting offenders and taking out restraining orders were not having the desired results.

It soon became evident that the enactment of legislation to deal with domestic violence was inadequate to deal with the nature and scope of the crime. Several shortcomings were identified in the legislation, as well as constraints to providing the necessary support and infrastructure for the legislation to be effective. Issues to be addressed were demands for further legislation, legal counseling and assistance, the inability of the court to deal with the heavy influx of cases, the need for additional personnel, the small fines imposed on the perpetrators, and the reluctance of the police to interfere in what seemed to be essentially a private matter.

In response to the shortcomings of the 1991 act, the Domestic Violence Act of 1999 was introduced. With the 1999 act, it became mandatory for police intervention in situations of domestic violence. The act also sought the following:

- To enhance the powers and jurisdiction of the Magistrate's Court

- To enlarge the ambit of the protection order

- To ensure that the response of the police is efficient and effective.

In addition to legislative reform, the government through its Ministry of Culture and Gender Affairs initiated the following projects: (1) establishment of a male support group to discuss and formulate solutions; (2) setting up of drop-in centers throughout the country; (3) 800-SAVE hotline; (4) Women's Second Chances group which focuses on the training and employment of women in agriculture, elderly care, and other fields; and (5) a women's leadership and enhancement institute, and a multisectoral team, including representatives of the University of the West Indies and various nongovernmental organizations (NGOs), to determine an integrated national policy on domestic violence and an action plan for social progress.

The existence of halfway houses, shelters for battered women, rape crisis centers, and counseling services provides additional support for victims of domestic violence. These initiatives resulted from the efforts of nongovernmental agencies. In Trinidad and Tobago, women's groups organized seminars on the issue and used the media to focus attention on the prevalence of violence.

Legal aid and advice are provided for battered women in Trinidad and Tobago, the cost of which is borne by the state. The aid is intended for persons of small or moderate means.

Groups Dealing with Domestic Violence

At the community level there are groups dealing with domestic violence, some of which are highlighted here:

- Citizens for a Better Trinidad and Tobago

- Women Working for Social Progress (WWSP)

- Men Against Violence Against Women (MAVAW)

- Families in Action

- Caribbean Association for Feminist Research and Action (CAFRA).

International Day Against Violence Against Women (November 22) is usually observed in Trinidad and Tobago.

In the past, most of the attention centered on women as the principal victims of domestic violence. However, the need for some sort of group equipped with the skills, the knowledge, and the experience to counsel and support dysfunctional males resulted in the formation of Men Against Violence Against Women (MAVAW). This group provides the necessary support for such men and has identified areas to eradicate violence against women, including anger management, and confronting internal conflict and negative and abusive beliefs. There is also a suggestion for a home for battered men since men are requesting equality of treatment in response to strategies for dealing with domestic violence against men.

In spite of efforts, the prevalence of domestic violence has increased, so there is a need for other intervention strategies and a change of focus to combat this difficult problem. Instead of dealing with the consequences of domestic violence, it was felt that there is a need for a better understanding of the issue and that more research, data collection, and compilation of statistics were needed.

Criticisms have been leveled against the strategies adopted for dealing with domestic violence. The view was articulated that there was the need to consider the multicultural, multiethnic composition of the society in which a one-size-fits-all approach was flawed.

Regional Strategies

Regional governments in 1991 adopted model legislation on violence against women, which was prepared by CARICOM. This is the basis for national legislation in many of the CARICOM countries. Most of the Caribbean states have enacted legislation dealing with domestic violence and sexual offences. In Antigua and Barbuda, there is the 1996 Domestic Violence Bill and the Sexual Offences Act. In Dominica, there is a similar Sexual Offences Act, and the Law Reform Committee is considering a Family Protection Against Domestic Violence Bill. In Jamaica, amendments to the Offences Against the Person Act and the Incest Act are intended to make changes in the law regarding evidence and procedure in relation to rape, carnal abuse, and incest offences. In St. Kitts-Nevis, there is a Law Reform Programme paying specific attention to women and the family.[16]

In addition to legislative reform, Caribbean governments have provided support to shelters for abused women and children, established a telephone hotline, and provided training for police officers. Nongovernmental organizations have been active in this area, operating most of the shelters for abused women and children, conducting radio programs, hosting public fora, and undertaking candlelight vigils. In spite of all these activities, domestic violence against women is on the increase according to the various NGOs and regional institutions monitoring the situation.

Caribbean ministers have agreed to "an urgent need to tackle the root cause of violence" and recommended that policy and program interventions be based on a better understanding of the issue.

These recommendations are consistent with recommendations of the Platform for Action, which came out of the Beijing Conference and called on governments and other actors to promote research, collect data, and compile statistics on domestic violence against women, as well as support and initiate research on the impact of violence. In 1997 the regional governments approved the Charter of Civil Society for the region, which promotes policies and measures aimed at strengthening gender equality and ensuring that all women have equal rights with men in the political, civic, economic, social, and cultural spheres.

Discourse, Documentation, and Direction

At the societal level, much of the discourse on domestic violence is facilitated by the media. Newspapers, radio, and television provide firsthand accounts of the consequences of domestic violence. Details are often gory and revolting, and it is argued that these scenes should not occupy the front pages of newspapers or be lead stories on television. However, relegating it to less prominent positions or playing it down will not eliminate it.

Newspaper articles, comments, interviews, editorials, and basic information tips all contribute to a heightened awareness of the problem. Radio and television programs keep the issue alive as they attempt to inform and educate the public. As a result there is a growing body of literature emanating from the media, which literature is useful for research purposes.

In the academic arena, the issue is receiving scholarly attention. The Centre for Gender and Development Studies of the University of the West Indies is engaged in research in the area. The Women and Development Studies Groups on the three campuses of the University of the West Indies are involved in activities aimed at improving gender relations in Caribbean societies. This group has published *Gender in Caribbean Development* as well as two other publications. The Library of the University of the West Indies, St. Augustine Campus, holds Caribbean studies theses on the issue of domestic violence, in addition to other regional and international publications. In addition, *Carindex* provides a useful bibliographic tool for researching the issue.

Added to this, the output of seminars, workshops, and conferences hosted by the Economic Commission of Latin America and the Caribbean, the University of the West Indies, Government Ministries, and other organizations contribute to the research literature. *The Caribbean Journal of Criminology and Social Psychology* devoted an entire issue to domestic violence. Some information is also available in electronic sources, for example, OCLC, which provides country reports.

Conclusion

Domestic violence is a complex phenomenon and requires a multifaceted approach for its elimination. Apart from social and legislative policy reform, instruments of change include homes, schools, religions, and the media.

Part of the solution can be to include men in sessions on treating domestic violence, rather than directing solution to women only. Men need to be included in the formulation of solutions since they are part of the problem. Education is seen as the key to addressing gender-relations conflict and enabling conflict resolution, mediation, and ideological change that would eventually lead to a reduction or an elimination of domestic violence.

NOTES

1. Miranda Davies, ed., *Women and Violence* (London: Zed Books, 1994), pp. 1–2.

2. Monica Williams, "Domestic Violence and Family Relationships: Policy Recommendations," *Caribbean Journal of Criminology and Social Psychology* 5, no. 1–2 (January/July 2000): 193.

3. R. Emerson Dobash and Russell P. Dobash, *Rethinking Violence Against Women* (Thousand Oaks, Calif.: Sage Publications, 1998), p. 16.

4. Dobash and Dobash, *Rethinking Violence Against Women,* pp. 12–13.

5. Roanna Gopaul et al., *Women, Family and Family Violence in the Caribbean: The Historical and Contemporary Experience with Special Reference to Trinidad and Tobago* (St. Augustine: UWI Women and Development Studies Group, Centre for Gender and Development, 1994), p. 61.

6. Eva Lundgren, "The Hand That Strikes: Gender Construction and the Tension between Body and Symbol," in *Rethinking Violence Against Women,* ed. Dobash and Dobash, pp. 169–198.

7. Bukkha Rennie, "Violence—A Gender Perspective," *Trinidad Guardian* (November 10, 1999): 9.

8. Dobash and Dobash, *Rethinking Violence Against Women,* p. 15.

9. Ricardo Welch, "Square Debates, Solutions to Domestic Violence," *Trinidad Guardian* (November 22, 1999): 10.

10. Donna Pierre, "Violence Against Women Increasing," *Trinidad Guardian* (October 7, 1999): 16.

11. Hulsie Bhaggan, "Sick Indian Men and Hypocrites," *The Independent* (November 6, 1998).

12. Jacquelyn C. Campbell, ed., *Assessing Dangerousness: Violence by Sexual Offenders, Batterers, and Child Abusers* (Thousand Oaks, Calif.: Sage Publications, 1995).

13. Joan M. Rawlins, "Domestic Violence in Trinidad: A Family and Health Problem," *Caribbean Journal of Criminology and Social Psychology* 5, no. 1–2 (January/July 2000): 165–180.

14. Peter Richards, "Are T & T Men Pressure Cookers?" *Trinidad Guardian* (November 29, 1999): 11.

15. Ann Marie Bissessar, "Policy Transfer and Implementation Failure: A Review of the Policy of Domestic Violence in Trinidad and Tobago," *Caribbean Journal of Criminology and Social Psychology* 5, no. 1–2 (January/July 2000): 57–80.

16. Richards, "Are T & T Men Pressure Cookers?" p. 11.

BIBLIOGRAPHY

Bhaggan, Hulsie. "Sick Indian Men and Hypocrites." *The Independent* (November 6, 1998).

Bissessar, Ann Marie. "Policy Transfer and Implementation Failure: A Review of the Policy of Domestic Violence in Trinidad and Tobago." *Caribbean Journal of Criminology and Social Psychology* 5, no. 1–2 (January/July 2000): 57–80.

Browne, Juhel. "The Common Factor: Archbishop Anthony Pantin Links Domestic Violence to Unions Outside of Marriage." *Trinidad Guardian* (October 11, 1999): 17.

Campbell, Jacquelyn C., ed. *Assessing Dangerousness: Violence by Sexual Offenders, Batterers, and Child Abusers.* Thousand Oaks, Calif.: Sage Publications, 1995.

"Citizens for Better T & T Blames Priests for Violence." *Trinidad Guardian* (November 30, 1999): 13.

Counts, Dorothy Ayers, Judith K. Brown, and Jacquelyn C. Campbell, eds. *Sanctions and Sanctuary: Cultural Perspectives on the Beating of Wives.* Boulder, Colo.: Westview, 1992.

Davies, Miranda, ed. *Women and Violence.* London: Zed Books, 1994.

Dobash, R. Emerson, and Russell P. Dobash. *Rethinking Violence Against Women.* Thousand Oaks, Calif.: Sage Publications, 1998.

Ellis, Pat, ed. *Women of the Caribbean.* London: Zed Books, 1986.

Gopaul, Roanna, et al. *Women, Family, and Family Violence in the Caribbean: The Historical and Contemporary Experience with Special Reference to Trinidad and Tobago.* St. Augustine: UWI Women and Development Studies Group, Centre for Gender and Development, 1994.

Kamugisha, Stephanie. "Violence Against Women." In *Women of the Caribbean,* edited by Pat Ellis. London: Zed Books, 1986. Pp. 74–79.

Khodabaks-Hasnoe, Rehanna, and Maureen Habieb. "Gender Issues in the Indian Joint Family System in Contemporary Rural Suriname." In *Matikor: The Politics of Identity for Indo-Caribbean Women,* edited by Rosanne Kanhai. St. Augustine: UWI, School of Continuing Studies, 1999. Pp. 32–39.

Leo-Rhynie, Elsa, Barbara Bailey, and Christine Barrow. *Gender: A Caribbean Multi-Disciplinary Perspective.* Kingston: Ian Randle Publishers, 1997.

"Licks for Children Leads to 'Licks' for Women." *Express* (November 27, 1999): 35.

Phillips, Daphne. "Domestic Violence and Public Policy in Trinidad and Tobago." *Caribbean Journal of Criminology and Social Psychology* 5, no. 1–2 (January/July 2000): 181–188.

———. "Men Should Also Be Present at Domestic Violence Sessions." *Trinidad Guardian* (November 30, 1999): 18.

Pierre, Donna. "Violence Against Women Increasing." *Trinidad Guardian* (October 7, 1999): 16.

Rawlins, Joan M. "Domestic Violence in Trinidad: A Family and Health Problem." *Caribbean Journal of Criminology and Social Psychology* 5, no. 1–2 (January/July 2000): 165–180.

Rennie, Bukhka. "Violence—A Gender Perspective." *Trinidad Guardian* (November 10, 1999): 9.

Report of the Ad Hoc Committee for the Reform of the Domestic Violence, 1991 and Related Legislation. *Trinidad Guardian Supplement* (November 9, 1997).

Richards, Peter. "Are T & T Men Pressure Cookers?" *Trinidad Guardian* (November 29, 1999): 11.

———. "Domestic Violence on the Rise in Caribbean." *Trinidad Guardian* (November 29, 1999): 11.

Strategies for Confronting Domestic Violence: A Resource Manual. New York: United Nations, 1993.

Welch, Ricardo. "Square Debates, Solutions to Domestic Violence." *Trinidad Guardian* (November 22, 1999): 10.

Williams, Monica. "Domestic Violence and Family Relationships: Policy Recommendations." *Caribbean Journal of Criminology and Social Psychology* 5, no. 1–2 (January/July 2000): 193–201.

Zellerer, Evelyn. "Domestic Violence in Trinidad and Tobago: Some Comments." *Caribbean Journal of Criminology and Social Psychology* 5, no. 1–2 (January/July 2000): 209–227.

11. Women in Trinidad and Tobago: Role of Education and Politics

Jennifer Joseph

Introduction

At the start of the twenty-first century, women of the Caribbean, and in particular the women of Trinidad and Tobago, can be proud of their achievements. They are well represented in every sphere of life and have made significant inroads into areas that traditionally had been the domain of men. Women are now active at the highest levels in business, politics, industry, the legal profession, and the public sector. Education has been the key to women's empowerment and attainment of status in the society, and women continue to utilize fully the opportunities that education provides as the vehicle for upward mobility and the route to self-sufficiency.

Indeed, the developments in education laid the foundation for the advancement of women in a society whose structures and systems had excluded women. This paper will attempt to highlight the achievements of women in Trinidad and Tobago, with some emphasis on their involvement in politics and education. However, any description or evaluation of the dynamics of the achievements and role of women in the sphere of education and politics in Trinidad and Tobago must be set against the background of colonialism, decolonization, the ethnic composition, and the cultural mores upon which modern Trinidad and Tobago has developed. The paper will therefore trace the historical development of women's achievements and activities in Trinidad and Tobago, and the concurrent efforts to document these achievements.

Women of the Caribbean: Current Status

Women of the Caribbean, specifically in Trinidad and Tobago, are seen as strong and independent. They are faced with a variety of challenges including poverty, unemployment, and racial and class differences and biases. However, in the face of all the challenges, women have been able to move into nontraditional areas and many have moved to the top of their professions. By the mid-1970s in Trinidad and Tobago, women represented about one-third of the labor force, whereas in 1960, they had represented only 23.79 percent (Reddock 1994, 186). Throughout the Caribbean, women hold senior management and administrative positions both within public and private sectors. In Trinidad and Tobago, women now hold the highest positions in the public service—out of a total of twenty-two permanent secretaries and heads of departments, fifteen are women. In addition, the solicitor general, the chief parliamentary counsel, the auditor general, the chief personnel officer, and the comptroller of accounts are women. Women predominate in the teaching and nursing professions. At the University of the West Indies, several key positions are held by women including the deputy principal (currently acting as the principal); the campus bursar and deputy bursar; the assistant registrars for Examinations, Student Affairs and Appointments; and the campus librarian and deputy librarian. The current president of the Public Services Trade Union is female. Some women also hold high office in regional and international organizations. Indeed, the achievements of women in the Caribbean are all the more significant since women have continued to fulfill the gender stereotype role and responsibility for child care and home management.

Developmental Issues

The special circumstances of women in Trinidad and Tobago are rooted in the unique events that have brought together people of different races and various cultures on these two small islands, which in a sense have even been socialized differently. Trinidad and its Amerindian population was discovered in 1498 by Christopher Columbus and remained as a dependency of Spain until it was captured by the British in 1797. Following the abolition of slavery in 1838, the demand for labor for the sugar estates opened the way for the arrival of indentured laborers from China, Portugal, and mainly from India. The history of Tobago evolved differently since the island did not change hands as frequently, neither did indentured laborers settle there. Tobago has therefore remained essentially with a population descended from African slaves. In 1899, the nearby island of Tobago was made into a ward of Trinidad, signifying the start of the union of Trinidad and Tobago as a single state (Mohammed 1987, 5).

The islands of Trinidad and Tobago are therefore populated by people of African descent who were converted to Christianity, a large number of Indians who are mainly Hindus, and a smaller number of Muslims. A small percentage of the Indian immigrants were later converted to Christianity. The blacks are essentially from the more urban areas and Tobago, while the Indians continue to live mainly in the rural areas. The developments in education eventually provided equal opportunity to all and opened the way for women of Indian descent to participate fully in national life, despite the constraints placed on their role as circumscribed by the Hindu and Muslim faiths (Mohammed 1987, 24–25).

The British way of life, political structures, and education system dominated the islands of Trinidad and Tobago for a long time. This social structure maintained the primacy of the foreign, white bourgeoisie over a colored middle class, a black urban working class, and the East Indian agricultural workers. The educational structure was imported from Britain and fully encompassed its philosophy, curriculum, methodology, textbooks, and certification (Reddock 1994, 52–56).

In the late-nineteenth century and early-twentieth century, the education system in place reinforced the biases of colonial society. That is, upper-class men were educated to become leaders, professionals, and senior officers within the colonial administration, while upper-class women were socialized for their role as "good wives and mothers" (Senior 1991, 46). Until then, elementary schooling for blacks was provided by small private schools established by plantation owners or Christian missionaries. A report of Lord Patrick Keenan in 1869 on the state of public education in Trinidad suggested that the responsibility for education should be shared between the state and the church. By 1885, there were sixty-one church-assisted schools and fifty-five government schools in Trinidad. The church schools were run by Roman Catholics, Wesleyans, Anglicans, Moravians, and Canadian Presbyterians (Reddock 1994, 50–53). Religion and religious institutions have played an important role in encouraging and facilitating the participation of women in the education system. For most women of African and East Indian descent, only a very basic form of education was available through the primary school system, which offered rudimentary education to all, dating back to 1835.

The missionaries of the Presbyterian Church were responsible for the entry of Indian women into education. Prior to this, East Indians had not made any significant attempt to take advantage of educational opportunities. Research has shown that illiteracy in English and fear of derision by the rest of the school population were factors that kept them from participating. The Canadian missions established special Indian schools, which were used to teach and convert the East Indians to Christianity. As a result, the Presbyterian East Indians were the first to enter the professions, business and politics (Rouse-Jones 1988, 174).

Gender-Specific Education

There was limited secondary education, mainly for the upper-class white males. In the mid-thirties to the early sixties, the existing education system facilitated the development of boys in the industrial and technical fields, while girls were prepared for a domesticated life—a relic of the colonial era. The only secondary school for girls in the nineteenth century, St. Joseph's Convent, was provided for whites and the elite coloreds. In practice, schools taught home economics, cookery, etc., to girls, while boys were taught woodwork and other handicraft (Reddock 1994, 49). This kind of "gender-specific" education was also the norm at the postprimary level. Schools channeled girls into traditional careers such as social work, teaching, and nursing. Indeed, girls who made it into secondary schools fell into the gender stereotype and chose the careers of teaching, social work, nursing, and secretarial work (Pasley 1999, 88).

Educational Reform

In the postwar years, educational reforms were closely linked with the expansion of the economic and political systems of the West Indies. Between the late-nineteenth and early-twentieth centuries, girls' schools were increasingly established, for example, Tranquility Girls' School, St. Hilary's College (later Bishop Anstey High School), and Naparima Girls College. In Tobago, the coeducational Bishops High School was established in 1927. However, many of these schools were fee-based secondary schools and effectively excluded the majority of the female population until the introduction of free secondary education in the 1960s. Intermediate schools were introduced to absorb those persons who could not go to secondary schools. By 1937, the number of girls receiving secondary education had risen from zero in 1903 to 922; for boys the increase was from 375 to 1215 (Reddock 1994, 50).

The year 1939 saw the start of revisions to the curriculum and the introduction of textbooks written for the Caribbean. A significant milestone in education in the Caribbean was the report of the West India Royal Commission, headed by Lord Moyne. The commission found that women were effectively debarred from participation in public life, in particular they did not hold office or administrative posts, and they did not have equal access to civil service jobs. The Moyne commission report recommended, inter alia, equality of educational opportunity and improved education for girls. Policies to democratize education replaced the more biased gender policies, which had discriminated against girls and women (Senior 1991, 50). In 1946, the number of school places available for girls was approximately 40 percent lower than for boys. The People's National Movement (P.N.M.) advocated equality in education, and by 1960 the introduction of the Common Entrance Examination facilitated entrance by both sexes to secondary and assisted secondary schools. Since the 1960s, there is a free, compulsory system of education at the primary and secondary school levels that offers equal opportunity for all. However, statistics have shown that there is a higher dropout rate among males (Reddock 1994, 55). The establishment of the University of the West Indies in 1948 opened the world of higher education to women who would later take full advantage of the opportunities offered.

The Growing Influence of Women in the Society in the 20th Century

Women began to play a greater role as educators, especially through their connection with churches. However, there were several barriers against female teachers. For example, married women were not allowed to be teachers. In 1950, women represented 26.6 percent of civil service employees, and there were no women in the police force. They served as civil servants, teachers, nurses, and social workers. Men predominated in the teaching service until the mid-1950s. However, women now outnumber men as school teachers and principals, although studies have linked the differences in the numbers of teachers in education with salaries, indicating that men generally leave teaching for higher paid jobs. At the university level, although many women hold key positions at the academic and administration level, men hold the vast majority of senior posts.

Women and Trade Unionism

The involvement of women in trade unionism was first linked to education. What appears to be the precursor to the Trinidad and Tobago Teachers' Union was the Assistant and Pupil Teachers Union, which apparently installed three women as officers on September 6, 1919 (Reddock 1994, 142). Women were also associated with the struggles of the Trinidad Workingmen's Association (TWA), which took place in the 1920s.

A few women are featured in Trinidad and Tobago's trade union history. Mrs. Ursula Gittens was the first female president of the Public Services Association. In addition, Ms. Daisy Crick headed the powerful Women's Auxiliary Arm of the Oilfields Workers Trade Union. Another significant person involved in the trade union was Ms. Elma Francois, who was the founder and principal leader of the Marxist-oriented Negro Welfare Cultural and Social Association (NWCSA), which strove for gender equality. The group assisted Tubal Uriah Buzz Butler in organizing the general strike and insurrection that began on June 19, 1937.

The riots of 1937 led by Butler signaled a new era in trade unionism and the labor movement. In this new scenario, trade union activity was to be transformed from direct confrontation with the employer/ruling class to dependence on a mediator from British institutions. Butler himself was expelled from the union. This period also signified a decline in the involvement of women in trade unions. After World War II, there was a resurgence of trade union activity and more women were actively encouraged to join (Reddock 1994, 142–146).

Women and Politics

The advancement of women in education and politics in Trinidad and Tobago is linked to the birth and development of the P.N.M., and the leadership of Dr. Eric Williams, the first premier and prime minister of Trinidad and Tobago. Williams paid particular attention to women's struggle for equality, especially in the sphere of education. Indeed, in his publication, *Education and the British West Indies,* he advocated the education of women, especially at the university level. Universal adult franchise was granted in 1946 and for the first time all women could vote. Williams assisted the League of Women Voters and spoke to the group whenever he was asked. Out of this group later came several of the foundation members of his party's Women's League. The P.N.M. Women's League became the vehicle by which women entered fully into the political landscape of Trinidad and Tobago (Reddock 1994, 297–306).

P.N.M. Women's League

After 1956, the P.N.M. Women's League was the base from which women entered politics. The inaugural meeting of the Women's League was held on May 19, 1956, at the headquarters of the Coterie of Social Workers. From the start, the league was established as a fixed part of the party structure. Membership was open to all women throughout the villages, and women of the lower end of the strata of society were encouraged to join. Williams gave working-class and middle-strata Afro-Trinidadian women a sense of importance. The league stressed the importance of women's role in the home. In this organization women were offered the opportunity to learn management and organizational skills (Reddock 1994, 306). The Women's League continues to be broad-based and is represented at the party's annual convention. The league, however, has remained a fairly conservative arm of the party, always openly supportive of the (male) leader's stance on party and national issues. The organization became known for its almost fanatical support of the leader.

Women in Politics: 1956 to the Present

Over the last half-century, women have always been involved in politics. However, their role has been largely supportive. Women have been active in the campaigns and as party workers. In comparison to men, however, few have put themselves forward for service at the highest level. The P.N.M. remained in power continuously from 1956 to 1986 and several women have held ministerial office and served in the Cabinet or as government senators. In the 1970s the prime minister coined the term "Kitchen Cabinet" when he named five women as ministers. While the appointment was a breakthrough for women, many persons viewed the use of the word "kitchen" as maintaining the gender stereotype of the woman's place being in the home. During the 1991–1995 term of the P.N.M., a woman was occasionally given responsibility as attorney general and minister for Legal Affairs in the absence of the appointed (male) attorney general. Another was appointed as the Speaker of the House. Under the government of the United National Congress (U.N.C.), which assumed power in 1995, a woman was actually appointed attorney general but served in that position for only two and a half months! More recently, for the first time in Trinidad and Tobago, a woman was allowed to "act" as prime minister for one week. Another was given that honor for a mere two days. However, it is clear that the highest level of politics in Trinidad and Tobago is still viewed as a man's domain since the various appointments seem to demonstrate a certain level of tokenism. No woman has ever been appointed to any of the traditionally tougher ministries such as National Security and Finance. Indeed, a comparison with other Caribbean countries would show that Trinidad and Tobago lags behind in the participation of women at the highest political level. The island of Dominica has had a female prime minister and the current deputy prime minister and minister for Foreign Affairs in Barbados is a woman.

Organizations Working for Women's Status

The Centre for Gender and Development Studies (CGDS) at the University of the West Indies was established in 1993, subsequent upon the development of Women and Development Studies Groups. These groups had been established on the three campuses of UWI in 1982 as a result of a regional meeting called by the Women and Development Unit (WAND), which had been established in 1977. The center is regional in scope and is committed to a program of teaching, research, and outreach that "questions historically accepted theories and explanations about society and human behaviour; seeks an understanding of the world which takes women, their lives and achievements into account; identifies the origins of power differences between men and women, and the division of human characteristics along gender lines." As a result, the center has introduced an integrated program of gender and development studies at both the undergraduate and graduate levels. In addition, research is conducted on women and gender-related issues in the Caribbean. Outreach includes linkages with and the empowerment of national and regional institutions concerned with gender and development (CGDS brochure). With the institutionalization of the Centre for Gender and Development Studies in 1993 at St. Augustine, a decision was taken to continue the work of the Women and Development Studies Group (WDSG). This group, which has over one hundred members, continues to exist as the support, staff development, and outreach arm of the center.

The Caribbean Association for Feminist Research and Action (CAFRA) is an organization of feminist researchers and activists committed to understanding the relationship between the oppression of women and other forms of exploitation in the society—and working actively to change the situation. CAFRA seeks, inter alia, to develop research priorities based on the needs of women and to develop a base of documentation on the women's movement in the Caribbean. CAFRA has national representatives in several Caribbean islands.

Documentary Sources

The success and progress of women in the society is now documented fairly well. The Centre for Gender and Development Studies at the three campuses of the University of the West Indies is responsible for a Caribbean region research program. The center at St. Augustine is responsible for several initiatives aimed at generating knowledge in the area. CGDS therefore has a growing body of literature that is being generated by staff, students, and other research persons. The Working Paper Series attempts to facilitate the discussion and debate on contemporary issues related to women and gender. The

Faculty of Humanities and Education is also a source for several postgraduate theses on the contribution of women in education.

As part of the Oral and Pictorial Records Programme (OPReP) of the University Libraries at St. Augustine, interviews have been conducted with some women on women's issues and challenges. Interviews were conducted as follows:

- Althea Lashley (nursing, West Indian)

- Adeline Dumas (nursing, Tobago)

- Ann Murray (teacher)

- Viola Gopaul Whittington (descendant of African-Indian)

- Stella Abidh (doctor, East Indian)

- Violet Thorpe (social welfare and political organizations)

- East Indian women

- Education of Muslim women.

Outside of the university, there have been several publications highlighting the work and contribution of women to the society. In 1991, the *Daily Express* published a collection of photographs and biographical data entitled *The 90 Most Prominent Women in Trinidad and Tobago,* highlighting the contribution of a select group of women. In 1993, there was yet another publication dedicated to women. This publication, *Why Not A Woman,* edited by Mrs. Radica Saith, provided profiles of women from all walks of life. At the time of publication, Saith's husband was a minister of government in the P.N.M. regime (1991–1995).

In 1996, the Bishop Anstey High School, a prominent girls' school in the capital city, Port of Spain, published a commemorative calendar for its diamond jubilee, profiling school graduates who had made a significant contribution to the society.

An annotated bibliography entitled *East Indian Women of Trinidad and Tobago* was published by Kumar Mahabir in 1992. It is the first book to be published in the Caribbean specifically about Indian women. It includes photographs and provides information on 236 successful Indian women who live in Trinidad and Tobago and abroad, as well as annotations of newspaper articles about East Indian women.

Shades of I-She is a dramatic production combining vocals, music, and dance with a collection of poetry/dramatic pieces about women written by Pearl Eintou Springer, director of the National Heritage Library. This production focuses on many of the issues that women have traditionally struggled against in silence, such as rape and incest.

The press has had a major role in highlighting the achievement and involvement of women in the society, signifying in particular their entrance into male-dominated occupations. For example, the *Trinidad Guardian* of April 5, 1966, reported on the first woman who was appointed as a meteorological assistant at the Meteorological Services. Again, in 1998, one daily newspaper highlighted women in public service.

On the website of the National Library and Information System Authority (http://www.nalis.gov.tt), "Women of Substance" in Trinidad and Tobago are also highlighted. The website includes biographical data on some of the earliest pioneers who have left their mark on education, politics, social services, and the police service.

Trinidad Women Speak, edited by Dr. Bori S. Clark, comprises seven interviews with women of different social and ethnic backgrounds, and serves to highlight and illustrate the social reality and changing status of women at a point in the society's history. It focuses on employed women who have a "life" beyond that of housewife and mother.

Women Achievers: A Sample

Audrey Jeffers was the founder of the Coterie of Social Workers in 1921. This organization comprised mainly respectable women of African descent. The aim of the organization was to assist the underprivileged and to raise the status of black middle-class women (and men) in the society. Jeffers came from the small, black property-owning class. In 1929, she was recommended by the Legislative Council to represent Trinidad and Tobago at the National Council for Women in Great Britain. In 1936, she was elected to the Port of Spain City Council, and in l946 she became the first woman to be elected to the Legislative Council.

Isabel Teshea, an early member of the P.N.M., was associated with several "firsts." She was the first woman to be elected to the House of Representatives, the first woman government minister, and the first woman to serve as an ambassador. She became chairman of the Women's League in 1956 as well as Lady Vice-Chairman of the P.N.M., and retained both posts for several years.

Gema Ramkeesoon was a leading voluntary social worker. She served as president of several voluntary social welfare services, the Caribbean Women's Association, the Young Women's Christian Association (YWCA), and the Soroptomists International. Ramkeesoon successfully balanced her social work with the nurturing of her six children. She was also active in politics and spoke on political platforms in the preindependence period. For her outstanding service to work, she was honored both locally and internationally. In 1950 she was presented with the prestigious award of Member of the British Empire (MBE) and was given a special award by the judges of the Guardian (newspaper) Women of Trinidad and Tobago Awards in 1996.

Dr. Anna Mahase, a product of the Presbyterian education system, has played a major role in education in Trinidad and Tobago as principal of the St. Augustine Girls' High School for thirty-two of her forty years in the teaching profession. Under her guidance, the St. Augustine Girls' School has maintained very high standards. Many of the school graduates continue to make a significant contribution to the society. On January 1, 1994, Mahase became chairman of the Campus Council for the University of the West Indies at St. Augustine, making a direct contribution to the developments in tertiary education. She was also awarded an honorary doctorate by the University of the West Indies for her contribution to education. She has served as board of director for several state corporations and has also been involved at the political level as an independent senator. She maintains the motto "blessed is the woman who knows what must be done, twice blessed is she who gets the job done."

Ms. Pat Bishop has achieved in several spheres. She is committed to the pursuit of scholarship, culture, and the arts (in particular painting and music); and service to her country in fields as diverse as environmental education, government economic policy, and the development of Carnival and the steel band. She is the holder of the country's highest award and was conferred with the Hon. D.LITT. by the University of the West Indies in 1994. She is the director of the Lydian Singers, one of the country's leading choirs. As a historian, Bishop is constantly working at gathering information about her country and identifying the sources of its cultural heritage.

Conclusion

Education has given women economic independence and entry into the professional strata, previously dominated by men. The reforms and developments in education have allowed women to take their place in society alongside men. Women with the highest levels of education have made significant breakthroughs while a large number of women still maintain the "feminine" occupations of teaching, nursing, and social work. However, education and the subsequent achievements of professional women have altered the relationship between men and women and have assisted women at all levels and in all occupations to assert their sexual equality and independence. The statistics show that there is a higher dropout rate among men in the education system. Women and girls seem to generally perform better in school and in examinations and earn more than their male counterparts. The question of male underachievement now arises.

Despite the advances and general achievement of women in the society, there are lingering prejudices. The status quo may have visibly changed, while psychologically it is not really evident that there has been any change. Women have managed to transcend the traditional expectations of the economy and the society, despite the fact that they maintain the role in the family as the nurturer. Indeed, the issue of gender relations in the home has now taken "center stage," perhaps in the wake of the changing occupational roles that educational opportunities have opened to women. At the same time, men seem to find it difficult to accept the independence of women. This situation has perhaps led to an increase in domestic violence in the society. The issue of domestic violence awaits further research.

SELECT BIBLIOGRAPHY

Ali, Shameen. 1993. "A Social History of East Indian Women Since 1870." Master's thesis, University of the West Indies.

Daily Express. 1991. *The 90 Most Prominent Women in Trinidad and Tobago*. Port of Spain, Trinidad: Inprint Caribbean.

Drayton, Kathleen. 1995. *Gender Issues in Education: A Review of the Major Gender Issues in Education and of Relevant Caribbean Studies*. Castries, St. Lucia: Organization of Eastern Caribbean States.

Ellis, Pat, ed. 1986. *Women of the Caribbean*. London: Zed Books.

Mahabir, Noorkumar. 1992. *East Indian Women of Trinidad and Tobago: An Annotated Bibliography*. Port of Spain, Trinidad: Chakra Publishing House.

Mohammed, Patricia. 1981. "Women and Education in Trinidad and Tobago, 1838–1930." Master's thesis, University of the West Indies.

———. 1987. *An Analysis of the Post World War II Educational Attainment of Women in Trinidad and Tobago*. St. Augustine, Trinidad: University of the West Indies.

Pasley, Victoria. 1999. "Gender, Race and Class in Urban Trinidad: Representations in the Construction and Maintenance of the Gender Order, 1950–1980." Ph.D. dissertation, University of Houston.

Reddock, Rhoda. 1988. *The NWCSA and the Workers' Struggle for Change in the Caribbean*. London: New Beacon Books.

———. 1994. *Women, Labour and Politics in Trinidad and Tobago: A History*. London: Zed Books.

Rouse-Jones, Margaret. 1987. "Recent Research in the History of Trinidad and Tobago: A Review of the Journal and Conference Literature, 1975–1985." In *Caribbean Collections: Recession Management Strategies for Libraries*, edited by Mina Jane Grothey. Papers of SALALM XXXII, Miami, Florida, May 10–15, 1987. Madison: SALALM, 1988. Pp. 169–194.

Saith, Radica. 1993. *Why Not A Woman*. Port of Spain, Trinidad: Paria Publishing.

Senior, Olive. 1991. *Working Miracles: Women's Lives in the English-Speaking Caribbean*. London: James Currey and Indiana University Press.

Taylor, Ewart. 1995. *Women in School Administration: Exclusion and Isolation*. St. Augustine, Trinidad: University of the West Indies.

Todd, Neila. 1999. *Legacy of the Coterie of Social Workers*. Port of Spain, Trinidad: Texprint.

Research Sources on Gender, Sexuality, and Ethnicity

12. Gay, Lesbian, and Transgendered Serials in Brazil

Robert Howes

The year 2001 marked the twentieth anniversary of the demise of the most famous Brazilian gay serial, *Lampião,* and nearly four decades of lesbian and gay journal publishing in Brazil. This paper will present an overview of the development of Brazilian lesbian and gay serials, attempting to categorize the various titles that have appeared over the years, and then note the titles that are currently available before concluding with some notes on sources for acquisitions and research.[1]

Journals have special characteristics that differentiate their cultural and historical significance from books. They are primarily a collective endeavor and generally presuppose a group of people with shared interests, both among the producers, those who write and publish them, and among the audience, those who subscribe to, buy, or read them. However ephemeral, journals represent and create a community of interests that extends over time. To their immediate readers, gay journals often provide the key to information about the physical location, lifestyle, cultural interests, and political views of the gay community, and so a chance to become a member of that community. For historians, they are a tangible resource but, as well as their utilitarian uses, they also serve to mold the culture they represent.

It is possible to identify three key factors in the development of the lesbian and gay press in Brazil:

1. Developments in the gay community itself—the last forty years have seen a growing visibility, self-confidence, and assertiveness among lesbians and gays worldwide, which has had its counterpart in Brazil. There has been a thriving gay subculture in the major cities, such as Rio de Janeiro and São Paulo, at least since the late-nineteenth century. Rapid urbanization, changes in gender relations, the influence of feminism and alternative lifestyle philosophies, and the increasing impact of international gay culture through globalization have encouraged the growth of a self-conscious gay community. At the same time many aspects of lesbian and gay life specific to Brazil, such as travestis, have continued to flourish.

2. The national political context—the growth of the international gay liberation movement in the early 1970s coincided with the most repressive period of the military regime in Brazil. Although gays were not directly

targeted, press censorship and the atmosphere of fear and intimidation effectively inhibited the development of a gay movement or gay press in this period. The foundation of *Lampião* and the explosive growth of the Brazilian lesbian and gay movement in the late 1970s formed part of the general political liberalization or "abertura" created as the military began to relinquish power.

3. Developments in printing technology—in Brazil, as elsewhere, developments in printing technology, such as the mimeograph, photocopying, offset litho, and desktop publishing, have made publishing cheaper and have allowed relatively small groups and organizations to publicize their views. The recent growth of the Internet is a further step in this direction.

Brazilian lesbian and gay journals can be grouped into six main categories:

1. Gay movement publications: bulletins and newsletters published by groups, whether formally or informally constituted, and intended primarily for their own members or individuals with an interest in the issues addressed by the group.

2. Community newspapers: titles intended for general circulation among the lesbian, gay, and transgendered community, with an emphasis on political comment, gay rights, news, and cultural matters.

3. Lesbian publications: serials published by and for lesbians.

4. Lifestyle magazines: glossy magazines published by commercial publishers for general sale, with an emphasis on fashion and culture.

5. Erotica: glossy magazines containing nude photographs but excluding explicit sexual activity.

6. AIDS: serials concentrating on issues relating to HIV and AIDS.

There is inevitably some overlap between these categories. Most of the groups publishing bulletins form part of the wider lesbian and gay movement, while advice on preventing AIDS also appears in commercial magazines. An important differentiator is the means of distribution. The commercial lifestyle magazines and erotica are now freely available on the newsstands in major cities and so are visible and accessible to a wide audience, both gay and nongay. The AIDS serials benefit from official support and subsidies, and reach health professionals as well as people directly affected by HIV and AIDS. The bulletins and community journals have the most precarious financial resources and distribution systems, yet some of these have the longest life spans. There are also a few journals that do not fall neatly into any of these categories.

The first wave of gay journals sprang up in the 1960s, thanks to the development of the mimeograph. These journals were published by informal groups of gay men who were generally identified as "bonecas" or queens. The contributors invariably used women's names. The journals contained news, gossip ("fofocas"), travel diaries, and some short articles, as well as line drawings of figures in female clothing. They used purple or black stencils, ran to several pages, and were usually numbered and dated, albeit somewhat erratically. The longest lasting was *O Snob,* produced in Rio de Janeiro from 1963 to 1969 by Agildo Guimarães. Others included *Baby, Darling, Le Femme, Gay Society, Le Sophistiqué,* and *O Tiraninho.* These journals were circulated among friends and acquaintances and were also distributed in gay meeting places. There was even an incipient Associação Brasileira da Imprensa Gay in the late 1960s. Most of these journals ceased publication in 1969, following the declaration of the repressive Institutional Act No. 5 or AI5, for fear of being mistaken for subversive publications. The background and development of these journals is described in some detail in James Green's *Beyond Carnival*[2] and the works by Peter Fry and Leila Míccolis.

As the repression was relaxed and abertura gathered pace, gay publishing resumed in 1976. The *Boletim Informativo da Caixinha* was produced by photocopying, with an electroset masthead. It published some ten issues about once a month throughout 1976. It contained some serious articles as well as social news and gossip, and the contributors now used masculine names. This was followed by *Gente Gay,* published by Agildo Guimarães, which continued publishing until the end of 1978, by which time it had adopted a tabloid newspaper format. These bulletins, together with the similar *Entender* and *Mundo Gay,* formed the precursors of *Lampião da Esquina.*

Lampião, as it was generally known, broke new ground in a number of ways. It was produced to professional standards as a tabloid-format newspaper. It appeared regularly at monthly intervals and was sold openly on the newsstands as well as having commercial subscription arrangements. The editors were a group of gay activists including journalists, academics, writers, and other intellectuals who were aware of developments in the international lesbian and gay movement. Articles covered the theoretical and political issues facing the gay movement; aspects of gay life, such as the gay scene, prostitution, attacks on gays, police repression, Carnival, religion, transsexuals and travestis; and the situation of gays in other Latin American countries, especially Argentina and Cuba. The paper attempted to reach out to lesbians, feminists, blacks, and the organized working-class movement, although remaining primarily concerned with gay men. *Lampião* succeeded in giving a new visibility to the lesbian and gay community in Brazil and helped provide the framework for the expansion of the Brazilian gay movement.

Lampião had a curious beginning. Winston Leyland, the editor of *Gay Sunshine,* a San Francisco–based cultural journal, wished to publish an anthology of Latin American gay writers (later published as *Now the Volcano*). He contacted João Antônio de Mascarenhas, *Gay Sunshine*'s only subscriber in South America at the time, for help. Leyland had a grant from the National Endowment for the Arts, which stimulated media interest, and when he arrived in September 1977 he was interviewed by reporters from the mainstream press. As a result of the publicity and contacts created by this visit, a number of activists decided to publish a gay newspaper. *Lampião* published an experimental number, thirty-seven monthly issues and four extras between April 1978 and June 1981, when it ceased publication. During 1978–1979, an unsuccessful attempt was made by the federal government to prosecute the paper for offences against morality and public order. *Lampião* was able to secure mainstream support and the protests led to the case being shelved.

The late 1980s and early 1990s were a period of political disenchantment and financial chaos in Brazil, which were compounded by the onset of the AIDS epidemic. The gay movement, which had burgeoned in the years 1978–1980, declined rapidly after 1982 and by the mid-1980s only a handful of groups continued in existence. Nevertheless, gay journals continued to appear and at least two were relatively long-lived. *Okzinho* was published by the Turma OK group in Rio de Janeiro run by Agildo Guimarães, who had been active in publishing since the 1960s. The magazine appears to have been produced using both photocopiers and mimeographs, and it consisted of a mixture of internal group news and newspaper clippings aimed at gay consciousness raising. It started in December 1984, continued through 1985 and 1986, and was still being published in 1991 under the title *Jornal Okzinho*.

In Salvador, the Grupo Gay da Bahia (GGB), founded in 1980 by Luiz Mott, professor of anthropology in the Federal University of Bahia, began publishing the *Boletim do Grupo Gay da Bahia* in 1981. This was initially produced by mimeograph and later by printing. The *Boletim do GGB* took a combative stance in support of the campaigns promoted by the GGB. From the first issue, it regularly published lists of gays who had been murdered, based on newspaper cuttings and research by members of the GGB. This provided Mott with the material to refute the widely held view abroad of Brazil as a sexual paradise and helped highlight the dangers of homophobia. The GGB was also one of the first organizations in Brazil to recognize the danger of AIDS and to campaign for greater government action.

Other gay groups throughout Brazil continued to publish bulletins and newsletters during the 1980s and 1990s. In Rio de Janeiro, the Triângulo Rosa group founded by João Antônio de Mascarenhas cooperated with the GGB campaigns and coordinated the unsuccessful attempt in 1987 to get discrimination on the grounds of sexual orientation outlawed in the Constitutional Revision. The Triângulo Rosa group produced a small *Boletim Informativo,* which was reproduced from typescript by photocopying, as well as a short-lived printed newsletter called *Triângulo Rosa*. Other examples included the *Folha de Parreira* of the Grupo Dignidade and *Turma da Batalha* of the Grupo Esperança, both in Curitiba; *Journal des Amis* of the Les Amis Club in São Paulo; and *O Grito* of the Comunidade Fratriarcal in Natal. *The Boletim GTPOS* (Grupo de Trabalho e Pesquisa em Orientação Sexual) in São Paulo and *Sexualidade: Gênero e Sociedade* of the Programa de Estudos e Pesquisas em Sexualidade in Rio de Janeiro were more academic, in contrast to the fanzine *Monänoz.*

Most of the publications were produced by men and show a distinct male bias. An exception to this rule was *Chanacomchana* published by the Grupo Ação Lésbica Feminista in São Paulo during the 1980s, which directly addressed the political and social concerns of lesbians. Other journals for lesbians published in the mid-1990s were *Um Outro Olhar, Femme, Elas & Elas,* and *Ousar Viver,* a newsletter supported by the Ministry of Health.[3]

Gay journal publishing revived in the 1990s as Brazil's economic situation began to stabilize. A notable publication was *Nós por Exemplo,* which was printed on good quality paper to the highest standards. It combined news and cultural articles with artistic black-and-white photographs by the Bolivian-born photographer Eduardo Velásquez. It was supported financially by a public health body as a vehicle for its AIDS information insert *Agaivê Hoje* (HIV today) and was distributed in Rio de Janeiro, São Paulo, and other major cities. During the same period, a small magazine called *Ent&* circulated in Rio de Janeiro and contained news, reviews, a gay guide, and personal ads.

A major innovation in late 1994 was the appearance of *Sui Generis,* on the newsstands. *Sui Generis* was a glossy color lifestyle magazine with an upbeat cosmopolitan and consumerist outlook. It contained articles and interviews with gay and gay-friendly personalities; news items from Brazil and abroad; male fashion features; and reviews of music, cinema, videos, and books; as well as articles about gay history, literature, and culture. *Sui Generis* ran for over five years, ceasing publication with no. 55 in March 2000, while its sister publication, *Homens,* which features male nudes, continued.

Besides the lifestyle magazines, there have been numerous examples of commercially published erotica, which feature male nudes and are available on the newsstands. An early example was *Pleiguei: o Jornal do Homo* and other similar titles included *Coverboy, Alone, Gato,* and *Sex Symbol.* Currently, the newsstands are dominated by *G Magazine.* This publication appears to have found a winning formula by combining the two great obsessions of the modern age, sex and celebrity. A series of well-known actors, singers, and dancers have been featured in full frontal nude color spreads. *G Magazine* hit the national headlines when Vampeta, a leading player with the Corinthians soccer team, revealed all, to be followed by his teammate Dinei. When the next player, Roger, a goalkeeper with São Paulo, appeared, however, he was thrown out of his team by the manager. The manager's attitude was considered unsporting by many people and Roger later returned to the team. Vampeta was reported to have been paid 120,000 *reais* for the photo session, a large sum which indicates the strength of the pink real and shows how far gay publishing has come since the little mimeographed journals of the 1960s.[4]

Other erotica titles featured prominently on the newsstands include *Homens,* mentioned above, *Gold,* and *Travestis,* a long-running magazine specializing in nude photos of Brazilian transvestites. *G Magazine* and, to a lesser extent, *Homens* contain a range of news, reviews, travel notes, fashion notes, and letters from readers. The other titles carry some text, including interviews, fiction, and health notes, but mainly concentrate on photographs. All contain advertisements for products and services aimed at gay men. Information about the gay scene can be found in *Jornal Grito G,* a monthly free tabloid newspaper published in Niterói. A similar paper, *Babado,* was published in Campinas. In the same city, there is *Zoom Mix Magazine* by and for drag queens, which also has its own website.

Amongst the gay groups, the Grupo Gay da Bahia is well established and has its own building in the historic center of Salvador. Official recognition of its AIDS prevention work has allowed it to undertake an active publishing program. It currently publishes *Homo Sapiens,* a bimonthly journal in newspaper format, containing news items, book reviews, useful addresses, and articles on gay issues, with an emphasis on the importance of gay pride and human rights. Other journals sponsored by the GGB are *Aláfia: Jornal do Povo do Axé,* a small quarterly aimed at a black readership, and *Princesa: Boletim da Associação de Travestis de Salvador,* intended for travestis. Both stress the AIDS prevention message. In Fortaleza, the AIDS prevention group GAPA-CE publishes a small glossy magazine aimed at gays called *IDentidade.* The main body concerned with AIDS prevention is the Associação Brasileira Interdisciplinar de AIDS (ABIA), based in Rio de Janeiro, which has helped Brazil achieve international recognition for its work in the AIDS area. The ABIA produces the *Boletim ABIA* and the *Boletim Arayê,* as well as translating and distributing the Brazilian edition of *Ação Anti-AIDS,* produced in London.

There are numerous gay websites, including some belonging to gay groups and magazines, which provide current information on the state of the lesbian and gay movement.[5] Although web access is still relatively limited, it is interesting to speculate whether websites will replace print as a means of communicating among the lesbian and gay community. The drag queens' website at Zoomgls is full of gossip, which is remarkably reminiscent of the small mimeographed magazines of the 1960s.

Acquisitions

As indicated above, the commercially published lifestyle and erotica magazines are freely available on the newsstands, the latter in plastic wrappers. Back issues of *Sui Generis* can still be found, but at present there is no widely available gay cultural magazine. The most prominent representative of the gay journal is now *G Magazine*. Its erotic photographs may make acquisition problematic but it is undoubtedly a publishing and cultural phenomenon, and its visible presence on the newsstands is an antidote to the effeminate stereotypes still common in Brazilian *telenovelas*. Copies of *Jornal Grito G* can be found in gay outlets, such as specialist video rental stores. There is a gay bookstore in São Paulo but it is not known whether it stocks journals. The publications of gay groups are best obtained through personal contacts or personal visits to their meetings. An approach via their website or by email could also be tried, although paying for postage can be a problem.

Research

There are a number of specialized collections in Brazil. The Arquivo Edgard Leuenroth at the University of Campinas holds copies of the little magazines of the 1960s and others. The documentation center of the ABIA in Rio de Janeiro has issued a listing of the gay serials that it stocks. Scattered holdings can be found in collections abroad, such as the Labadie collection of the University of Michigan and Canadian Gay Archives in Toronto. Finally, some serials have been microfilmed for Brazil's *Popular Groups Collection on Microfilm* project.

NOTES

1. I am grateful to Luiz Mott, the late João Antônio de Mascarenhas, James Green, Aquiles Brayner, and the staff of the Arquivo Edgard Leuenroth and the Associação Brasileira Interdisciplinar de AIDS for their help in the research for this paper. An expanded version is scheduled to appear in a forthcoming issue of the *Revista Iberoamericana.*

2. James N. Green, *Beyond Carnival: Male Homosexuality in Twentieth-Century Brazil* (Chicago: University of Chicago Press, 1991), especially chapters 4 and 6. There is a list of the small journals on p. 326, footnote 115.

3. Sérgio Barcellos, "I Forum de Mídia Gay e Lésbica," *Nós por Exemplo* 3, no. 18 (dezembro [1994]): 14–15.

4. "O mecenas de Nazaré," *Revista Época Online,* February 7, 2000, http://epoca.globo. com/edic/ed07022000/cult1.htm, accessed on October 4, 2001.

5. See accompanying list of serials and websites.

BIBLIOGRAPHY

Associação Brasileira Interdisciplinar de AIDS. *Homossexualidade e AIDS no Brasil. Catálogo do Centro de Documentação e Recursos.* Rio de Janeiro: ABIA, 2000.

Brayner, Aquiles Ratti Alencar. "Lampião: um Bandido Social? Análise Discursiva da Revista Lampião da Esquina." Ph.D. dissertation, University of Leiden, 1998.

Fry, Peter. "História da Imprensa Baiana." *Lampião da Esquina* 1, no. 4 (agosto 25– setembro 25, 1978): 4.

Green, James N. *Beyond Carnival: Male Homosexuality in Twentieth-Century Brazil.* Chicago: University of Chicago Press, 1999.

———. "Desire and Militancy: Lesbians, Gays and the Brazilian Workers Party." In *Different Rainbows,* edited by Peter Drucker. London: Gay Men's Press, 2000. Pp. 57–70.

———. "The Emergence of the Brazilian Gay Liberation Movement, 1977–81." *Latin American Perspectives* 21, no. 1 (winter 1994): 38–55.

———. "'More Love and More Desire': The Building of a Brazilian Movement." In *The Global Emergence of Gay and Lesbian Politics: National Imprints of a Worldwide Movement,* edited by Barry D. Adam, Jan Willem Duyvendak, and André Krouwel. Philadelphia: Temple University Press, 1999. Pp. 91–109.

Leyland, Winston, ed. *Now the Volcano: An Anthology of Latin American Gay Literature.* San Francisco: Gay Sunshine, 1979.

Macrae, Edward. *A Construção da Igualdade: Identidade Sexual e Política no Brasil da "Abertura."* Campinas: Editora da UNICAMP, 1990.

Mascarenhas, João Antônio de. Interview by author. Rio de Janeiro, October 2, 1997.

Míccolis, Leila. "'Snob', 'Le Femme' . . . Os Bons Tempos da Imprensa Guei." *Lampião da Esquina* 3, no. 28 (setembro 1980): 6–7.

Míccolis, Leila, and Herbert Daniel. *Jacarés e Lobishomens: Dois Ensaios sobre a Homossexualidade.* Rio de Janeiro: Achiamé, 1983.

Moreira, Antônio Carlos. *Só para Cavalheiros: Crônicas Urbanas do Jornal Lampião.* Rio de Janeiro, 1997.

Mott, Luiz Roberto. *Epidemic of Hate: Violations of the Human Rights of Gay Men, Lesbians, and Transvestites in Brazil. A Joint Report of Grupo Gay da Bahia, Brazil and the International Gay and the Lesbian Human Rights Commission.* Salvador and San Francisco, 1996.

———. *Homofobia: A Violação dos Direitos Humanos de Gays, Lésbicas and Travestis no Brasil. Relatório elaborado pelo Grupo Gay da Bahia e Comissão Internacional de Direitos Humanos de Gays e Lésbicas.* Salvador and San Francisco, 1997.

Trevisan, João Silvério. *Devassos no Paraíso: a Homossexualidade no Brasil, da Colônia à Atualidade.* 4th ed. Rio de Janeiro: Record, 2000.

Websites

Arquivo Edgard Leuenroth. http://www.arquivo.ael.ifch.unicamp.br.

Associação Brasileira Interdisciplinar de AIDS. http://www.alternex.com.br/~abia/.

Edições GLS. http://www.edgls.com.br.

Galeria Mídia Gay, PUC Campinas. http://puccamp.aleph.com.br/midiagay/.

Gente do Bem. http://www.gentedobem.com.br (see Entidades page).

Grupo Gay da Bahia. http://www.ggb.org.br.

Movimento Gay de Minas. http://www.artnet.com.br/~mgm (see Links page).

Zoomgls. http://www.zoomgls.com.br.

Serials of the Brazilian Lesbian, Gay, and Transgendered Community: A Provisional Listing

This listing contains details of serials published by or for the lesbian, gay, and transgendered community in Brazil. The entries comprise the place of publication, publisher, and dates for which issues are known to exist. These may not represent the entire time span of the title. The entries are also classified according to the following categories:

- AIDS: serials concentrating on issues relating to HIV and AIDS.

- Community newspaper: titles intended for general circulation among the lesbian, gay, and transgendered communities, with an emphasis on political comment, gay rights, and news items.

- Erotica: glossy magazines containing nude photographs but excluding explicit sexual activity.

- Gay movement: serials published by lesbian, gay, or transgendered groups and intended primarily for their own members or individuals with an interest in the issues addressed by the group.

- Lesbian: serials published by and for lesbians.

- Lifestyle: glossy magazines published by commercial publishers for general sale, with an emphasis on fashion and culture.

An online version of the list, which is updated from time to time, can be found at http://www.sul.stanford.edu/depts/hasrg/latinam/sergay.htm.

Ação Anti-AIDS. Rio de Janeiro: Associação Brasileira Interdisciplinar de AIDS, 1988–2001. AIDS.

Aláfia: Jornal do Povo do Axé. Salvador: Centro Baiano Anti-Aids—Quimbanda-Dudu, 2000–2001. Gay movement and AIDS.

Alone. São Paulo: Motivo Editorial, 1989 or 1990. Erotica.

Auê: Jornal de Sexualidade. Rio de Janeiro, 1981. Community newspaper.

Babado: Informativo do Grupo Expressão. Campinas: Expressão: Grupo de Defesa dos Direitos Humanos de Homossexuais, 1996–1997. Community newspaper.

Boletim ABIA. Rio de Janeiro: Associação Brasileira Interdisciplinar de AIDS, 1994–2001. AIDS.

Boletim Arayê. Rio de Janeiro: Associação Brasileira Interdisciplinar de AIDS, 1996–2000. AIDS.

Boletim da ABGLT. N.p.: Associação Brasileira de Gays, Lésbicas e Travestis, 1995. Gay movement.

Boletim do Grupo Gay da Bahia. Salvador: Grupo Gay da Bahia, 1981–1997. Gay movement.

Boletim do Quimbanda-Dudu. Salvador: Quimbanda-Dudu—Grupo Gay Negro da Bahia; Grupo Gay da Bahia, 2001. Gay movement.

Boletim GTPOS. São Paulo: Grupo de Trabalho e Pesquisa em Orientação Sexual, 1995–1996. Gay movement.

Boletim Informativo. Rio de Janeiro: Triângulo Rosa, 1986–1988. Gay movement.

Boletim Informativo. São Paulo: Lambda, Movimento pela Livre Orientação Sexual, 1988. Gay movement.

Boletim Informativo da Caixinha. Rio de Janeiro, 1976. Gay movement.

O Caso. Rio de Janeiro: Atobá—Movimento de Emancipação Homosexual, 1992. Gay movement.

O Centro. N.p.: Diretora: Betty Taylor, 1967. Mimeograph. Gay movement.

CGI: Orgão Informativo da Central Gay de Informações. São Paulo: Círculo Corydon, 1979. Gay movement.

Chanacomchana. São Paulo: Grupo Ação Lésbica Feminista, 1981–1987. Lesbian.

O Corpo. São Paulo: Grupo Somos, 1980–1983. Gay movement.

Coverboy. São Paulo: Editora Acti-Vita, 1982? Erotica.

Darling. N.p., 1968–1969. Mimeograph. Gay movement.

Ent&. Rio de Janeiro: 2AB Editora, 1994–1995. Community newspaper.

Entender. São Paulo: Corydon, 1977. CGA. Community newspaper.

Os Felinos (Suplemento d' O Snob). Rio de Janeiro, 1967–1968. Mimeograph. Gay movement.

Le Femme. Rio de Janeiro, 1968. Mimeograph. Gay movement.

Folha de Parreira: Boletim Informativo. Curitiba: Grupo Dignidade—Conscientização e Emancipação Homosexual, 1992–1995. Gay movement.

Freedom Jornal. Rio de Janeiro: Freedom Club, 1995? Gay movement.

G Magazine. São Paulo: Fractal Edições, 1999–2001. Erotica.

G Magazine Collection. São Paulo: Fractal Edições, 2000 or 2001. Reprint. Erotica.

Gato. São Paulo: Edições Kent, 1994? Erotica.

Gay Society. Bahia, 1968. Mimeograph. Gay movement.

Gente Gay. Rio de Janeiro: Direção Agildo B. Guimarães, 1976–1978. Gay movement.

Gold. São Paulo: Editora Marfe, 1999. Erotica.

O Grito. Natal: Comunidade Fratriarcal, 1994. Gay movement.

Grupo Somos. São Paulo: Grupo Somos de Afirmação Homosexual, 1981. Gay movement.

Homens. Rio de Janeiro: SG Press Editora, 2000–2001. Erotica.

Homo Sapiens. Jornal do Grupo Gay da Bahia. Salvador: Grupo Gay da Bahia, 1997–2001. Gay movement.

IDentidade. Fortaleza: Projeto Homens—GAPA-CE, 2001. Gay movement and AIDS.

Informativo del SLAGH. Salvador: Secretariado Latino-Americano de Grupos Homosexuales, 1985. Gay movement.

Jornal do Gay. Noticiário do Mundo Entendido. São Paulo: Círculo Corydon, 1978–1980. Gay movement.

Jornal For Gays. [São Paulo?] 1980. Lifestyle.

Jornal Gay Internacional. São Paulo: Liga Eloinista, 1980. Gay movement.

Jornal Grito G. Niterói, 2001. Community newspaper.

Jornal Okzinho: Informativo da Turma OK. [Rio de Janeiro]: Diretor fundador: Agildo B. Guimarães, 1991. Gay movement.

Jornal World G. News. São Paulo, 1996. Community newspaper.

Journal des Amis. São Paulo: Les Amis Club, 1994–1995. Gay movement.

Lampião da Esquina. Rio de Janeiro: Esquina Editora de Livros, Jornais e Revistas, 1978–1981. Community newspaper.

Mix Magazine. São Paulo: Club Mix, 1995. Lifestyle.

Monänoz Info. São Paulo? 1995. Gay movement.

Mundo Gay: o Jornal dos Entendidos. 1977. Community newspaper.

News from Brazil. Curitiba: Grupo Dignidade—Conscientização e Emancipação Homosexual, 1993. Gay movement.

Nós por Exemplo. Rio de Janeiro: Editora Leviatã, 1991–1996. Community newspaper.

OK Magazine. São Paulo: Zás Estúdio, 1996. Lifestyle.

Okzinho: Orgão Oficial da Turma OK. Rio de Janeiro, 1984–1986. Gay movement.

Ousar Viver. Publicação da Rede de Informação Um Outro Olhar. São Paulo: Um Outro Olhar, 1995. Lesbian.

Um Outro Olhar. São Paulo: Rede de Informação Lésbica, 1990–1991. Lesbian.

Pleiguei: o Jornal do Homo. Rio de Janeiro: A.S. Produções Artísticas, 1981–1982. Erotica.

Previna-se. São Paulo: Grupo de Apoio à Prevenção à AIDS, 1989–1990. AIDS.

Princesa: Boletim da Associação de Travestis de Salvador. Salvador: Associação de Travestis de Salvador, 2001. Gay movement and AIDS.

Revista Carnaval do Milênio 2001 Gay. São Paulo: Gallery Editores Associados/Editora Escala, 2001. Lifestyle.

Sex Symbol. São Paulo: P.R. Editora e Produções, 1999. Erotica.

Sexualidade: Gênero e Sociedade. Rio de Janeiro: Programa de Estudos e Pesquisas em Sexualidade, Gênero e Saúde—CEPESC/IMS/UERJ, 1995. Gay movement.

O Snob. Rio de Janeiro: Diretora: Gilha Dantas Veiga, 1963–1969. Mimeograph. Gay movement.

Le Sophistiqué. Campos: RJ, 1966. Mimeograph. Gay movement.

Spartacus. São Paulo: Edição Ki-Bancas, 1988–1990. Erotica.

Sui Generis. Rio de Janeiro: SG-Press Editora, 1994–2000. Lifestyle.

O Tiraninho. N.p., n.d. Mimeograph. Gay movement.

Travestis. São Paulo: Editora Ondas, 2000. Erotica.

Triângulo Rosa. Rio de Janeiro: Triângulo Rosa, Grupo de Liberação Homosexual, 1986. Gay movement.

Turma da Batalha. Curitiba: Grupo Esperança, 1994–1995. Gay movement.

13. The Feminist Movement in Latin America as Part of Our Collection Design Tapestry

Lourdes Vázquez

> In my class in Collection Development and management, I like to bring in, on the first day a vase of flowers. While this may sound more of a decorative than instructive gesture, I use the flowers as an emblem of what I want to say about the subject. I have long held the view that "collection building" and other related terms of "development" and "management" are too masculine.[1]

The Missing Thread

Through the slogan *lo privado es público,*[2] Latin American feminist organizations question among other matters, the organization of the world, its economy and its politics, the sexual labor division, and the normative parameters of a culture that excludes diversity. As a consequence the feminist movement organizes in multiple and diverse nongovernmental organizations (NGOs) in order to reclaim their rights.

The feminist NGOs in Latin America are highly organized groups. One of their constant battles is the lack of information that may affect women in the region, where repressive governments and mainstream media often hide the facts on economic and social conditions, health, and habitat. These NGOs plan and evaluate campaigns and policies, research and design projects, develop gender training, and organize resource centers and libraries. In this process plenty of grey literature is developed. Some examples are posters, videos, films, audio, radio scripts, brochures, minutes, internal correspondence, conference papers, campaign strategies, training manuals, press releases, reports to local and national governments, reports to international organisms, and proposals to funding agencies. On the Internet, URL and list-servs are developed where the feminist movement can spread their campaigns.[3] The majority of these NGOs have organized informal exchange programs with similar NGOs, governmental offices, research centers, and international organizations. The materials received are researched and repackaged in the form of bulletins, newsletters, and new action plans. As a consequence, the area of women's and gender studies in Latin America with its multidisciplinary perspectives presents a challenge to the bibliographer, either from the area studies perspective or from the gender one.

Although in the United States and abroad the academic and commercial presses continue publishing more titles on the topic of gender and women's studies, in Latin America gender documents must be actively sought from NGOs, feminist private presses, and religious and political organizations. The continuous search for this information is not through the regular library approval plans, but through frequent scrutiny of the women's movement information production. Some examples are the many journals, bulletins, and newsletters produced by these organizations: *Cotidiano mujer* (Uruguay), *Lola Press* (Uruguay-Germany), *Fem* (Mexico), *CAFRA Newsletter* (Trinidad-Tobago), *Magin* (Cuba), *La otra bolsa de valores* (Mexico), *La correa feminista* (Mexico), *Atajos* (Peru), *Fempress* (Chile), the radio scripts of Radio Fire (Costa Rica) and the women's department of AMARC (Colombia), and the dossiers and publications of ISIS-Chile and Flora Tristán (Peru).

How to Design the Tapestry

Certain goals need to be defined by the library: What type of information are we looking for? What will be the parameters to collect such information? These questions will probably be answered through the scope of the gender and women's studies or area studies program in the institution. In the case of Rutgers University, the gender and women's studies program wants to bring to their students issues such as the following:

> 1. How women's studies research queries disciplinary boundaries and addresses the relationship between power and knowledge in the development and institutionalization of knowledge claims;
> 2. the theoretical and empirical innovations produced through women's studies debates on difference which have questioned the boundaries between social categories and identities such as gender, race, class and sexuality;
> 3. the range of women's studies research exploring the cross-cultural study of women, the gendered international division of labor and transnationalism;
> 4. an understanding of the history and diversity of feminist discourses and debates.[4]

By studying the goals of this program, it can be concluded that the complexity and multidisciplinary components of gender and women's studies at Rutgers goes beyond the traditional curriculum. As a consequence, a gender and women's studies collection development strategy cannot exclude the wealth of the literature produced by the women's movement in the Southern Hemisphere.

Besides the regular women's studies program, there are five more components involving research and service: the Institute for Research on Women, the Center for Women's Global Leadership (with its resource center), a Women's Rights Litigation Clinic, the Center for Women and Work, and the Center for American Women and Politics. Finally, a consortium of all these groups was organized under the name of Institute for Women's Leadership. What is indicative in the development of some of these research centers is the urgent need for nontraditional information.

In November 2000, as part of the Dialogue of the Americas, the Rutgers Latin American Studies Program (RULAS) invited women from the Mothers of the *Plaza de Mayo,* the Mothers Organization of Colombia, the Mothers of Guatemala, and the Mothers Against Violence of the United States, and representatives from twenty-five leading newspapers from Latin America and Spain. The impact that the platforms of the Latin American gender movement have today is such that RULAS considered that the dialogue was and is still necessary. In a two-day symposium, the media, the feminist, political, and human rights advocates, as well as faculty and students were immersed in a knowledge-building dialogue that crossed traditional, disciplinary, and geographic boundaries. This vision is well reflected in RULAS mission statement:

> In order to consider Latin America we must move beyond our traditional regional screen and include in the picture the dynamics of globalization, particularly the rapid back-and-forth movements of people, ideas and capital across borders, particularly across the US border. Therefore, Latin American studies, in order to be salient and relevant to our needs as a multicultural society has to reshaped its approach to be more Hemispheric in scope.[5]

Weaving the Network

In Latin America, there are many examples of organizations and coalitions that produce such literature. Flora Tristán and ISIS-Chile are two of the best examples. As pioneers in the publishing industry in their countries, utilizing desktop publishing applications or commercial printing companies, the publications in their catalogs are the result of the research work of their programs or research directly related with their objectives. Their catalogs include monographs, series, periodicals, and in the case of Flora Tristán, women's literature. Their libraries are highly sophisticated operations devoted to the compilation, processing, analysis, and dissemination of gender information. They have extensive gender collections of books, periodicals, theses, conference reports, bibliographies, and newspaper clippings about health, technology, labor, sexuality, development, feminism, media, literature, human rights, women's rights, and violence against women. The emergence of documentation centers, resources centers, and libraries that specialize in women's issues throughout the world can be explained by the need expressed first and foremost by women and their organizations. Groups such as Manuela Ramos (Peru), SOSCorpo (Brazil), Centro de Estudios de la Mujer (Argentina), Colectivo feminista sexualidade e saude (Brazil), Centro de información para la acción femenina or CIPAF (Dominican Republic), CAFRA (Trinidad and Tobago), and REPEM (Network of Popular Education between Women) are also good examples.

REPEM is a *red,* a network and a coalition of 140 organizations from Latin America and the Caribbean. These organizations have formed national groups that operate regularly implementing REPEM's general and specific activities. In order to have more country participation, five regional coordinations have been determined: Mexico, Brazil, Andean countries, the southern cone, and countries from Central America and the Caribbean. REPEM develops programmed activities and projects at three levels: national, regional, and international. The main interests of REPEM are incorporating gender to the citizenship and equity dialogue with consideration to the contributions of feminist theory and practice; and contributing to the development and implementation of global strategies in order to improve women from the gender and education perspective.[6] REPEM is today one of the most important redes in Latin America, together with Articulación de Mujeres Brasileiras (Articulation of Brazilian Women), CLADEM (Latin American Committee of Defense of the Rights of the Woman), the network DAWN (Alternative Development for Women), Women and Habitat, Red Feminista de América Latina en contra de la Violencia Doméstica y Sexual (Feminist Coalition Against Domestic and Sexual Violence), the Coalición en Contra del Tráfico de las Mujeres (Coalition Against Trafficking of Women), and the Red de Salud de las Mujeres Latioamericanas y del Caribe (Latin American Women's Health Network).

REPEM emphasizes an education system with a gender perspective, oriented towards developing leadership among women. Some of REPEM's objectives are to strengthen the popular education movement in Latin America from the gender theoretical and practical point of view; to teach human rights as well as the duties of government and institutions; to design educational programs for children that promote the sensibility and knowledge of human sexuality, gender equity, and cultural diversity; to promote programs and literacy projects within the cultural specifications of the region; and to contribute to the training of popular educators in Latin America.

As an NGO, REPEM creates workshops, strategizes regional meetings and plans of action, and lobbies in the international arena. The publications (see addendum) produced by REPEM include results of workshops, debates, monographs, strategic plans, campaign results, conference papers, case studies, gender work methodologies, and a bulletin *La red va.* In the digital society, REPEM is easily connected and the Internet has provided a medium for the social cohesion of its members. *La red va* is an electronic bulletin that circulates throughout the network of the Institute for Global Communications. It is the most powerful communication tool of this network. In December 2000, I interviewed one of the editors of the bulletin.[7] In the interview, a major concern on the part of the editor is the sharing of information with its members. *La red va* began in a very informal way. In 1997 the editors received some information from Sweden related to a specific workshop and they thought that REPEM's affiliates needed to know this information immediately. The first bulletin came into existence. From that moment the writing and editing of the bulletin has been organized around the wealth of information the editors received; and since then they have engaged in mastering the electronic medium, and have invited their affiliates to take hold of the Internet capabilities. A section within the bulletin "Consejos útiles para mujeres y hombres al borde de un ataque de nervios" (Advice to Women and Men in the Verge of a Nervous Breakdown) was developed to educate their affiliates in this new and exciting form of communication.

The table of contents of the bulletin contains book reviews, a calendar of activities, monographs, and conference and project reports. The editors receive around fifty messages per day from the affiliates, NGOs and networks, plus the print information received in their offices. It is this information that they repackage and present to their affiliates. In special circumstances, like international conferences, the editors publish special bulletins directly from the conferences serving as parallel diplomatic officers. In this bulletin, one can read about negotiations and bargaining of agreements, as well as the forming of international agreements within the context of a nonterritorial space. The editors wanted to create a bulletin made by nonjournalists, presented in an edition and format that could be read by any person. The REPENAS create, analyze, translate, and repackage information that is later published in the bulletin. It is a quick, assertive way of maintaining their membership on target.

As of May 2001, *La red va* was in its fourth year and had circulated 150 bulletins. The bulletin is sent every Wednesday and it is published in a bilingual edition of Spanish and Portuguese. *La red va* goes to nine hundred email addresses and is published in Uruguay in the main offices of REPEM. Other communications networks like ARACA and APC resend it to their members. The example of *La red va* has created similar cases; but most of all it has created trust in the REPENAS and now other redes are engaging with the REPENAS for production of their materials in English, Spanish, and Portuguese. A second version of the bulletin is published in English, *Voices Raising*. This version is produced for their partners in the United States, Europe, Africa, and Asia. REPENAS even collaborates in a regional nonsexist children's literature contest as well as a didactic game for children.

Conclusion

Publications by Latin American feminist NGOs have become important sources of information, but they remain hard to obtain. Not even book fairs such as the Guadalajara or Buenos Aires book fairs have much of these materials, and more faculty and graduate students are desperately trying to locate these resources. The nature of the subject and the variety of information that is needed challenges the traditional library. I have been selecting and researching information on feminist NGOs for the last eight years. Much had changed since 1994 in the way information is produced and the way information can be found on the topic. As the Internet spreads, there will be more access to some of these extraordinary resources. The impact of this medium is clearly demonstrated when the publisher of the electronic database *Contemporary Women's Issues* included more grey and fugitive literature of the women's movement in the Southern Hemisphere; one good example for others to follow.

ADDENDUM

REPEM

List of Publications

This list of publications is in chronological order.

Taller latinoamericano sobre feminismo y educación popular. Quito: REPEM, 1987.

Educación popular y liderazgo de las mujeres en la construcción de la democracia latinoamericana. Quito: REPEM, 1990.

Lagarde, Marcela. *Metodología de trabajo con mujeres.* Quito: REPEM, 1991.

Liderança e participação das mulheres na construção da democracia latino-americana. Quito: REPEM, 1991.

Tres historias y un mismo camino de mujer. Montevideo: PLEMUU, 1991.

Modelo de desarrollo y políticas sociales para la mujer (Mimeo). Bogotá: REPEM, 1992.

Relación madre-hija. Curso de la Dra. Marcela Lagarde (Mimeo). México, D.F.: REPEM, 1992.

Jaque al rey. Memorias del Taller de Participación Política de la Mujer. [Quito]: REPEM, 1993.

Lagarde, Marcela. *Democracia genérica.* México, D.F.: REPEM, 1994.

Microemprendimientos, mujeres y políticas de ajuste. Montevideo: Red Mujer Uruguay, 1994.

Mujeres y tecnologías alimentarias. Quito: UNIFEM; Lima: REPEM, 1994.

Ciudadanía, género y educación. Montevideo: REPEM, 1995.

Construcción de liderazgos femeninos. Montevideo: REPEM, 1995.

Gender, Education and Popular Economy. Montevideo: REPEM, 1995.

Género, educación y economía popular. Montevideo: REPEM, 1995.

More than Goodwill Is Needed to Help Poor Women in Income Generation. Montevideo: REPEM, 1995.

Orellana, Inocencia. *Aprendiendo a ser líderes. Ciudadanía y desarrollo.* Venezuela: REPEM, 1995.

Para ayudar a las mujeres pobres a generar ingresos se precisa algo más que buena voluntad. Montevideo: REPEM, 1995.

Taller: Estrategias de Participación Política de las Mujeres en la Región Andina. REPEM, 1995.

La educación en movimiento. Acuerdos sobre educación y género en las conferencias mundiales de los 90'. Uruguay: REPEM, octubre de 1996.

Education in Motion. The Agreements on Gender and Education at World Conferences in the Nineties. Uruguay: REPEM, octubre 1996.

Memoria Foro Género y Ciudadanía, La Paz, 18 al 21 de julio de 1996. La Paz, Bolivia: CIDEM-REPEM, octubre de 1996.

Educación con igualdad de oportunidades. Montevideo: REPEM, 1996.

Experiencias exitosas de mujeres en microempresas rurales de alimentos. Directorio: Bolivia, Colombia, Ecuador, Perú, Venezuela. Lima: UNIFEM-REPEM, 1996.

Confintea v. Hamburgo 1997. Enmiendas propuestas—enmiendas aprobadas (Mimeo inglés). Montevideo: REPEM-GEO, setiembre de 1997.

Anderson, Jeanine. *Programa de formação em gênero.* Montevideo: CEAAL-REPEM, noviembre de 1997.

―――. *Programa de formación en género. "Sistemas de género, redes de actores y una propuesta de formación."* Montevideo: CEAAL-REPEM, noviembre de 1997.

Dibujando la agenda. Género, educación y economía popular. Montevideo: REPEM, noviembre de 1997.

Traçando a agenda. Gênero, educação e economia popular. Montevideo: REPEM, noviembre de 1997.

Las mujeres microempresarias rurales en la región andina. Lima: UNIFEM-REPEM, 1997.

Sein, Gita. *Los desafíos de la globalización.* Montevideo: DAWN-REPEM, junio de 1998.

Programa de Formación en Género: Seminario Virtual "Una propuesta de formación, extensiones, implicancias y segundos pensamientos." CEAAL-REPEM, setiembre de 1998.

Así se hace: 9 emprendimientos exitosos liderados por mujeres y un manual de lobby propositivo. Montevideo: REPEM, 1998.

Educación popular y feminismo. Santiago: REPEM, Red Mujer Uruguay, 1998.

Género y ciudadanía una construcción necesaria. La Paz, Bolivia: CIDEM-REPEM, 1998.

Education in Motion: Monitoring the Implementation of World Conferences on Gender and Education. REPEM-GEO, mayo de 1999.

It's Done this Way: 9 Successful Income Generating Projects Led by Women (Summary of: Así se hace, 9 emprendimientos exitosos liderados por mujeres y un manual de lobby propositivo). Montevideo: REPEM, mayo de 1999.

Index of Accomplished: Commitments on Gender & Education. Regional Report for Asia-Pacific. Manila, Philippines: REPEM-GEO and DAWN SEA, 1999.

Valenzuela, Malú y Tere Garduño. *El juego de las posibilidades. Juego didáctico para niños y niñas.* México, D.F.: REPEM, 1999.

El Banco Mundial. Mujeres y educación. Montevideo: REPEM, febrero de 2000.

Para abrir agendas. Propuesta y estrategias desde los emprendimientos exitosos liderados por mujeres de los sectores populares de América Latina (in English and Spanish). Montevideo: REPEM, marzo de 2000.

Memoria del II Seminario Regional de Poderes y Saberes: debates sobre reestructura política y transformación social (in English and Spanish). Montevideo: DAWN-REPEM, mayo de 2000.

No nos vengan con cuentos. Primer Concurso Latinoamericano de Cuentos Infantiles No Sexistas. Montevideo: REPEM, agosto de 2000.

Marketización de la governanza. Translated by REPEM. Uruguay: REPEM, diciembre de 2000.

NOTES

1. Anne Lunding, "A Delicate Balance: Collection Development and Women's History," *Collection Building* 14, no. 2 (1995): 42–48.

2. A possible translation could be "let's get out the dirty laundry."

3. Lourdes Vázquez, "Mujer y Sida en América Latina y el Caribe: ong's e información," *FEM* 23, no. 97 (agosto 1999): 22–25.

4. Rutgers University, Women's Studies program, http://womensstudies.rutgers.edu/home/about.html.

5. Rutgers University, Program in Latin American Studies, http://www.rci.rutgers.edu/~rulas/.

6. Vera M. Britto, Hablando sobre desarrollo: un proyecto de entrevistas, http://www.personal.umich.edu/~fiatlux/td/eccher/ctc.html.

7. Marcela Mazzei, co-editor of *La red va,* electronic interview with author, December 2000.

14. La Red de Información Etnológica Boliviana REDETBO: una experiencia en información indígena

Eloisa Vargas Sánchez

Introducción

Bolivia se caracteriza por ser un país multicultural, multiétnico y multilingüístico, así lo ratifica la Constitución Política del Estado que en el Art.1° la letra dice: "Bolivia, libre, independiente, soberana, multiétnica y pluricultural . . .". La población indígena y originaria de Bolivia está constituida por 4.210.946 millones de personas (monolingües nativas y bilingües nativo-español), pertenecientes a 37 diferentes pueblos indígenas y originarios del Occidente, Oriente, Amazonía y Chaco. Residentes en nueve departamentos, 314 municipios, 50% asentados en comunidades y Tierras Comunitarias de Origen, 47% en ciudades intermedias y mayores de Bolivia y 3% en áreas de colonización.[1] Dentro de este contexto expondremos una experiencia de trabajo cooperativo de nueve unidades de información de Bolivia, especializadas en el área etnológica.

Antecedentes de la Red de Información Etnológica Boliviana REDETBO

La Red Etnológica (REDET) regional La Paz, inicialmente surge de un convenio suscrito entre tres unidades de información: el Servicio de Información y Documentación para Movimientos Indígenas (CEDOIN/SIDMI),[2] el Centro de Información y Promoción del Campesinado (CIPCA) y el Museo Nacional de Etnografía y Folklore (MUSEF).

La REDET nace el 1° de abril de 1996 (con la firma de una Carta de Intenciones entre CEDOIN/SIDMI, CIPCA y MUSEF) con el objetivo de llevar a cabo un trabajo conjunto y cooperativo, como es el Catálogo Etnológico "Pueblos Indígenas de las Tierras Bajas de Bolivia". A partir de esta experiencia de trabajo colectivo con resultados altamente positivos fue constituida formalmente la Red Etnológica el 2 de abril de 1997. Posteriormente, se incorporan el Taller de Historia Oral Andina (THOA) y el Ministerio de Asuntos Campesinos Pueblo Indígenas y Originarios (MACPIO).

Con estos elementos y gracias al apoyo financiero de la Fundación Programa de Investigación Estratégica en Bolivia (PIEB), en junio del 2000 se amplía el radio de acción a nivel nacional y se incorporan a la Red otras cinco unidades de información de otros departamentos de Bolivia, todas especializadas en información de pueblos indígenas del Occidente, Oriente, Chaco y Amazonía de Bolivia (Tierras Altas y Tierras Bajas), adquiriendo así, la denominación de REDETBO.

Estructura de la REDETBO

La REDETBO es una red de información temática y abierta en la especialidad de etnología, de estructura celular, constituida por un Centro Coordinador Nacional (MUSEF-La Paz) y ocho centros participantes (CIPCA, THOA, MACPIO-La Paz; Biblioteca Etnológica-Cochabamba; APCOB-Santa Cruz; CIDDEBENI-Beni, CEPA-Oruro y CERDET-Tarija).

- *Apoyo para el Campesino Indígena del Oriente Boliviano. Santa Cruz (APCOB):* Cuenta con un centro de documentación especializado en pueblos indígenas de tierras bajas y medio ambiente con más de doce años de funcionamiento. Dispone de un ambiente especialmente asignado en el local de la sede central de la Institución en la ciudad de Santa Cruz. Pertenece a la red de bibliotecas y centros de documentación sobre la región Amazónica, UNAMAZ, que alimenta periódicamente la base de datos local, nacional e internacional. También participa en la Red de Forestería Social de Santa Cruz. Recientemente se han contactado con la red de FTPP y el Programa Regional de Bosques Nativos Andinos del Ecuador.

- *Biblioteca Etnológica. Universidad Católica de Cochabamba:* Biblioteca especializada en etnología, dependiente de la Universidad Católica Boliviana, Regional Cochabamba. Es coordinador regional de la REDOC (Red de Documentación de Cochabamba) y actualmente centro participantes de la REDETBO.

- *Centro de Ecología y Pueblos Andinos. Oruro (CEPA):* Centro de documentación especializado en antropología, ecología, medio ambiente e historia andina. Tiene por objetivo sensibilizar sobre la problemática ecológica, la temática étnica y las culturas andinas, así como promover un desarrollo sostenible en el altiplano que favorezca la calidad de vida de la población.

- *Centro de Estudios Regionales para el Desarrollo de Tarija (CERDET):* El Centro de Documentación CERDET ha enfocado sus esfuerzos, desde sus inicios, a concienciar a la población regional sobre temas que fomenten el desarrollo democrático y equilibrado en el departamento. Parte de esta filosofía ha sido la formación de una biblioteca especializada que responda al objetivo central de proporcionar información y bibliografía especializada en temas relativos a pueblos indígenas, género, medio ambiente, desarrollo sostenible y reformas estatales.

- *Centro de Investigación y Documentación para el Desarrollo del Beni (CIDDEBENI):* Centro de Documentación especializado en pueblos indígenas de la Amazonía, medio ambiente, desarrollo sostenible, recursos naturales, desarrollo regional y ecología. Lo representativo de la colección bibliográfica está constituido por investigaciones realizadas en la institución.

- *Centro de Investigación y Promoción del Campesinado. La Paz (CIPCA):* Biblioteca especializada en ciencias sociales con énfasis en temas rurales e indígenas. Su formación, crecimiento y consolidación están ligados a la acción y a las actividades de investigación que desarrolla la institución cuyo producto son las publicaciones propias con que cuenta.

- *Museo Nacional de Etnografía y Folklore. La Paz (MUSEF):* Biblioteca especializada en antropología, etnología, etnografía, etnolingüística, etnohistoria, folklore y cultura popular. Es parte del Departamento de Extensión y Difusión Cultural del Museo y constituye una de las bases estructurales del mismo. La biblioteca tiene sus orígenes en la antigua biblioteca especializada, creada el año 1971 con el objetivo de apoyar las investigaciones de la Institución. En una primera etapa, la biblioteca acumuló materiales bibliográficos y documentales para su consolidación. A partir de 1982 se constituye en un subsistema del Sistema de Información y Documentación Científica.

Entre una de las publicaciones más importantes con que cuenta la colección está la Serie *Anales de la Reunión Anual de Etnología* que es producto de los trabajos de investigación presentados en la Reunión Anual de Etnología que se realiza cada año en el mes de agosto.

La Reunión Anual de Etnología (RAE) es considerada como el único espacio, a nivel nacional, donde se realizan debates y discusiones de carácter horizontal. Es un evento respaldado institucionalmente, donde nuevos investigadores interactúan dentro de este foro idóneo con cientistas sociales que llevan años de productiva labor académica, logrando resultados meritorios para la investigación en general.

- *Taller de Historial Oral Andana. La Paz (THOA):* A partir de su fundación y en base al trabajo de investigación, comunicación y formación sobre historia, cultura, identidad, idioma aymara, quichwa y uru, fue reuniendo información valiosa que dio origen a la creación de un centro de documentación especializado en ciencias sociales y el mundo andino.

- *Ministerio de Asuntos Campesinos Pueblos Indígenas y Originarios. La Paz (MACPIO):* Centro de documentación especializado en pueblos indígenas de Tierras Altas y Tierras Bajas. La importancia de su colección radica en los informes de consultorías y resultados de trabajos de campo: Tierras Comunitarias de Origen (TCO), Registros de Programas de Cursos de Capacitación (RPG's); cuenta también con la colección del Instituto Lingüístico de Verano.

Misión de la REDETBO

Impulsar democráticamente el uso y acceso de la información etnológica de Bolivia para apoyar el desarrollo nacional.

Objetivos

Objetivo general

Consolidar la Red de Información Etnológica Boliviana para impulsar y desarrollar tareas conjuntas, dentro de un marco de trabajo colectivo y cooperativo, en el procesamiento y difusión de la información etnológica.

Objetivos específicos

- Apoyar y asesorar esfuerzos de organismos de base de los sectores indígenas de Bolivia que deseen organizar sus propios recursos documentales por medio de talleres piloto dirigidos por especialistas de la Red.

- Ampliar los beneficios de la Red a nivel nacional invitando a otras instituciones y organizaciones que trabajan con información referida a pueblos indígenas del Occidente y Oriente de Bolivia.

- Recopilar, sistematizar, accesibilizar y difundir información en diversos soportes (escritos o impresos, magnetofónicos u orales, visuales o gráficos), y versiones (originales, duplicados, copias o versiones en borrador), para su disposición al servicio público.

- Impulsar y apoyar trabajos tendientes al desarrollo de nuevas tecnologías informáticas para el procesamiento de la información entre los centros participantes de la Red.

- Realizar actividades conjuntas para el desarrollo de bases de datos comerciales destinadas al mercado mundial a través de Internet u otros medios convencionales.

- Contactar el apoyo de instituciones nacionales e internacionales para lograr el financiamiento de los trabajos de la Red, así como para apoyar programas de tecnificación en nuevas tecnologías, sobre la base de programas y proyectos de cooperación existentes actualmente en el mercado profesional.

Proyecto de Fortalecimiento de la Red de Información Etnológica Boliviana (PIEB/REDETBO[3])

A partir de la convocatoria pública de la Fundación PIEB, para la elaboración de proyectos en su segunda fase, intitulada "Apoyo a Redes Documentales Temáticas o Regionales", la REDETBO presenta el proyecto denominado "Fortalecimiento de la REDETBO", que se centra en dos actividades puntuales: la Reunión de Coordinación Nacional y la elaboración de dos productos colectivos.

Reunión de Coordinación

En enero del presente año se realiza una reunión nacional en la ciudad de Cochabamba, donde se definen los instrumentos técnicos que permitan la edición de dos productos y la definición de las bases operativas de la Red (Cooperación interbibliotecaria, convenios interinstitucionales, etc.).

Producto Colectivo

Se editarán dos catálogos en formato electrónico CD Rom: la 2ª edición del *Catálogo Etnológico de Pueblos Indígenas de las tierras bajas de Bolivia,* y la 1ª edición del *Catálogo Etnológico de las Tierras Altas de Bolivia.* El tema escogido son los recursos bibliográficos sobre pueblos indígenas que existen en las unidades de información de la Red.

Servicios

Entre los Servicios especializados que ofrecen las unidades de información de la Red, están el préstamo en sala (estantería cerrada y abierta), acceso a bases de datos referenciales, referencia, email, teléfono, correo, reprografía, DSI (diseminación selectiva de la Información), asesoramiento bibliográfico y préstamo interbibliotecario.

NOTAS

1. Fuente: MACPIO.

2. Actualmente CEDOIN/SIDMI ya no presta Servicios de Información.

3. Programa de Investigación Estratégica en Bolivia. Ampliación Fortalecimiento de la Red de Información Etnológica Boliviana REDETBO.

Latin American and
Latino Collections

15. The Borderlands, Then and Now: Manuscript and Archival Sources at the University of Texas at Austin

Adán Benavides

There are two parts to this presentation that focus on the archives and manuscripts at the University of Texas at Austin regarding the southwestern borderlands. Both parts perhaps relate more to the collection development policy enjoyed by the University of Texas rather than to specific content as exemplified in the theme of these meetings, "Latin American Identities: Race, Ethnicity, Gender, and Sexuality." The first part of this paper focuses on building research collections about those areas of New Spain/Mexico with proximity to contemporary Texas. This policy was especially active through the second third of the twentieth century. The second part of the presentation is the shift that occurred, about 1970, to collecting documentary collections regarding the *mexicano* experience in Texas.

Manuscript Collections from Mexican and Spanish Sources

The insistence on writing history in the United States based on primary sources in the Germanic tradition of Leopold von Ranke, for example, coincided *(más or menos)* with the founding of the University of Texas in 1883. The history department from then until the early-twentieth century determined that one area they could claim as their own was the Spanish and Mexican eras of Texas history. In 1899, it was a coup to rescue from the Béxar County Commissioner's Court in San Antonio what is now called the Béxar Archives. These records of some quarter-million pages cover the period 1717 to 1836. The Béxar Archives is an accumulation of several archival sources: civil and military principally, and ecclesiastical only by way of exception.[1] Herbert E. Bolton's tenure at the university immediately after that acquisition enabled him to pursue a new tack—away from his medieval history courses and in a new foreign language, Spanish. His success in that endeavor founded a new historical tradition, the Boltonians, and of course those who now view that trajectory as an incorrect one, the anti-Boltonians. Others of his contemporaries who recognized his promise were able to hire him away from the University of Texas—a feat that has occurred more than once by California universities.[2]

The Béxar Archives has been a source for scholarship for over a century, yet all its treasures have yet to be exhausted. Early theses and articles on town government, church and state conflict, and Indian relations provided many narrative historical works. In more recent decades, the "social science" in history has resulted in, for example, Frank de la Teja's fine study on the formation of San Antonio in the eighteenth century, and a demographic analysis of census records first by Alicia Vidaurreta de Tjarks in the 1970s and later by Tina Meacham in her dissertation based on almost all of the surviving Texas census records.[3] Elizabeth John, in her classic work *Storms Brewed in Other Men's Worlds,* certainly used the Béxar Archives to better understand the interaction and accommodation undergone within the Spanish and Indian worlds.[4]

Evolving technology benefited the first generation of twentieth-century documentary collection building at the university. The typewriter allowed wholesale copying of records. Great accumulations of typescript copies from the Archivo General de Indias (Seville), the Archivo General de la Nación (Mexico City), the Nacogdoches Archives, and Texas county courthouses ensued. The second generation of building collections to study northern New Spain would collect in another new medium, photostatic copies. Carlos E. Castañeda working with his brother provided several U.S. institutions (for example, the University of California–Berkeley and the Library of Congress) with surviving civil and ecclesiastical records from the Mexican border towns of Matamoros and Reynosa, Tamaulipas, and from the Coahuila State Archives then located in Saltillo, which had been the capital of Texas for much of its Spanish and Mexican past. These early collections of copies are now housed at the university's Center for American History.

The purchase of the formidable Genaro García Collection in 1921 brought to the university an exquisite collection of 25,000 volumes of books and periodicals relating to Mexico, the Americas, the West Indies, and Spain, as well as over 250,000 pages of manuscripts on Mexican history, education, and law at a time of rising interest in the United States in Latin American studies. The Genaro García manuscripts number some forty subcollections. These are principally concerned with central Mexican politics, history, and culture; but many contain valuable information on, for example, the Texas question. Indeed, one of the most important manuscripts is the holograph memoir of Antonio López de Santa Anna. The Genaro García Collection's first curator was Lota May Spell, who produced studies on the early history of music in Mexico City, Texas, and New Mexico. One of her chief contributions was her work on Samuel Bangs, the first printer active in Texas, in what is now northeastern Mexico, who was "taken" to Monterrey about 1817 by Joaquín de Arredondo. Spell's work on Bangs remains a standard work in Texas historiography since its appearance forty years ago.[5]

The García Library purchase paved the way for a commitment by the university to establish a Latin American Collection in 1926 and to name Carlos Castañeda its first head librarian. He assumed the position in February 1927. Thus, the academic year 2001–2002 provided the Nettie Lee Benson Latin American Collection an opportunity to celebrate its seventy-fifth anniversary.[6]

The first twenty years of the Latin American Collection brought to it great collections for the study of northeastern Mexico, that is, what had been the Spanish Provincias Internas—especially those areas in its eastern division. These collections include the following:

1. 1936: A significant portion of the records of a Spanish (later, Mexican) garrison at Janos, Chihuahua, covering the years 1706 to 1858 (8 linear feet). These records came to the university through its ad hoc agent, J. Evetts Haley. (J. Evetts Haley wrote *A Texan Looks at Lyndon* many years later.[7])

2. 1938: The W. B. Stephens collection of 1,300 printed items and 20,000 pages of manuscripts on Mexico and the Spanish Southwest. Many of these items, especially the printed materials, include rare newspapers and periodicals that reported the activity in Texas during the 1830s.

3. 1941: The Alejandro Prieto library of complete and partial files of thirty-one early Mexican newspapers, over 3,000 pages of manuscripts, and a large number of books on the culture of the Mexican state of Tamaulipas.

4. 1943: The Sánchez Navarro family papers of some 75,000 pages (seventeenth–twentieth centuries) containing much socioeconomic information on the northern Mexican states, especially Coahuila. The Sánchez Navarro papers have been used as the basis for the study of matriarchal inheritance by Ida Altman and the comprehensive study of the development and maintenance of one of the great latifundios of all of Latin America by Charles Harris.[8]

Nettie Lee Benson assumed the position as head librarian of the Latin American Collection in 1942. Her vision greatly expanded the collection in all directions and in all formats.[9] Extensive runs of microfilm from the AGN particularly expanded the primary sources available at the university for historical research. The two most significant archival collections directly related to the southwestern borderlands to be acquired by Miss Benson were the following:

1. 1967: The Lázaro de la Garza papers elucidating the activities of his employer, General Francisco "Pancho" Villa, and the Revolutionary Army of the North (bulk 1913–1920).

2. 1969: The Pablo Salce Arredondo papers on northern Mexico and the U.S. Southwest, 1594–1965. These papers contain many original documents and printed decrees regarding local affairs in the communities of Nuevo León, but I hasten to add that many items are typescript copies.

Technological innovation, westward expansion, and the articulation of a political philosophy embodied in Manifest Destiny had emboldened the citizenry of the United States. By the latter part of the nineteenth century, their efforts left the landscape marked, and political maps forever changed. The opening of the West and Southwest brought railroads and telegraph lines linking the U.S. East with its West. The events on land were but harbingers of U.S. dominance in transportation and communications on the North American continent. They further reinforced U.S. shipping, which had flourished from the nation's earliest days. The acquisition of immense Mexican territory was not enough, however. Capital formation in the United States allowed for adventurous investments deep within the boundaries of its southern neighbor. Mining, cattle ranching, and foreign investments in Mexico were directly affected by U.S., British, and other European interests. Among the several mining and hacienda papers at the Benson Collection are the papers of the Ferrocarril Noroeste de México. Documentation also exists for the displaced Native American in the Felipe and Dolores Latorre collection on the Kickapoo Indians.

Manuscript Collections Regarding the Mexicano Experience

By the early 1970s opportunities became available for the Benson Collection to carve out new areas in its collection development. This happily (paradoxically?) coincided with the increased difficulty of acquiring manuscript materials from Latin America out of respect for *patrimonio nacional* and because of the great expense of such collections that may come up for sale legally. In 1974 the Mexican American Library Program (MALP) was established by the General Libraries as a unit of the Benson Collection to support the educational needs of students of Mexican American and U.S. Hispanic culture and history. It also now supports the research activities of the faculty of the Center for Mexican American Studies, a national leader in teaching, research, and publications. MALP has worked to enhance the understanding of the Mexican American experience and to strengthen the Mexican American presence in the intellectual terrain.

Library materials obtained initially through MALP relate to the history, politics, and culture of the mexicano experience in Texas and the U.S. Southwest. Given the rapid demographic changes in the U.S. Latino population, however, a concerted effort has been made to represent other groups in the collection, notably those of Caribbean and Central American origin.

The archival and manuscript collections under MALP consist primarily of organizational records, personal papers, and literary manuscripts. These form a rich variety of resources. Some archival collections, such as the Carlos Villalongín Dramatic Company Archives, the journal of Catarino Garza, and the personal papers of historian Carlos E. Castañeda[10] were acquired before the organization of MALP. A comprehensive acquisition program has brought to the Benson Collection other primary sources. These include the literary manuscripts of Rolando Hinojosa-Smith, the records of Austin's Economy Furniture Company strike, and the archives of the League of United Latin American Citizens (LULAC). Today, the ninety archival and manuscript materials total over 1,151 linear feet and include information in a rich variety of formats: photographs, slides, or other visual documentation; taped conferences, lectures, and interviews; and memorabilia such as campaign buttons, bumper stickers, and posters. An online exhibit of the Eleuterio Escobar Papers is available at the Benson Collection website.

Other collections include the personal and professional papers of renowned scholars Américo Paredes, George I. Sánchez, and Julián Samora illuminating important facets of the history of American anthropology, education, and civil rights. The Paredes Papers are one of the most recent acquisitions: over 100 linear feet of material including notes and correspondence on music, especially *corridos,* and his writings based on his childhood home of the lower Rio Grande Valley. Still other papers and collections record the lives of *hispanas:*

1. The Hispanic Network of Women in Texas papers that record the activities of an organization promoting the development of hispanas in the professions, scholarship, and education. Most, but not all, activities relate to Mexican American women.

2. The Estela Portillo Trambley papers of an El Paso native who was an early successful Chicana playwright noted for her novel and poetry.

3. The Carmen Tafolla papers, which reflect the life of a performance artist, writer, and playwright. This is a collection to which additions are irregularly acquired. Reared in south Texas, Tafolla's work sometimes reflects rough aspects of life in south Texas, especially the harsher aspects of machismo and domestic violence.

The Benson Collection also serves as the depository for several organizations and productions. There is the previously mentioned LULAC archives. One may also mention the nationally syndicated radio program, *Latino U.S.A.,* which airs on National Public Radio and which is UT-sponsored and produced. The Benson Collection maintains copies of all of its taped programs. LLEGO, the National Latino/a Lesbian, Gay, and Transgender Organization (Washington, D.C.), has also named the Benson Collection as the recipient of its records and newsletters.

Audiovisual resources acquired through MALP are significant aids to the study of the humanities in the U.S. Southwest. Among these are the following:

1. The Rio Record Shop and Joe Nicola collections of Mexican and Mexican American music containing sound records dating from the late 1930s through the 1970s.

2. The photographic collections of Manuel "Chaca" Ramírez, María Flores, and Bendi Photographics.

3. Chicano art collections of Texas and Southwestern artists Amado Peña and Carmen Lomas Garza; the East Los Angeles Self-Help Graphics silkscreen prints; and works by renowned Chicano artists Malaquías Montoya, Gronk, and Rupert García from the Ricardo Romo papers.

These and other collections along with some 22,500 monographs, 350 serial titles, and 2,500 reels of microfilm combine to provide rich resources for students, faculty, and scholars of Hispanic life in the U.S. Southwest.

Summary

Now, I have overdrawn the distinction between past collection development of manuscript materials by the Benson Collection and contemporary practice. Indeed, unique materials in historical, literary, and photographic collections continue to be acquired for all of Latin America, but there has been greater growth among the Mexican American materials. It may be noted that all of the head librarians of the Benson Latin American Collection, including Lota May Spell, have been scholars deeply interested in their native Texas, particularly in its Spanish and Mexican past. Spell, Castañeda, and Benson have all contributed their personal notes, correspondence, and papers to the Benson Collection. These serve as rich resources for the history of the Benson Collection, the history of the U.S. and Mexican borderlands, the history of Mexico, and as testaments to their lives dedicated to creating one of the finest resources for the study of all of Latin America and to those regions in the United States that once formed part of the Spanish Empire.

Bolton arrived in Texas at a propitious time. He took advantage of the primary sources at hand and made a lasting contribution. There is much to be learned from this example of looking back while moving forward.

NOTES

1. Chester V. Kielman and Carmela Leal, eds., *The Béxar Archives at the University of Texas Archives,* 172 reels (Austin: [University of Texas Library], 1967–1970); Adán Benavides, comp. and ed., *The Béxar Archives, 1717–1836: A Name Guide* (Austin: University of Texas Press for the University of Texas Institute of Texan Cultures at San Antonio, 1989).

2. John Francis Bannon, *Herbert Eugene Bolton: The Historian and the Man, 1870–1953* (Tucson: University of Arizona Press, 1977), pp. xvi, 33–34, 58–64.

3. Jesús F. de la Teja, *San Antonio de Béxar: A Community on New Spain's Northern Frontier* (Albuquerque: University of New Mexico Press, 1995); Alicia Vidaurreta de Tjarks, "Comparative Demographic Analysis of Texas, 1777–1793," *Southwestern Historical Quarterly* 77, no. 3 (January 1974): [291]–338; Tina Louise Meacham, "Population, Family, and Community: A Socio-demographic History of Texas, 1685–1836" (Ph.D. diss., University of Texas at Austin, 2000).

4. Elizabeth John, *Storms Brewed in Other Men's Worlds: The Confrontation of Indians, Spanish, and French in the Southwest, 1540–1795* (College Station: Texas A&M University Press, 1975).

5. Lota May Spell, *Pioneer Printer: Samuel Bangs in Mexico and Texas* (Austin: University of Texas Press, 1963), p. 34. Appendix II (pp. 167–199) is a bibliography of Bangs imprints.

6. Adán Benavides, ed., *The Nettie Lee Benson Latin American Collection* (Austin: General Libraries, University of Texas at Austin, 2001).

7. J. Evetts Haley, *A Texan Looks at Lyndon: A Study in Illegitimate Power* (Canyon, Tex.: Palo Duro, 1964).

8. "A Family and Region in the Northern Fringe Lands: The Marqueses de Aguayo of Nuevo León and Coahuila," in *Provinces of Early Mexico: Variants of Spanish American Regional Evolution,* ed. Ida Altman and James Lockhart (Los Angeles: UCLA Latin American Center Publications, University of California, 1976); Charles H. Harris, *A Mexican Family Empire: The Latifundio of the Sánchez Navarros, 1765–1867* (Austin: University of Texas Press, 1975).

9. Laura Gutiérrez-Witt, "Benson, Nettie Lee," *The New Handbook of Texas,* 6 vols. (Austin: Texas State Historical Association, 1996), 1:493–494. The growth and development of the collection is aptly described in Nettie Lee Benson, "Latin American Collection," *Discovery* (UT Centennial issue, 1983): 54–61.

10. Castañeda's papers at the Benson Collection relate principally to his activities as professor and librarian at the University of Texas at Austin; the University Archives also houses some materials related to his work while at the university. The greater part of his historical research materials are at the Catholic Archives of Texas, Austin, and at the Center for American History, UT-Austin.

16. La recuperación de material documental regional que realiza la Red de Bibliotecas del Banco de la República

Carlos Alberto Zapata Cárdenas

Introducción

Colombia es un país multicultural; nuestro territorio está dividido en 30 departamentos que representa 6 regiones, agrupadas así por compartir una cultura e identidad comunes y las cuales de cierta forma, representan la multiculturalidad de nuestra gente. Producto de esta variada composición racial, étnica social y cultural, son muchas y muy diversas las manifestaciones culturales de nuestras regiones, una parte de las cuales se consideran patrimonio bibliográfico de la nación. Es así como en las diferentes regiones se producen de manera permanente todo tipo de materiales (libros, videos, registros sonoros, etc.) los cuales debido a diferentes razones no alcanzan a llegar a todo el público y, en algunos casos, su circulación es tan restringida que resulta difícil acceder a ellos. Consciente de la importancia que reviste para preservar y promover nuestra cultura nacional, la Biblioteca Luis Ángel Arango, viene adelantando desde hacer varios años la recuperación sistemática de toda la producción impresa, gráfica, visual y sonora que se produce en las diferentes regiones de Colombia.

La Red de bibliotecas del Banco de la República

El Banco de la República es el Banco Central de Colombia y está organizado como una persona jurídica de derecho público con autonomía administrativa, patrimonial y técnica, sujeto a un régimen legal propio, según lo expresado en la Constitución Política de Colombia de 1991. El Banco ha mantenido viva la herencia cultural que forja la memoria colectiva de nuestro país, en donde las manifestaciones culturales que conserva en sus diferentes colecciones patrimoniales se convierten en símbolos vivos que le permiten al colombiano reconocerse, forjarse y apropiarse de su identidad.[1]

Además de las funciones que constitucionalmente le corresponden como banco central (emisión de moneda legal, banquero de bancos, administrador de las reservas internacionales, manejo de la política cambiaria y banquero, agente fiscal y fideicomisario de Colombia), el Banco viene desarrollando desde hace muchos años actividades orientadas a la promoción del desarrollo científico, cultural y social del país, a través de la creación de fundaciones destinadas a seleccionar, estimular y financiar investigaciones en las áreas de las ciencias, la tecnología, las humanidades, la antropología, la arqueología, la educación y la salud. Además, ha participado en el rescate y preservación del patrimonio cultural y en la creación de estímulos a su desarrollo mediante la administración y creación de bibliotecas y museos especializados en todo el país. El Museo del Oro y la Biblioteca Luis Ángel Arango, forman parte del Banco de la República y tienen amplio reconocimiento nacional e internacional por la labor que desarrollan.

Estas bibliotecas prestan servicios presenciales como biblioteca pública en Bogotá (Biblioteca Luis Ángel Arango) y en 12 ciudades del país. En el curso del año 2001 se abrirán 6 nuevas bibliotecas en otras ciudades, al norte y sur del país. Además de estas bibliotecas, existen 5 Centros de Documentación Regional, con colecciones de autores locales y relacionadas con el área; en otras ciudades existen pequeños centros de documentación económica. En Bogotá, además de la sede de La Candelaria, existe la colección Alfonso Palacio Rudas, situada en la Casa Ricardo Gómez Campuzano, en el norte de la ciudad. La red de bibliotecas del Banco constituye la principal red de bibliotecas públicas del país, y atiende aproximadamente 6.000.000 de usuarios presenciales por año.[2]

Además de los servicios propiamente bibliográficos, las bibliotecas del Banco de la República (ver cuadro 1), realizan una actividad cultural centrada en las áreas de música, artes plásticas y cultura regional.

En muchas de sus sedes existen salas de conciertos o salas de música, con programación musical y audiovisual permanente, y salas de exposiciones de arte. En sus aulas múltiples o especializadas se realizan talleres y actividades culturales, usualmente centradas en el estudio del patrimonio cultural, histórico, literario o artístico, de la región y del país. Una información detallada sobre los servicios que se prestan en cada sucursal y sus horarios se encuentra en la página de la biblioteca (www.banrep.gov.co/blaa).

Para aquellas regiones en donde el Banco no cuenta con biblioteca o en las que solo existe un área cultural, que desarrolla actividades en áreas distintas a las de la actividad bibliotecaria o de información, se ha asignado a las bibliotecas más cercanas la función de recuperación de los materiales regionales producidos en dichas regiones (ver cuadro 2).

La política de desarrollo de colecciones

Con el fin de desarrollar las colecciones en las diferentes bibliotecas y centros de documentación, la Subgerencia Cultural definió dentro de la política de adquisiciones, la obligación por parte de las áreas culturales del Banco en las sucursales, la adquisición de todo el material documental producido en la región (de autores regionales o que traten temas regionales), abarcando diferentes tipos de materiales.

Cuadro 1: Sucurales de la Red

Sucursal	Fecha Creación	Centro de Documentación	Biblioteca con Fondo Regional	Región de Cubrimiento
Armenia	1896	X		Quindío
Buenaventura	2001		X	Municipal
Cali	1984	X		Valle
Cartagena	1981		X	Bolivar
Cúcuta Norte	1985	X		Santander y S/
Florencia	2001		X	Caquetá
Girardot	1981		X	Municipal
Honda	1998		X	Municipal
Ibagué	1984		X	Tolima
Ipiales Frontera	1984		X	Municipal /
Leticia	1986		X	Amazonía
Manizales	1981		X	Caldas
Montería	1988	X		Córdoba
Pasto	1984		X	Nariño
Pereira	1983		X	Risaralda
Popayán	2001		X	Cauca
Quibdo	1987		X	Choco
Riohacha	1981		X	Guajira
San Andrés	1985	X	X	San Andres Islas
Santa Martha	1980		X	Magdalena
Sincelejo	2001		X	Sucre
Tunja	1983		X	Boyacá
Valledupar	2001		X	César

Cuadro 2: Sucursales responsables de otras regions

Sucursal	Dpto. de Cubrimiento Principal	Dpto. de Cubrimiento Complementario
Cartagena	Bolívar	Atlántico
Cúcuta	Norte de Santander	Santander Arauca / Venezuela
Florencia	Caquetá	Guaviare
Ibagué	Tolima	Huila
Leticia	Amazonas	Vaupés/ Guainía/ Vichada
Pasto	Nariño	Putumayo
Tunja	Boyacá	Meta/ Arauca / Casanare

Las colecciones responden a las cuatro funciones básicas de la Red de Bibliotecas del Banco. Es una colección patrimonial, que pretende ser exhaustiva en la adquisición de los libros y publicaciones periódicas colombianas o sobre Colombia, y que incluye colecciones documentales y de manuscritos.

Es una colección universitaria (biblioteca de investigación), para atender un publico que está compuesto en un 70% por estudiantes y profesores universitarios, atender a los funcionarios del Banco, y para complementar las actividades de los dos museos del Banco de la República: El Museo del Oro y la Colección de la Biblioteca Luis Ángel Arango (colección permanente de arte, donación Botero, colección numismática, colección de instrumentos antiguos). Es una colección general para atender a todos los diversos sectores de la comunidad. En varias regiones es una colección infantil con salas especiales de atención para los niños. La colección patrimonial se concentra en Bogotá, aunque en cada región la biblioteca local busca formar una colección también exhaustiva sobre el área de influencia correspondiente.[3]

La orientación en el desarrollo de las colecciones que cumplen el componente patrimonial de la política de adquisiciones de la Red de Bibliotecas y Centros de Documentación, se centra en la adquisición, a través de diferentes mecanismos (compra, donación o canje), de los siguientes tipos de materiales:

- Libros y folletos de autores que traten exclusivamente temas de la región.

- Periódicos regionales y artículos que se publiquen dentro y fuera de la región que traten sobre temas de la región.

- Revistas sueltas cuyos números hayan sido dedicados a la región o tengan artículos sobre la región. Se podrán adquirir colecciones completas de revistas, siempre que el tema central de la publicación sea sobre aspectos de la región.

- Mapas y planos que ilustren los cambios políticos y geográficos de la region.

- Hojas sueltas con información sobre hechos de importancia local y regional.

- Fotografías que permitan descubrir la memoria gráfica regional.

- Materiales audiovisuales y grabaciones sonoras que registren temas o acontecimientos regionales, con énfasis en la memoria oral.

- Documentos institucionales como informes, estudios, investigaciones, que puedan dar testimonio del desarrollo científico, económico, social, educativo, productivo, empresarial, etc., de la región, que no sean de reserva por su contenido.

- Documentos y materiales de eventos académicos, sindicales, políticos, etc., los cuales por lo general son de circulación limitada, y siempre que obedezcan a temas o asuntos regionales.

- Documentos oficiales y en general todo tipo de material bibliográfico que contribuya a la identificación y aceptación de la personalidad cultural de la región.

La recuperación de la Bibliografía Nacional

En el desarrollo de la política de adquisiciones, las bibliotecas y centros de documentación de las sucursales desarrollan las siguientes funciones:

- Rescatar, mantener, preservar, controlar, analizar y difundir el acervo documental colombiano y colombianista producido en la región, que sirva de base para el crecimiento y desarrollo regional.

- Elaborar diferentes instrumentos para el ordenamiento de la producción intelectual de la región, que contribuya a la compilación de la bibliografía colombiana.

- Proveer las fuentes para la investigación de los diferentes aspectos regionales (historia, geografía, grupos étnicos, economía, manifestaciones culturales, etc.) y difundirlos con fines de estudio y conservación.

- Registrar, sin importar el soporte, la historia de la región, sus gentes, tradiciones y leyendas con el fin de conservarlas y contribuir a revivir las fiestas tradicionales y el folclor.

- Establecer vínculos con otras instituciones con las que se compartan objetivos e intereses comunes, y que puedan realizar proyectos conjuntos.

- Proveer servicios especializados para los investigadores acreditados antes el CDR, con el fin de contribuir a la investigación de la tradición y la memoria regional.

Con el fin de desarrollar adecuadamente las colecciones regionales, las bibliotecas y centros de documentación, la Subgerencia Cultural del Banco asigna los recursos económicos necesarios para la compra de la producción editorial regional. Para lograr el objetivo de recuperar el patrimonio regional se desarrollan las siguientes estrategias.

Participación en ferias regionales del libro

Las ferias regionales del libro son acontecimientos culturales de especial importancia en las regiones. Estos eventos se constituyen en un escenario propicio para identificar y adquirir los materiales regionales que por razones de diversa índole no se adquieren por los canales tradicionales del comercio del libro. Este tipo de ferias en general son utilizadas por los autores inéditos para presentar su producción intelectual. La importancia de participar en estas ferias radica en la baja cantidad de materiales que se exponen, muchos de los cuales se agotan rápidamente, por lo cual la presencia de funcionarios de la red de bibliotecas del Banco garantiza la adquisición de estos materiales. Otra particularidad es precisamente la relacionada con los temas regionales, atributo que hace de la feria regional un mecanismo adecuado para la adquisición de todo tipo de producción regional.

Visitas institucionales

Una función primordial que deben cumplir los directores de las bibliotecas y centros de documentación es la relacionada con los contactos institucionales. De hecho, la producción bibliográfica institucional en Colombia ha mejorado notoriamente, tanto en la calidad de las ediciones como en el contenido. Este hecho tiene especial significado para los propósitos de la red, toda vez que el ejercicio de canje que realiza la Biblioteca Luis Ángel Arango ha permitido incrementar las colecciones de la red de manera dramática. Como la cantidad de instituciones que potencialmente producen material bibliográfico y documental regional es muy grande, se definió una estrategia de visitas apoyadas en una programación anual que permitan centrarnos en aquellas que resultan de mayor interés para el cumplimiento de los objetivos de nuestra red de bibliotecas. De manera complementaria, fue necesario fijar unos criterios para la selección de las instituciones como:

- Hacer énfasis en entidades gubernamentales cuya producción institucional generalmente no se adquiere a través del mercado del libro.

- Fortalecer el vínculo con las instituciones universitarias, académicas y de investigación con el objeto de detectar las líneas de publicación de cada una y definir una estrategia para la adquisición de sus materiales.

- Identificar los organismos no gubernamentales que por su naturaleza produzcan información sobre la región, con el fin de acceder a estas fuentes documentales.

Las visitas institucionales se realizan tanto en la Luis Ángel Arango, a través de la coordinación de Canje como en las sucursales a través de los Directores de las Areas Culturales. Esta información se ingresa a una bases de datos que permite tener un control sobre las producción bibliográfico o documental de las diferentes instituciones, así como sobre las líneas de información que manejan. Actualmente se encuentran registradas en dicha base de datos 1415 instituciones localizadas en diferentes regiones del país.

Contactos con editoriales

El trabajo directo con las editoriales es una de las formas más efectivas para lograr la recuperación del material documental regional. Debido al desconocimiento de nuestra política de adquisiciones y en particular del componente patrimonial de ésta, las librerías y editoriales, solamente nos ofrecían materiales orientado a un público académico y a cubrir las necesidades habituales de los usuarios de una biblioteca pública y desechaban la presentación de ofertas de material colombiano por considerar que estaba por fuera de nuestra línea de adquisiciones. Una vez advertida esta situación, se diseñó una estrategia de acercamiento a editores y libreros, con el fin de explicarles el alcance de la política de adquisiciones en forma global, pero enfatizando en nuestro interés por qué nos ofrecían los materiales regionales, sin importar la calidad de los mismos o el tema que traten, siempre que fueran de autores colombianos y desarrollaran temas propios de cada región o del país en general. De esta forma, se comenzaron a adquirir materiales de valor patrimonial que han fortalecido nuestra colección y nos han permitido crear una comunicación constante con los editores y libreros, quienes de alguna forma se han convertido en una extensión de nuestras bibliotecas para el desarrollo de las colecciones.

Contactos con los autores

El contacto permanente con los autores colombianos ha sido otra preocupación permanente de la Biblioteca Luis Ángel Arango y su red de sucursales. Por definición, adquirimos toda la producción intelectual de autores colombianos, incluyendo autores nacionales que residen en otros países del mundo. En las regiones, el acercamiento a los autores es más prolífico y genera vínculos indisolubles de estos con nuestras bibliotecas y centros de documentación. En la programación cultural que desarrollan las diferentes áreas culturales del Banco, están presentes encuentros con autores regionales, ferias regionales del libro, y otras actividades que contribuyen a recuperar los materiales que de otra forma podrían perderse de manera irremediable. No son pocas las ocasiones en que los autores producen materiales de gran calidad pero que por razones económicas tienen un bajo tiraje, por lo que creemos que es una obligación nuestra adquirir dichos materiales. En algunos casos, los mismos autores conscientes de la trascendencia que tiene la red de bibliotecas del Banco, donan sus obras para que éstas no solo sean conocidas, sino como un mecanismo de promoción de su producción literaria o técnica.

Establecimiento de convenios de canje

El canje se constituye en uno de los mecanismos más efectivos para el desarrollo de colecciones de la red de bibliotecas, y tiene la característica de ser el medio a través del cual se adquieren aquellos materiales que se encuentran fuera del mercado tradicional del libro. En el caso de la actividad de adquisiciones de la Biblioteca Luis Ángel Arango y la red de sucursales, el canje representa un 40% del total de las colecciones que ingresan anualmente a las bibliotecas y centros de documentación (ver cuadro 3). Durante el año 2000, la red recibió por canje un total de 33.192 publicaciones, de las cuales aproximadamente el 65% corresponde a material regional colombiano. En este mismo año, la actividad de canje representó un incremento de las colecciones equivalente a $280.000 dólares por concepto de ingresos (80% más que durante 1999).

Cuadro 3: Resultado de la actividad de canje año 2000

Tipo de Publicación	No. de Títulos	No. de copias
Libros	18.152	23.455
Seriadas	2.865	2.865
Folletos, afiches, fotografías, láminas, postales	3.277	5.824
Material cartográfico	35	50
Material audiovisual	580	998
Total	24.909	33.192

Con el fin de garantizar que esta actividad no sea un simple ejercicio marginal, el canje se maneja a través de convenios interinstitucionales y se realiza un seguimiento individual sobre cada una de las instituciones con las cuales tenemos convenio, además de visitas periódicas de acuerdo con un cronograma previamente establecido. Adicionalmente, se fijan metas anuales de crecimiento de dichos convenios, lo que genera resultados positivos en cuanto a la adquisición de materiales de utilidad para nuestra comunidad de usuarios. Con el fin de lograr los resultados antes mencionados, el área de canje cuenta con recursos presupuestales para la compra de materiales para canje, la administración de la base de datos de canje, la verificación de materiales, los costos de correo, la contratación de personal externo, etc. Como una línea de adquisición que maneja el área de canje, se encuentra la donación de colecciones, lo que ha permitido adquirir valiosas colecciones de material colombiano (archivos fotográficos, archivos de prensa, manuscritos, archivos privados, partituras, etc.) preservando así nuestra memoria colectiva.

Proyectos de cooperación

Aunque esta es una actividad que corresponde a la Dirección General de la Biblioteca, quien fija las directrices sobre este asunto, y la cual abarca no sólo proyectos bibliotecarios, sino además de arte, música, museología, capacitación, asesoría, etc., la red de bibliotecas del Banco adelanta con frecuencia convenios de cooperación con otras instituciones afines para recuperar el patrimonio documental; dentro de estas actividades de cooperación conviene resaltar la recuperación de colecciones de prensa antigua y contemporánea, a través del mecanismo de microfilmación, descripción de archivos históricos, restauración de fuentes patrimoniales de interés histórico, reproducción de materiales en otros soportes, etc.

NOTAS

1. Catalina Gómez y Verónica Uribe, *La biblioteca Luis Ángel Arango: Patrimonio que se desaprovecha en su proyección* (Bogotá: Universidad Javeriana, 1995). Diagnóstico.

2. Banco de la República, Servicios de la Biblioteca Luis Ángel Arango y la red de bibliotecas del Banco de la República (Bogotá: La biblioteca, 2001). Documento Interno.

3. Banco de la República, Servicios de la Biblioteca Luis Ángel Arango y la Red de Bibliotecas del Banco de la República (Bogotá, marzo de 2001). Tomado del documento preparado por el doctor Jorge Orlando Melo, Director del Departamento de Bibliotecas y Artes del Banco de la República.

17. Relevance of Academic Libraries' Hispanic-American Collections in a Diverse Society

Nelly S. González

"Do we understand how to live in a pluralistic society where social, economic, and linguistic differences among racial, ethnic groups can become a source of [strength rather than] mistrust, jealousy, and intergroup hostility?"[1] Henry Der, executive director of Chinese for Affirmative Action, posed this question in his introduction to *Developing Library Collections for California's Emerging Majority*. The same question continues to haunt academic and public libraries today. The importance of developing collections of Spanish titles being published in Latin America, Spain, and the United States in libraries across the nation is well stated by Adriana López: "In contrast to other immigrant groups in this country, Latinos will never stop speaking and reading in their native language. By the end of the decade, the United States will be the second largest Spanish-speaking country, behind Mexico."[2] Fortunately, institutions, librarians, and scholars are working together and beginning to see its importance; they are taking steps to address this problem.[3] Public and academic libraries are building their collections to be able to serve the needs of their clientele. In the past, bookstores and libraries overlooked these materials, especially those written by Latino/a authors writing in English. Furthermore, they were inadequately reviewed in the mainstream media. Aware of this deficiency, *Publishers Weekly, Library Journal*, and *School Library Journal* joined efforts to create *Críticas,* which is an English speaker's guide to the latest Spanish titles.

Teaching institutions play a major role in the intellectual life of the community since their responsibility is the education of its members in order to achieve a positive interaction between the diverse groups that comprise American society. Public libraries also have the same responsibility to their clientele, gathering publications which will educate both Hispanics and non-Hispanics in Hispanic culture and issues. School libraries play an even greater role in this process, "[since] education is often cited as the primary solution to our collective woes."[4]

All libraries serve as providers of information on ethnic minorities, thus educating the general community about its varied cultural groups and preparing each community to address the challenge of living in a pluralistic society in harmony and with respect. The information revolution has enormously benefited the access to sources of information on Hispanic Americans available on the Internet, as libraries provide timely dissemination of current research relevant to Latino/a populations in the United States. There are numerous search engines devoted to Latino/a subjects providing websites in English and Spanish. The Internet is in a state of constant development. There are numerous search engines and they open a whole universe of sites and information. Also, there are additional Spanish search engines, for example, Yahoo en español. Besides them, academic institutions have web pages with Hispanic-American and/or Latino/a information sources providing excellent links to a myriad of centers, agencies, nonprofit organizations, etc., that complement in finding these materials.

My work deals with the manner in which the academic library would support Hispanic Americans and the university community in general through development of a rich and varied collection of Hispanic-American literature. In the past, bookstores and libraries have overlooked Spanish-language books. It is essential that the university library collection complement the academic curriculum, particularly for courses dealing with all the characteristics of the human experience, stressing its diversity, its cultural heritage, and its steady evolution through the history of the United States.

The need for this kind of collection became clear during the 1970s and 1980s, which witnessed strong movements to achieve social justice, to fight discrimination and racism, and to have equal employment and educational opportunities for the various minority groups in the United States. The large Hispanic population in America, which became "foreigners in their native land" as David J. Weber stated,[5] also felt the need to come to terms with the disregard that it faced as an ethnic group. As more minority Hispanic students reached higher education, universities were challenged with the necessity to modify their curriculum, providing courses and programs that teach the history of this ethnic group and its long-standing presence in the United States. Hispanic-American youth demanded information about their background, contributions to American society, prominent writers, educators, and political leaders.

During the same period academic libraries were making efforts to develop Hispanic-American collections to support programs for and about Hispanics in the United States. There are more than 31,000,000 Hispanics from over twenty-one countries making the United States the fifth largest Spanish-speaking country in the world. The majority of Hispanic Americans are Mexican-American, Puerto Rican, or Cuban-American (even though, there are sizable groups that come from Central and South America). Consequently, it is reasonable that these collections should place special emphasis on the three largest subgroups of Hispanic Americans in order to adequately support a balanced research on the varied types of experiences of this diverse ethnic group. One must not forget that to study this increasingly important part of the demographic composition of the United States, the origin of its culture must also be researched. To support Hispanic-American studies, there is a need for a bibliographic apparatus that would "reflect the ample harvest of books, journals, newspapers, government documents, pamphlets, theses, dissertations and other publications which are relevant to Hispanic-American cultures."[6]

New York is the preferred area of immigration for all of the Caribbean nations, and this is particularly true for Puerto Ricans, as is demonstrated by the massive scale of people from Puerto Rico who have emigrated to the New York area.[7] This preference is due to three reasons: (1) their status as American citizens; (2) the ease of travel to this metropolis; and (3) the relatively plentiful opportunities for work.[8]

The Spanish tradition is part of the American life, because historically some areas of the nation have had large Hispanic populations, even before these areas were incorporated into the United States. The Southwest and West in particular are populated by Mexicans and Mexican-Americans.[9] Thus, Chicano collections in those areas have flourished in academic and public libraries to serve their needs. Excellent collections on Mexican-Americans have flourished in California's universities as well as in their public libraries. Texas has developed excellent collections, followed by New Mexico and Arizona. In comparison, the East Coast has large Puerto Rican populations and it is no surprise that large collections on Puerto Rican materials are also concentrated in this area.[10] One must also not forget the depositories of materials in Puerto Rico itself, both in academic institutions as well as public libraries. New York contains the largest repository of Puerto Rican publications in the United States at the New York Public Library, which is dispersed between the main metropolitan library and the individual borough libraries.[11] An even more important collection is the one in the Library of Congress, which has holdings on Hispanic materials that are very extensive. Its collection holds over 2,000,000 books and periodicals.[12]

The University of Florida Libraries have a long history of interest in collecting Cuban materials as well as publications from and about the Caribbean region. As early as the late 1920s, scholars interested in Cuba turned to the Florida libraries for assistance in researching Cuban publications.[13] Afterwards, the coming of Castro and the Cuban Revolution sent into exile over 1,000,000 Cubans, who settled in the United States, primarily in Miami and other parts of Florida, as well as the New York–New Jersey area.[14] As a result, the majority of Cuban-Americans are in Florida. Thus, the most comprehensive collections of Cuban and Cuban-American materials are found in Florida, both in university and public libraries. These are the three largest Hispanic subgroups; the rest may be located in different regions of the country, generally around the big cities.

The Midwest also has its share of the Hispanic population (mostly Mexican-Americans and Puerto Ricans). According to the 2000 census, the Hispanic population in the United States is 35,305,818 out of a total population of 281,421,906.[15] It is estimated that the Hispanic population in Illinois will increase from 8 percent in 1990 to 14 percent in 2025.[16] Rough estimates of growth of the Hispanic population indicate a 25 percent increase since 1980, with Hispanics ages 15–24 numbering around 160,000.[17] It is therefore easy to understand the concern of the University of Illinois regarding the collection development of materials to service this resident population, as well as the faculty and students of the university itself.

The Latin American and Caribbean studies holdings of the University of Illinois Library are among the most extensive collection in the country, and are the largest of the Midwest region. This makes it the library of resource for Hispanic materials for the area. Therefore, support for a core collection of Hispanic culture has been developed.[18] An important part of this work is the list of basic references for current sources on Hispanic-American literature. Many of the basic works are invaluable for collection development decisions in libraries. The selection criteria for the acquisition of Hispanic-American literature materials at the University of Illinois Library is in accordance with the emphasis placed by the University of Illinois Library on primary research materials and/or those works that are suitable for academic scholarship. This is natural since the library serves a large student body and must provide sources to support the varied curricula and diverse interdisciplinary courses taught at the university.

Basic General Resources

Academic libraries support the teaching and research needs of university faculty, researchers, and students, making it necessary to pursue a sound collection development policy to acquire the right materials and to establish a strong Hispanic-American collection. These materials are unique since they are primary source materials, manuscripts, and archival holdings that support scholarship and are one of a kind.[19] A core collection of general reference sources consists of the following:

Handbook of Latin American Studies: Humanities and Social Studies, 1935–.
   This annotated bibliography is published annually with alternating volumes devoted to the humanities and the social sciences. It has been and continues to be a de rigueur reference work for Latin American, Caribbean, and Latino/a studies. It is available online as well as in print.

Hispanic-American Periodicals Index (HAPI), 1975–.
   This index is as valuable as the handbook described above, especially for current materials, which are mainly found in serial publications. Articles are indexed from a comprehensive list of Latin American and Caribbean journals as well as journals published in the United States, Canada, and Europe that cover Latin American, Caribbean, and Hispanic-American topics. *HAPI* also includes references to book reviews that are published

in the journals that it indexes. Over 250 journals are indexed. *HAPI* is also available online through the UCLA Latin American Center.

Bibliographic Guide to Latin American Studies, 1978–.

The timeliest bibliography among bibliographies, this important reference work is published yearly, with coverage of all Latin American, Caribbean, and Latino/a studies works that are held in the library of the University of Texas at Austin, as well as some books in the Library of Congress. It is arranged in dictionary format, and can be searched by author, title, or subject.

There are several other noteworthy sources to mention which cover more specialized topics. Here are some examples:

MLA International Bibliography on CD-ROM. Coverage since 1963.

This is the best index to use for searching topics relating to literature. It indexes books, journal articles, and dissertations in modern languages, literature, folklore studies, and linguistics. It includes citations dealing with literary criticism, literary theory, comparative literature, etc.

UMI's Dissertation Abstracts on CD-ROM. Covers from 1861 to the present.

This is a computerized dissertation database indexing bibliographic citations of masters and doctoral theses presented at American and Canadian universities. Information can be retrieved by subject classification or by keyword, as well as by author, institution granting the degree, and date of awarded degree.

The Chicano Database on CD-ROM. Published semiannually (July 1991–).

"Portions of the database were published and sold separately as the *Chicano Periodical Index; The Chicano Index; Arte Chicano; Chicano Anthology Index;* and *The Chicana Studies Index.*" The CD-ROM edition includes publications on Puerto Ricans, Cuban-Americans, and Central American refugees as well as persons of Mexican heritage.

A Guide to Latin American, Caribbean, and U.S. Latino Made Films and Video. Karen Ranucci and Julie Feldman, eds. Lanham, Md.: Scarecrow Press, 1998.

The editors are associated with LAVA (Latin American Video Archive) and the titles listed in the above guide are available through the International Media Resource Exchange. This media is being developed in all academic institutions since it is well used by the academia as well as students.

Methodology

This search for materials on Hispanic-American works was conducted by referring to several of the basic reference works mentioned above, along with sources that focus specifically on Hispanic Americans. These sources are the following:

- *Handbook of Latin American Studies*

- *Hispanic-American Periodicals Index (HAPI)*

- *Bibliographic Guide to Latin American Studies*

- *MLA International Bibliography* on CD-ROM

- *University of Illinois online catalog* (LCS/FBR).

The *MLA International Bibliography* on CD-ROM retrieved the largest number of relevant entries for searches in the belles-lettres compared to the other indexes consulted. Therefore, this is the best index to use for studies in literature. An added bonus in this database is the inclusion of dissertations that cover literature topics presented at American and Canadian universities.

Special bibliographies consulted are the following:

Covington, Paula H., ed. *Latin America and the Caribbean: A Critical Guide to Research Sources*. Westport, Conn.: Greenwood, 1992.

This "is intended to bring relevant bibliographic and research sources and methods relating to the study" of the region. Although the title does not include the term "Latino/a studies," it covers this topic under the term "Hispanic-American."

Robinson, Barbara, and J. Cordell Robinson. *The Mexican-American: A Critical Guide Research Aids*. Greenwich, Conn.: JAI Press, 1980.

A basic scholarly reference, which includes bibliographies, guides, directories, dictionaries, biographical and statistical sources, and newspaper, periodical, and audiovisual sources. The second part comprises subject bibliographies for education, folklore, history, labor, linguistics, literature, women, and social and behavioral science. There are 668 entries, which have been selected for inclusion after examination of over 2,000 works. Works included date from 1857 to 1980. This work is a de rigueur reference work of Hispanic-American studies.

Chabrán, Richard. "Latino Reference Sources: A Bibliographic Essay." In *Latino Librarianship: A Handbook for Professionals,* edited by Salvador Güereña. Jefferson, N.C.: McFarland, 1990. Pp. 35–57.

A scholar in Latino bibliography, Richard Chabrán gives an excellent overview of the state-of-the-art tools necessary for Latino research.

Güereña, Salvador, ed. *Latino Librarianship: A Handbook for Professionals.* Jefferson, N.C.: McFarland, 1990.

Aimed at Latino librarianship in public libraries, Richard Chabrán's articles on Latino reference sources provide an excellent overview of works on the subject.

Selected Recent Acquisitions. Mexican-American Research Collections, Stanford University Libraries. No. 1 (September 1985–). Stanford, Calif.: The Collections.

This is an important list of the holdings of the Stanford University Chicano Collection, which is among the largest in the country.

Bilindex: A Bilingual Spanish-English Subject Heading List. Oakland: California Spanish Language DataBase, 1983. *Bilindex Supplement I, 1985–1986.*

Over 15,500 Library of Congress subject headings that are useful for reference and cataloging.

Appropriate search strategies for finding information on Hispanic Americans include the following:

- Mexican-Americans[20]

- Mexican-Americans—Politics and Suffrage

- Mexican-Americans—Illinois . . . etc.

- Mexicans in Arizona (and other geographical areas)

- Mexicans-Americans Studies

- Mexican-Americans—Case Studies

- Puerto Ricans—United States

- Cuban-Americans (subdivided by subject and geographical areas)

- Hispanic Americans (subdivided by subject and geographical areas)

- Assimilation (Sociology)

- Civil Rights

- Discrimination

- Ethnic Attitudes

- Ethnic Barriers

- Ethnic Groups[21]

- Ethnic Press

- Ethnic Studies

- Ethnicity[22]

- Minorities

- Race Awareness

- Race Discrimination[23]

- Race Questions

- Race Relations

- Segregation

- Spanish Americans in the United States.

The above subject headings are only examples for the strategy to follow in the search. There are other subjects that the user could search following the pattern provided.

The Reference and Adult Services Division's Committee on Library Service to the Spanish Speaking of the American Library Association has heightened the awareness of the significant cultural and linguistic differences present in the varied Hispanic community by providing a document known as the "RASD Guidelines for Library Services to Hispanics." This work helps library professionals to understand the importance of Hispanic Americans as a large ethnic group, particularly in regard to developing a collection that will support the needs of Hispanic Americans. There are several works and bibliographies written on Latino collections and libraries. Special and excellent bibliographies were written particularly through the 1970s. Chabrán states that there is no one Latino bibliographic source that contains the entire universe of Latino resources.[24] There is a present need to update these reference works to facilitate the search for current sources of information.

Conclusion

The Hispanic community in the United States contributes a vast creative potential to society. The source of this creativity can be traced back to the fruitful combination of Hispanic cultures and peoples, each with a unique background and heritage. The various subgroups of Cuban-Americans, Puerto Ricans, Mexican-Americans, as well as other cultures have interwoven to form a vibrant tapestry of life. Their works present a dynamic expression and outgrowth of this mixture. This is what makes Hispanic-American culture an exciting area of study for many researchers. Updating the resources available on this subject will make a contribution toward the further discovery of rich jewels hidden in the treasure trove of the Hispanic-American experience.

NOTES

1. Henry Der, "Introduction: Building Our Future Through Diversity," in *Developing Library Collections for California's Emerging Majority,* ed. Katharine T. A. Scarborough (Berkeley, Calif.: Bay Area Library and Information System, 1990), p. 2.

2. Adriana Lopez, *Críticas* 1, no. 1 (spring 2001): 2.

3. E. J. Josey and Marva L. DeLoach, eds., *Ethnic Collections in Libraries* (New York: Neal-Schuman, 1983), p. viii.

4. Salvador Güereña, ed., *Latino Librarianship: A Handbook for Professionals* (Jefferson, N.C.: McFarland, 1990), p. 4.

5. David J. Weber, comp., *Foreigners in Their Native Land: Historical Roots of the Mexican Americans* (Albuquerque: University of New Mexico Press, 1973).

6. Fay Fowlie-Flores, comp., *Annotated Bibliography of Puerto Rican Bibliographies* (New York: Greenwood, 1990).

7. Eugene V. Mohr, *The Nuyorican Experience: Literature of the Puerto Rican Minority* (Westport, Conn.: Greenwood, 1982).

8. Ibid.

9. Iliana Sontag, Shelly E. Phipps, and Ross W. McLachlan, comps., *Guide to Chicano Resources in the University of Arizona Library* (Tucson: University of Arizona Library, 1980).

10. Brigitte T. Darnay, ed., *Subject Directory of Special Libraries and Information Centers,* vol. 4, Social Sciences and Humanities Libraries (Detroit, Mich.: Gale Research, 1983).

11. MODOC Press, comp., *Special Collections in College and University Libraries* (New York: Macmillan, 1989), pp. 445–446.

12. Guy Lamolinara, "The Hispanic Division: Center of Latin American Scholarship," *Library of Congress Information Bulletin* 49, no. 18 (September 10, 1990): 299.

13. David Geggus, *The Caribbean Collections at the University of Florida: A Brief Description* (Gainesville: University of Florida Libraries, 1985), p. 1.

14. Danilo H. Figueredo, "Cuban American Literature: Authors and Resources," in *Latino Librarianship,* ed. Güereña, p. 92.

15. U.S. Census Bureau, "2000 Census of Population and Housing," *American Factfinder,* *Geographic Comparison Table,* 2001, http://factfinder.census.gov/servlet/BasicFactsServlet, accessed on May 16, 2001.

16. *Illinois Population Trends from 1980 to 2025* (Springfield: State of Illinois, Bureau of the Budget, 1987).

17. Ibid.

18. Carl Deal, "A Survey of Latin American Collections," in *Latin American Studies into the Twenty-First Century: New Focus, New Formats, New Challenges,* ed. Deborah L. Jakubs. Papers of SALALM XXXVI, San Diego, California, June 1–6, 1991 (Albuquerque, N.Mex.: SALALM, 1993), pp. 315–334.

19. Roberto G. Trujillo and Linda Chávez, "Collection Development on the Mexican American Experience," in *Latino Librarianship,* ed. Güereña, p. 79.

20. Under the subject heading "Mexican-Americans" are works on American citizens of Mexican descent or works concerned with "Mexican-American minority groups." Works on immigration from Mexico, braceros, etc., are under "Mexicans in the United States."

21. Under this subject heading are theoretical works on groups of people who are bound together by common ties of ancestry and culture.

22. Under this subject heading are works on the subjective sense of belonging to an individual ethnic group.

23. Under this subject heading are works limited to overt discriminatory behavior directed against racial or ethnic groups. Works on discrimination directed against Mexican-Americans are under "Mexican-Americans—Social Conditions."

24. Richard Chabrán, "Latino References Sources: A Bibliographic Essay," in *Latino Librarianship,* ed Güereña, p. 43.

18. The Covers Are the Story: The Artwork of Ediciones Botas, Mexico

Claire-Lise Bénaud
Sharon Moynahan

There is a strong interest at the University of New Mexico (UNM) in Latin American visual arts and photography. One of UNM's strengths is Mexican popular graphic art from the nineteenth and twentieth centuries. The acquisitions of the Taller de Gráfica Popular Archive several years ago reflect this interest. The recent purchase of the archive of the Librería y Ediciones Botas, a prominent twentieth-century Mexican publishing house, also coincides with faculty interests in this area. This collection was bought primarily for the books' illustrated covers, which are a good representation of Mexican graphic art from this period. Content was secondary.

The Ediciones Botas Archive at the University of New Mexico

The University of New Mexico purchased the Botas collection from Karno Books. This collection was part of an archive, presumably bought from an individual who worked for the Botas publishing house. The UNM General Library acquired a small portion of this archive. There are three parts to this collection: the books, the original artwork for the covers, and some manuscripts. Each part is valuable in its own right.

Books

The books are the most valuable part of the collection and were acquired because of illustrations on their covers. The collection consists of some 150 books, ranging in subjects such as Mexican literature, history, philosophy, politics, botany, medicine, hypnotism, spiritualism, cooking, and translations of European authors. The library already owned some books published by the Botas publishing house, but most of them were bound and the covers were discarded in the process. The original covers are striking. They epitomize the flavor of the time. It was for this aspect that UNM purchased the collection.

Original Artwork

The original artwork includes 600–700 drawings, including mock-up covers in varying sizes. Some mock-ups are smaller than the original, while others are larger. In several cases, it is possible to trace the creation of the image from start to finish: pencil drawing, pen and ink drawing, and the same drawing with colors added. In some instances, there are two mock-ups for a cover, one ultimately abandoned and one chosen. This part of the archive is very pertinent for artists interested in book covers. However, the cover illustrators are not well-known artists. The library may not want to keep all the artwork, perhaps keeping only the best examples.

This part of the archive also includes many interesting photographs that were used, or were planned to be used, as illustrations. Many of these photographs represent scenes of rural Mexico, especially festival scenes. There are also drawings by F.A.G., one of the most prominent cover artists working for Botas. Included are also some of this artist's medical and technical drawings, which are unrelated to the Botas illustrated covers.

Manuscripts

The archive also contains two boxes of manuscripts and assorted correspondence between Gabriel Botas and various authors published by Botas. The manuscript portion consists of several handwritten or typed book manuscripts and some proofs, but they do not necessarily correspond to the titles purchased in this collection. The correspondence section includes royalty receipts signed by authors, in some cases notarized, as well as lengthy book contracts. There are also some interesting letters discussing submission, withdrawal, or disposition of manuscripts between authors and the publisher. This part of the collection provides a great example of the workings of the editorial and publishing process.

Brief History of Ediciones Botas

The history of publishing in Mexico at the turn of the twentieth century is the history of people rather than the history of books. At this time, it was the norm for renowned publishing houses to have corresponding bookstores. This is certainly true of the Botas publishing house. At the turn of the century, the three major publishers were Porrúa, C. Bouret's widow, and Herrero. It was around this time that Andrés Botas became involved in the Mexican book business, and eventually in publishing.

Andrés Botas, originally from Spain, moved to Cuba where he became a landowner. At the end of the nineteenth century, he moved to Mexico City because of bad economic times in Cuba. There, on Calle de Vergara, he established a cigar shop. In 1906, a friend from Spain asked him to sell a number of books. Realizing that the book business was profitable, Andrés Botas opened "Librería Botas" in 1907 in his cigar shop. In 1911, the publishing house began its distinguished history. By the time it reached its heyday in the 1940s, it had published some 2,000 titles.

During this period, a century after its independence, Mexico enjoyed a literary renaissance. For the first time, Mexican writers assumed their own identity rather than following styles, fashions, and themes developed by Spanish writers. The love of country and Mexican nationalism are reflected in plays, novels, and poetry as writers began to look for new ways of expressing these ideas. Literature as well as other art forms—especially muralist art—contributed to the creation of a militant nationalist Mexico. The Botas publishing house belongs to this revival.

In 1910, Andrés Botas's son, Gabriel Botas, left Cuba to join his father's publishing house. He took over the business in 1916. Thus begins the golden age of Editorial Botas. Over the decades, it published the works of some of the most renowned writers and intellectuals of the time: Mariano Azuela, the most popular writer of the Mexican Revolution; Dr. Atl, who played a momentous role in Mexican public life; and José Vasconcelos, Minister of Education. Also included were Federico Gamboa, Carlos González Peña, Gregorio López y Fuentes, Julio Jiménez Rueda, and Mauricio Magdaleno—all friends of Gabriel Botas and all participants in the literary salons that he organized. Ediciones Botas was an important outlet for authors in Mexico in the 1920s, 1930s, and 1940s. It flourished during the presidencies of Cárdenas, Camacho, and Alemán, and it helped disseminate programs of national culturalism. It represented the official ideology of the Mexican Revolution in the 1930s and promoted national unity and national conscience using art and architecture in a systematic way. This was an all-out effort. Even the book covers helped advance these ideas. Cover art was used as a tool for advertisement, education, and propaganda. It targeted middle-class audiences during those years.

As business flourished, Gabriel Botas acquired another bookstore, the Librería Hispania in 1921. By 1933, the scope of the Ediciones Botas expanded and the editor began to publish two journals, *Criminalia* and *El Libro y las Letras,* as well as law textbooks. In 1943, the bookstore moved from its original location to Calle Justo Sierra. Gabriel Botas died in 1968 and the business was handed over to his son, Andrés Botas. Andrés Botas, a lawyer by profession, continued to practice law and the book business declined. Finally, in 1973, the journal *Criminalia* moved to Porrúa where it continued to be published. In 1988, Andrés Botas retired. The two bookstores, the Librería Botas and the Librería Hispania, which was renamed Librería México, are now operated by Andrés Botas's children: Ernesto, Andrés, Gabriela, and Laura. They are considering reprinting out-of-print Mexican classics.

Cataloging, Access, and Preservation

Due to the brittle paper and the general fragility of the books, the collection had to be housed in specially constructed boxes in the Special Collections Department. While this method of storage is good at preserving the covers, it makes it nearly impossible to view all the covers at once. Excessive handling, copying, or photographing would further damage the books. In this environment, the best way to view all the covers, and to provide the proper level of access to researchers, was to place them in a database mounted on the Internet. The records would contain, in addition to scanned images of the covers, bibliographic information and artist identification.

Controversy arose concerning whether the individual items should be cataloged on OCLC. Some catalogers felt they should just break away from the MARC format and do a stand alone database. Others felt they should provide individual catalog records in the OPAC. Still others felt it was all in a day's work and it was only a matter of how much staff time catalogers wanted to devote to this collection. In the end, it was decided to provide full cataloging for each piece, but not to do NACO level authority work on names or to upgrade description to current AACR2 rules.

While most titles had cataloging copy, much of it was minimal level (level K cataloging) using old cataloging rules. However, since most books were literature, few needed subject headings, and, fortunately, only a couple needed series treatment. A local made-up series, "Ediciones Botas book covers collection," was added to each catalog record to bring together this collection in the OPAC. The call number for the classed-together series was also used to bring together the file for the book and its two or three corresponding images (thumbnail image, larger image, and signature image). A collection level record in the OCLC database will eventually link the URL to the website.

A Microsoft Access database was created, which included the author, title, publisher, place, and date, along with the artist's initials/signature if available, a thumbnail image, a full-screen image, and notes. Clicking on the thumbnail brings up the larger image. Authors' names in the database were entered in direct order, as they appeared on the piece. Similarly, the text of each field in the database reflects the information found on the title pages or covers. All text fields are searchable, and the transcription of the artist's initials/signature is positioned immediately above the image of the signature, providing a best guess of the spelling. Whether or not this guess proves correct, this positioning allows the user to search for other instances of that artist.

Two problems plague the database. Diacritics were deemed necessary, but most users are not accustomed to producing accents and tildes on their keyboards. Without the diacritics, Microsoft Access will not recognize the name or word. A program or looping software will need to be found to allow all incidences of a letter, regardless of diacritics, to work. Also adding dropdown tables for authors is being considered, since a user has no way of knowing which authors are included in the collection without going through the whole list.

Direct transfer of MARC records was too cumbersome, since the MARC record contains too many fields to directly import into the database. Since the number of fields in the Access database is so small, it was more productive to input the data manually for individual records. Rekeying was still deemed a waste of time. Copying and pasting seemed to be most feasible, but OCLC diacritics are not recognizable to most software products. Fortunately, the diacritics in the OPAC translated perfectly into the database. The fields were copied and pasted from the OPAC record, which process occurred relatively quickly. Images were scanned by a student, and then linked to the database records. The database is simple and easy to use and to implement. The database is not yet accessible to the public, because it has not yet been mounted on the server.

Conclusion

The Botas collection was a perfect database for a first try at manipulating images for presentation to the public via the Internet. It was large enough to provide a good representation of the problems but small enough to be manageable and to allow changes in direction. It also proved that the cataloger involved should be familiar with the software and graphics programs. When creating a database, it is not advisable to rely entirely on technical staff for solutions. The subject specialists should be able to ask intelligent questions and understand the answers. Sound decisions as to the depth of information, searching capabilities, and arrangement of relational databases need informed participants. Catalogers are good database planners, since they spend their lives organizing information. Most catalogers enjoy breaking out of the MARC format once in a while, and doing so provides an understanding of different options for information control. The UNM General Library is acquiring a collection of book covers from Cuba from the 1970s and 1980s and a large poster collection from Latin America. The Botas model will be used to provide access to these and future collections.

BIBLIOGRAPHY

Historia de las empresas editoriales de América Latina, siglo XX, edited by Juan Gustavo Cobo Borda. Bogotá: CERLALC, 2000.

Pedersen, Wendy. "Artifact, Preservation, and Access: UNM's 'Editorial Botas Book Covers Collection.'" *Collection Management* (October 2001).

Rodríguez Díaz, Fernando. *El mundo del libro en México.* México: Editorial Diana, 1992.

Stern, Peter A. "Art and the State in Post-Revolutionary Mexico and Cuba." In *Artistic Representation of Latin American Diversity: Sources and Collections,* edited by Barbara J. Robinson. Papers of SALALM XXXIV, Charlottesville, Virginia, May 31–June 5, 1989. Albuquerque, N.Mex.: SALALM, 1993. Pp. 17–32.

Zahar Vergara, Juana. *Historia de las librerías de la Ciudad de México.* México, D.F.: Universidad Autónoma de México, 1995.

Access and Bibliographic Control
of Latin American Resources

19. From Subsidy to Market to Consortium(?): A Retrospective on Latin American Newspapers

David Block

> To date there has been no unified effort made to inaugurate a program
> envisaging the preservation on microfilm of even the most significant
> of this type of material.[1]

In literate societies, newspapers are a central feature of cultural expression. Their breadth and depth allows them to straddle the primary/secondary source divide and to provide fodder for a wide range of scholarship. Despite their indisputable research value, newspapers have always presented difficulties to those who collect them. Their size, their frequency, and their poor paper quality (since around 1880) make large-scale newspaper access troublesome and expensive. As background to the contemporary discussion of Latin American newspapers, this essay offers a survey of the literature and some observations on what a retrospective offers us.

Two Essential Concepts

Although there were newspapers in Latin America at the end of its colonial period, the genre really catches hold only in the period of independence struggles. Virginia Betancourt's description of the UNESCO-funded filming project of nineteenth-century Latin American newspapers lays out the importance of newspapers as a vehicle for the scientific and political ideology of the Enlightenment.[2] Early newspapers also reflect the regionalism that characterized nineteenth-century Latin America. In an age before reliable communication off sea-lanes and river courses, newspapers represented local concerns and likely a single political point of view. Stephen Charno's monumental union list, *Latin American Newspapers in United States Libraries* (1968), stands in testimonial to the wide geography of the genre and to the scattered holdings of the 5,500 titles he identified. Collection of early Latin American newspapers was largely an individual, as opposed to an institutional, activity. The acquisition of personal libraries from the region in the twentieth century often included newspaper holdings, and this is the way that most reached libraries in North America and Europe.

I have not been able to document the onset of subscriptions in the Latin American periodical press. (Those who look at invoices in the here and now know that subscriptions are not yet fully instituted, as some periodicals continue to bill as they are published.) But the change from issue-by-issue purchase to regular delivery is a key concept in collection development. For it is this regularity, in need of monitoring, to be sure, that supports research across time. Subscriptions for Latin American newspapers date largely from the 1950s, a topic to which I will return.

The second key concept in the research use of newspapers is that of microfilming. Readers hate film, but they accept it when applied to newspapers, and for good reasons. Film conserves both information and space. The first half of this proposition has lately drawn criticism from authors and collectors, prominently in the pages of *The New Yorker*.[3] But while Baker and Zinman call attention to the unanticipated consequences of destroying paper files, they have not altered the preservation community's conviction that wood-pulp paper is a slow fire and that bound newspapers in hard copy will not sustain the use that researchers put them to.[4] Thus, the most reliable science continues to intertwine newspaper and microfilm, although savants are certainly attracted by the potential of digital preservation and are experimenting feverishly with it.

Acquisitions

Foreign newspapers have long been a part of research collections in the United States. For instance, the Library of Congress began to list its foreign newspapers as early as 1929.[5] And though it is not specifically documented, their collection chronology probably follows that of the development of area studies, with a few institutions pioneering procedures and a post-Sputnik boom, which applied them broadly. I have not located a broad-based survey of Latin American papers between the publication of Charno's union list and the email inquiry prepared for the 1994 SALALM in Salt Lake City. So the following analysis of subscriptions is only a tentative starting place.[6]

The table compiles information on Latin American newspaper holdings from two sources, the informal survey done for a paper presented under the inauspicious title of "Results of Newspaper Holding Survey" at the 1994 SALALM and the compilation of current news sources prepared by Fernando Acosta-Rodríguez for the Latin America North East Libraries Consortium (LANE). While it hides the details of titles, backfiles, periodicity, and format, the numeric compilation supports two important observations. First, the number of subscriptions, 263 in the 1994 survey and 154 in the LANE survey, and their geographic distribution are quite impressive. It seems safe to assert that North American researchers could find some examples of newspapers of record for every country in the region. As to their costs, using the mean of $1,100 per subscription established by the Library of Congress would inflate expenditures, since some of the subscriptions in the table are for Sunday-only subscriptions.[7] Nevertheless, these figures represent a substantial investment in Latin American newspapers.

Newspaper Titles Held by Selected SALALM Libraries

	Total Number of Subscriptions		Number of Titles Held		Number of Titles Held (Four or More)	
	1994 Survey	LANE	1994 Survey	LANE	1994 Survey	LANE
Argentina	30	18	10	7	2	3
Bolivia	6	4	3	4	0	0
Brazil	38	18	12	4	4	3
Chile	22	11	9	4	1	1
Colombia	19	5	9	2	1	1
Costa Rica	4	5	2	3	0	1
Cuba	20	18	4	5	2	3
Dominican Republic	6	2	2	2	0	0
Ecuador	4	2	3	1	0	0
El Salvador	4	1	3	2	0	0
Guatamala	3	2	3	2	0	0
Haiti	4	2	3	2	0	0
Honduras	2	2	2	1	0	0
Jamaica	5	4	2	2	0	0
Mexico	45	21	12	7	4	3
Nicaragua	9	17	3	5	2	3
Panama	0	3	0	0	0	0
Paraguay	3	0	3	0	0	0
Peru	8	8	4	5	1	1
Puerto Rico	9	8	3	2	2	2
Trinidad and Tobago	5	2	4	2	0	0
Uruguay	6	0	6	0	0	0
Venezuela	9	4	4	2	1	0

Sources: "Results of 1994 Newspaper Holding Survey," unpublished paper presented at SALALM 39 (USC, Yale, Library of Congress, University of Florida, University of Georgia, Emory University, University of Illinois, Harvard, Duke, Cornell, Princeton, Rutgers, NYPL, Columbia, Dickinson, Penn, Brown, University of New Mexico, and University of Texas). LANE Union List is available at www.nypl.org/research/LANE/unionindex.htm.

One of the reasons for the LANE survey was to share information on the source of paper subscriptions. The sources are varied—newspaper publishers in Latin America, their branch offices in the United States, library subscription agents, SALALM Libreros, and periodical distributors in large cities all appear at the LANE website. And, I expect, there are other variations on this theme that the LANE documents did not identify. The major reason for such source variability is the corresponding variability in newspaper prices. Postage costs traditionally comprise two-thirds of subscription prices, and these have increased briskly as Latin America brings its rates into line with the developed world. Thus air expediters and, increasingly, international periodical jobbers in cities with substantial Latin American populations serve as alternatives to the post.

A second significant observation comes from the table's last two columns. While there is some duplication in the titles subscribed, especially for Brazil and Mexico, the title overlap, relatively and absolutely, is quite small. Even taking the conservative "four or more subscriptions" as a measurement threshold yields only 20 titles in the 1994 compilation and 21 in the current LANE list. Nowhere does the number of subscriptions to a single newspaper total more than six. This is not good news for potential vendors of Latin American newspapers in any format, unless the market is somehow elastic.

Microfilming Latin American Newspapers

I will not present a timeline showing twenty highlights of microphotography and a schematic of the optics that enable it. Suffice it to say that the technologies and their application to newspapers predate SALALM by nearly thirty years and have always been part of SALALM's agenda. In fact, the quote that opens this essay comes from Nettie Lee Benson's paper, "Microfilm Programs with Emphasis on Latin American Periodicals and Newspapers," given at the Chinsegut Hill meeting.[8]

A while ago the conversion of paper to film was relatively simple. It was never adequate to cover the variety of regional newspapers from Latin America, but it was straightforward. Paper subscriptions were held by research libraries. Filming took place in those libraries or through trusted suppliers. Delivery was reliable, although a bit slow. Paper issues were discarded when film arrived. Harvard's filming, chronicled by David Weber, which was eventually folded into the Center for Research Library's Foreign Newspaper Microfilming Project (FNMP), the Library of Congress, and the University of Chicago became major suppliers of newspaper microfilm.[9] All of these were "cost recovery" operations, which, undoubtedly, meant "institutionally subsidized."

The first shock to this stable system came in the early 1990s when Brazilian newspapers revoked their permission to sell microfilm of their publications. One paper, *Folha de São Paulo,* subcontracted its filming to a Brazilian company that produced microfilm at a very high price. Others simply revoked permissions without providing an alternative supply. The second shock emerged from economic neoliberalism that banishes subsidy in the name of efficiency. Chicago closed its filming lab in 1987. The Library of Congress severely reduced its photoduplication efforts.[10] FNMP remains vital but is being nibbled by commercial filmers who see mercantile possibilities and offer publishers higher royalties in exchange for exclusive distribution rights.

Enterprise operations have long operated alongside institutional film-ers. Bell and Howell and UMI, now one but once separate, offered microfilm subscriptions to several Latin American dailies well into the 1990s. But these subscriptions ceased abruptly and now appear in Bell and Howell catalogs as historical artifacts, that is, backfiles only.[11] While commercial enterprises are under no obligation to divulge proprietary information, they have, occa-sionally, shared some of their insights. In discussing the prospects for a Latin American newspaper CD in 1994, Dan Havercamp—then represent-ing Research Publications International—summarized the critical elements of business decision-making in this area as market niche (what else is out there?), rights (exclusive rights preferred), and market size (number of subscribers).[12] These are formidable criteria in today's market, criteria more likely to decrease than increase newspaper filming. Faced with declining microfilm sales, some former micropublishers have changed their business plans and gone digital. Others have repositioned themselves, becoming more North American repre-sentatives of projects done in Latin America than original filmers or digitizers.

Conclusion

I believe that the end of the technological cycle has arrived that began with breakthroughs in micro-optics in the 1920s. Because digital technology is not yet a preservation medium, microfilm remains the most viable format for long-term information storage. However, this legacy system has very little purchase, either in the marketplace or in the information community. So, as traditional microfilming sources—the Library of Congress, FNMP—decline, and it seems unlikely that commercial sources will be able to provide afford-able replacement products, librarians find themselves in difficult straights.

I believe that there will be a digital solution, not because librarians want it, but because there is such enormous commercial potential for it—microfilm-ing boomed to archive canceled bank checks. But in the next five to ten years, librarians will need to find the means to preserve newspapers so that the vital information they contain will still be in place when the promise of digital pres-ervation becomes reality.

NOTES

1. Nettie Lee Benson, "Microfilm Programs with Emphasis on Latin American Periodicals and Newspapers." *SALALM Papers I* (1956), Working Paper No. IV–1.

2. Virginia Betancourt, "Memory of Iberoamerica: Rescuing 19th Century Latin American Newspapers, 1993–1997," *IFLA Journal* 24, no. 4 (July 1998): 233–236.

3. For accounts that present pleasant reading but dubious preservation science, see Nicholson Baker, "Deadline," *The New Yorker* (July 24, 2000): 42–56; and Mark Singer, "The Bookeater," *The New Yorker* (February 5, 2001): 62–69. Baker's breathless *Double Fold* was published too late for me to incorporate it into this paper, but reviews suggest that it contains more of the same.

4. A part of the history of newspaper use before the onset of microfilming involved the production of a cost-ineffective rag-paper edition of the *New York Times* and the use of Japanese tissue to reinforce bound pages by the New York Public Library.

5. Henry S. Parsons, comp., *A Check List of Foreign Newspapers in the Library of Congress* (Washington, D.C.: U.S. Government Printing Office, 1929).

6. I hasten to point out that individual libraries faithfully prepared helpful finding aids. The Library of Congress' *Newspapers Received Currently in the Library of Congress* (1980–1993) and an early number of *Biblio Noticias* from the University of Texas are exemplary. Scott Van Jacobs' "Latin American Periodical Price Index," published annually in the *SALALM Newsletter,* began in 1991. Another interesting approach is provided by Laura Gutiérrez, who followed up the Charno compilation by soliciting additional newspaper titles from Colombia, Ecuador, and Venezuela. See Laura Gutiérrez, "Newspaper Titles from Colombia, Ecuador, and Venezuela Unavailable in U.S. Libraries: A Survey," in *Eighteenth Seminar on the Acquisition of Latin American Library Materials* (1973): 435–456.

7. Terry C. Peet reported an average cost of $1,100 per print newspaper in 1997. Terry C. Peet, "Back to the Future: An Immodest Proposal," in *Religion and Latin America in the Twenty-First Century,* ed. Mark L. Grover. Papers of SALALM XLII, Rockville, Maryland, May 17–21, 1997 (Austin, Tex.: SALALM Secretariat, 1999), p. 251.

8. Final Report 1 (1956): IV–l, no pagination.

9. David Weber's essay, "The Foreign Newspaper Microfilm Project, 1938–1955," was originally published in the *Harvard Library Bulletin* (spring 1956). I consulted the reprint in *Studies in Micropublishing 1853–1976,* ed. Allen B. Veaner (Westport, Conn.: Microform Review, 1976), pp. 415–422. Other useful histories include Herman H. Fussler, "A New Pattern for Library Cooperation," in *Studies in Micropublishing,* pp. 405–416.

10. In calling for shared responsibility for foreign newspaper microfilming, Peet revealed in 1997 that the Library of Congress had reduced production from 41 to 20 cameras in "a few years." Peet, "Back to the Future," p. 251.

11. For instance, see the Mexican papers *El Universal, El Universal Gráfico,* and *Excelsior* which UMI filmed until 1994, 1995, and 1996 respectively. *Newspapers in Microform Catalog* are available at http://www.lib.umi.com/nim/results.

12. Dan Havercamp, "Latin American Newspapers: Considerations in CD-ROM Publishing," in *Modernity and Tradition: The New Latin American and Caribbean Literature, 1956–1994,* ed. Nelly S. González. Papers of SALALM XXXIX, Salt Lake City, Utah, May 28–June 2, 1994 (Austin, Tex.: SALALM Secretariat, 1996), pp. 402–405.

20. OCLC, Vendor Records, and Cataloging Triage

Laura D. Shedenhelm

The issue of vendor records in the bibliographic databases has been a continual topic of discussion during the annual conferences of SALALM. Some SALALM members have been less than enthusiastic about them, while others have offered compelling reasons for their utility. Following the 1998 meeting in Puerto Rico, Bartley Burk and I conducted a small study of vendor records in the OCLC database, using materials ordered for the Hesburgh Library at Notre Dame. The results were published in the January 2001 issue of *Library Resources and Technical Services*.[1] Here, I will give you a brief description of our study and then discuss reactions and commentary.

The Study

Our hypothesis was that these records posed several problems for catalogers, even though they may be useful in the acquisition process. These records are created to advertise a product for sale. They serve that purpose very well. They do not, however, serve the purpose traditionally expected of a library's catalog record. We believed that it was easier and more cost-effective to create an original cataloging record than to convert the minimal-level acquisition record to a full cataloging record. While we only looked at Spanish-language records in our study, this was solely due to the fact that we were looking at a Latin American collection. No particular emphasis should be placed on any given vendor. To illustrate this point, note that many non-English vendor records would need to have the descriptive and subject fields translated into English. Further, most vendor records, including the North American and British vendors, would need to be expanded with an appropriate classification and subject analysis. Therefore, it is rarely the case that any vendor-produced record could be accepted as fulfilling long-established library standards.

Beyond the amount of upgrading vendor records needed in order to meet our requirements for library catalogs, we also looked at duplication of records in the OCLC database. Jay Weitz, Consulting Database Specialist at OCLC, was very helpful in explaining the Duplicate Detection and Resolution software OCLC uses.[2] The algorithm uses fourteen descriptive elements in the cataloging record on which to form a match before merging records. There are about ten conditions that prevent the merge, including exact publication date and choice and form of author.[3] Weitz brought to our attention the fact that OCLC tends to "err on the side of adding or leaving duplicates rather than merging away unique records whenever there is uncertainty."[4] We had noted that our initial search of the 64 titles in our sample yielded a duplication rate of 26.6 percent: 17 of the 64 titles had at least one other record. By the end of our study, the duplication rate had risen to 37.5 percent, or 24 out of 64 titles. It is possible that there is a higher incidence of duplication with Spanish-language records because there are two major suppliers for these records. Research would have to be done to verify if this high rate of duplicated records is consistent across all vendor-provided records.

A duplication rate of between one-fourth and one-third concerns the technical processing community because of the resulting increase in labor costs these records create. In the ideal world, a bibliographer gives a clerk, or a student worker, a citation to order a particular work. That clerk looks for the title in OCLC, finds one record, preferably with full cataloging, downloads the record to a local integrated library system (ILS), and produces an order to be sent to the vendor. The vendor sends the book, it is received against the record already in the ILS, is marked, and sent to the shelves. The whole process should be quick and cost less than a dollar. However, when the clerk has to decide among several records that may or may not have complete cataloging, the level of expertise needed to complete the job goes up and the timeliness goes down. The entry-level worker may have to send the various records to a higher-level employee to determine which one to use, resulting in higher labor costs and delays in ordering, receiving, and processing the item.

The corollary here, though, is that if one-third of the records are duplicates in the system, two-thirds are new or unique. It can be asked, then, would there have been more or less full-level cataloging in the database if the vendor records did not exist? Since materials go through the acquisition process more quickly because there are minimal-level vendor records, they get into the cataloging workflow more quickly. Does this correspond to more full-level cataloging being completed more quickly?

While we did not attempt to answer this particular question, we did track how quickly full cataloging appeared for the titles in our study. Slightly more than 20 percent of the titles had full cataloging at the initial search following receipt of the item. Three months later, this had risen to almost 47 percent. Within eight months, over 81 percent had full cataloging. While we were in the final stages of writing our article, Jeffrey Beall, who was then at Harvard, published an article about the impact of vendor records on cataloging. He noted the need for research into the percentage of vendor records enhanced to full-level cataloging after one year in OCLC, then after two years.[5] We already had the answer to the first question and the timing was right to provide data about the second question. In July of 2000, exactly two years after we originally started, we searched all of the titles again and found that 95 percent had full cataloging.

Finally, our study looked at costs of processing records through the system from ordering to completion of cataloging. Using Notre Dame's labor and network access prices on which to calculate our costs, the processing ranged from about seventy-nine cents for a title that had full cataloging at the time of ordering through just under twenty-five dollars for a title needing full cataloging by a professional. This last price was calculated after the title had gone through three searches of the database over a period of about eighteen months. While we were not able to do any comparative costs because of the fluctuations in regional labor costs and network pricing, our results provide a benchmark.

Based on our results, we made five recommendations. (1) OCLC should initiate a training campaign for all vendors adding records to the utilities, concentrating on bibliographic description standards used by the majority of OCLC's constituency. (2) OCLC should make the authority files available to vendors, and the vendors should receive training in the construction and application of the records in these files. (3) OCLC should initiate financial credit to libraries reporting duplicates in the database. (4) OCLC should significantly increase financial credits to libraries adding original records and upgrading or enhancing existing records. (5) Vendors should provide value-added information to their records, for example, tables of contents, through digital means such as scanning.

Reactions and Commentary

I contacted William J. Crowe, chair of the OCLC Board of Trustees; Larry Alford, president for 2000–2001 of the OCLC Executive Committee; Jay Weitz, Consulting Database Specialist at OCLC; and Judith Nadler, coordinator for the ALCTS (Association for Library Collections and Technical Services) Research Initiative; for reaction to our article. Crowe is the Spencer Librarian at the University of Kansas and Alford is at the University of North Carolina-Chapel Hill. Since both libraries have strong Spanish-language and Latin American collections and have consistently been represented at SALALM, I thought that both of these leaders for OCLC policy-making groups might have relevant commentary. Neither, however, has had the opportunity to respond to my inquiry.

Judith Nadler, at the University of Chicago, reported in January of 2001 on the progress of the task force of the ALCTS' Technical Services Directors of Large Research Libraries Discussion Group, commonly known as "Big Heads," charged to look at "records from external sources in general."[6] The second question formulated by the task force is looking specifically at "the use of records from outside sources [such as vendor records] and the required standards for these records to make them acceptable to libraries without additional local work."[7] While Nadler was not able to share with me any information the task force has gathered, she did invite interested parties to attend the Big Heads meeting during the summer 2001 at the American Library Association meeting in San Francisco where their report will be given.

Jay Weitz, though, was able to give brief comments about each of our recommendations. Following are summaries of his comments and my related thoughts.

Training

With regard to the suggestion for rigorous bibliographic training for vendors, Weitz was "not sure how practical this would be"[8] or that vendors would be interested in having this type of training. I cannot speak to the interest level of vendors or of the practicality issues related to offering training sessions. However, based on OCLC's own principles of cooperation adopted in 1996 by the OCLC Users Council, "accuracy and completeness"[9] are one of the four factors of the usefulness of WorldCat. This document goes on to indicate that the regional networks and other partners make a commitment to "provide high quality, cost-effective training, consultation, and support to encourage the efficient use of OCLC records."[10] These statements would tend to indicate a level of obligation on the part of OCLC toward providing the recommended training.

Authority Files

Weitz was not certain if vendors currently have access to the national authority file or if they would use it.[11] He also noted that the form of name was only one element in the duplicate detection algorithm, which might or might not cause a record to merge or be considered unique. Again, I cannot guess what vendors would do, but my assumption is that any element that would help them sell their products would be of interest to vendors. Having an authorized form of name that would help connect a title to other works by or about a particular person would seem to be a useful tool. Since the form of corporate names is much more difficult to predict, even for professional catalogers, the authority file would be a wonderful source of information. In particular, it may help in identifying acronyms and initialisms which often appear on title pages and covers of Spanish-language books.

Financial Credit for Reporting Duplicates

Weitz correctly pointed out that there have been several innovations since 1981 that have made the reporting of duplicates easier and less expensive than during the study done by Johnson and Josel.[12] However, he noted the distressing fact that "OCLC tries to discourage the reporting of books duplicates because we would be simply overwhelmed by the volume."[13] They currently have multiyear backlogs of duplicate reports in most formats (visual materials and computer files being the exceptions). Weitz indicated that they receive thousands of reports each month for the same duplicate records, some of which turn out to not really be duplicates, thus making assignment of credit to any particular library extremely difficult. Knowing that the vendor records have a 26 to 37 percent chance of creating duplicate records, one tends to wonder why OCLC insisted on loading vendor records into the main database instead of creating a separate database of vendor records as has been advocated in SALALM's Cataloging and Bibliographic Technology Subcommittee, among others. Weitz suggested that catalogers may make a more lasting contribution in this area through advocating an increase in staff at OCLC dedicated solely to resolving the duplication problems.

Increase Financial Credits for Upgrades, Enrichments, and Enhancements of Records

We had noted in our recommendations that, on average, it cost almost twenty-five dollars per title to fully upgrade an acquisition-level record.[14] This falls within the range of fifteen to thirty dollars suggested by Elizabeth Steinhagen and Sharon Moynahan.[15] Weitz pointed out that OCLC has increased the value of credits several times over the years, and that any further increase would have to be determined by OCLC management and their advisors.[16] Toward this end, the Cataloging and Bibliographic Technology Subcommittee of SALALM sent a letter dated March 7, 2001, to Glenn Patton of OCLC requesting a modest increase in the credit for upgrading vendor records.[17] I applaud this request, yet hope that OCLC may consider reimbursing libraries for the work of their employees at a rate closer to the reality of the costs incurred in providing the product OCLC sells.

Value-Added Content in Vendor Records

Weitz concluded his comments regarding our recommendations by agreeing that any value-added content in the vendor records would be good, but he wondered if the vendors would be interested in doing "the considerable extra work."[18] I, too, would not think that vendors would be interested in adding information that only came from a significant increase in labor. However, I believe that the ease of scanning the title page and any other relevant information and running optical character recognition software is much less work than Weitz anticipates. Further, this activity could help increase the accuracy of transcription for both the title and publication fields in all vendor records.

Conclusion

Bartley Burk and I recognized that vendor records are part of the modern cataloging world. Librarians need to be able to utilize them as efficient and effective parts of their work. During the earliest years that these records appeared, there was varying and unpredictable levels of accuracy and fullness. We believe that the quality is improving, but the current situation remains more like a field hospital than a state-of-the-art surgery. Catalogers would like to stop performing triage on the casualties coming across their desks, and get back to what they were trained and hired to do: create original cataloging records.

NOTES

1. Laura D. Shedenhelm and Bartley A. Burk, "Book Vendor Records in the OCLC Database: Boon or Bane?" *Library Resources and Technical Services* 45, no. 1 (January 2001): 10–19.

2. Jay Weitz, email to author, June 9, 2000, 11:09 A.M. and 11:58 A.M.

3. Jay Weitz, email to author, June 9, 2000, 11:58 A.M.

4. Ibid.

5. Jeffrey Beall, "The Impact of Vendor Records on Cataloging and Access in Academic Libraries," *Library Collections, Acquisitions and Technical Services* 24 (2000): 236.

6. ALCTS Technical Services Directors of Large Research Libraries Discussion Group, "Minutes of Big Heads Meeting, January 12, 2001," http://www.acsu.buffalo.edu/~ulcjh/bhmin0101.html, accessed May 2, 2001.

7. Ibid.

8. Jay Weitz, email to author, May 22, 2001.

9. OCLC, OCLC WorldCat, Principles of Cooperation, http://www.oclc.org/oclc/uc/coop.htm, accessed March 19, 2001.

10. Ibid.

11. Jay Weitz, email to author, May 22, 2001.

12. Judith J. Johnson and Clair S. Josel, "Quality Control and the OCLC Data Base: A Report of Error Reporting," *Library Resources and Technical Services* 25, no. 1 (January/March 1981): 40–47.

13. Jay Weitz, email to author, May 22, 2001.

14. Shedenhelm and Burk, "Book Vendor Records in the OCLC Database," p. 19.

15. Elizabeth N. Steinhagen and Sharon A. Moynahan, "Catalogers Must Change! Surviving Between the Rock and the Hard Place," *Cataloging and Classification Quarterly* 26, no. 3 (1998): 12.

16. Jay Weitz, email to author, May 22, 2001.

17. The contents of this letter may be found by searching the Archives of Latin Americanist Librarians' Announcements List, http://listserv.uga.edu/archives/lalal.html, accessed May 23, 2001.

18. Jay Weitz, email to author, May 22, 2001.

21. The Caribbean Newspaper Index Project at the University of Florida Libraries

Richard F. Phillips

Overview

The Caribbean Newspaper Index Project (CNIP) at the University of Florida Libraries is the product, in part, of years of focus by UF Libraries on the acquisition, cataloging, and preservation of information materials related to the Caribbean and circum-Caribbean. These years of activity have resulted in, according to some scholars, the strongest accumulation of Caribbean-related library holdings anywhere.[1] This paper will review CNIP at the UF Latin American Collection.

Funded by a 1994 grant from the Andrew Mellon Foundation, CNIP was developed as a selective indexing and abstracting database to UF's microfilmed copies of two major Caribbean newspapers: Haiti's *Le Nouvelliste* and Cuba's *Diario de La Marina*. Teams worked to scan and digitize all filmed images of these newspapers as well. The following years are covered in the CNIP index:

- *Le Nouvelliste*—years 1899–1979—14,090 articles indexed/abstracted

- *Diario de La Marina*—years 1947–1961—9,102 articles indexed/ abstracted.

Background

As stated, the University of Florida Libraries have logged years of concentrated effort to gather, make accessible, and preserve information materials related to the Caribbean. UF first offered classes in tropical agriculture in the 1890s, and has certainly attracted recognition from interested specialists in many quarters of the Americas. The libraries thus initiated work to support such academic programming, and as time went by and university curriculum expanded, library holdings at UF on Latin American and Caribbean subjects rapidly grew.

A 1954 article written by Irene Zimmerman, former UF Latin American Collection librarian, traced the development of the Farmington Plan, a federal program designed to ensure that U.S. scholars had access to critical information sources throughout the world.[2] The University of Florida Libraries were given the Farmington assignment and received support of the federal government to take responsibility for the Caribbean and circum-Caribbean region.

In the 1950s, UF also received a grant from the Rockefeller Foundation to microfilm in the major libraries and archives of that area. Many of the unique Caribbean books, newspapers, documents, journals, and manuscripts held by UF are the results of that work. Subsequent grants in the 1990s from NEH and Mellon have also been received.[3]

Mellon Foundation interest in furthering development of and better access to Latin American information sources attracted a proposal from UF Libraries in 1994. A grant was written by the libraries seeking support to scan, digitize, and index the two Caribbean newspapers (as already mentioned). The rationale for selection of these newspaper titles grew from several points. One was the rapidly changing nature of Florida's population statewide. Large numbers of Cubans, Cuban-Americans, Haitians, and Haitian-Americans have settled in Florida's diverse regions. Therefore, service to their information needs was deemed a priority by the libraries. Another reason was the critical geopolitical nature of these two Caribbean islands, both in proximity to Florida. Lastly, input by scholars from UF identified *Le Nouvelliste* and *Diario de La Marina* as the two principal news sources from those nations.

Methodology to develop CNIP followed simple logic. It was determined that, given the timelines of the grant, work would concentrate on indexing and abstracting only selected articles from each issue covered in the UF microfilm holdings. The Haitian paper's run was much longer than the Cuban title, therefore it was decided that only one article from each issue would be included in the database. On the other hand, the Cuban holdings covered in the project are only the years after World War II, with special attention paid to the rise of Fidel Castro, his revolution in the 1950s, and the turn to Marxism by his regime. CNIP picked up more articles per issue in this case.

Access

CNIP is currently available via a CD-ROM. The original intention of linking scanned images to each indexed article is yet to be totally fulfilled due to technical problems. A web-based version is being developed, and that may well create the linkages desired.

It should be pointed out that some gaps are present in the coverage. For example, years 1915–1923 are missing from CNIP's indexing of *Le Nouvelliste*, because no known copies of microfilm for those years exist.

Editing of the database still needs to be done, because there are some misspelled entries. For the most part, however, the indexing serves well as a guide to many important articles, speeches, letters, interviews, and commentaries on Haitian and Cuban affairs in the twentieth century.

CNIP is unique—there exists little access to information contained in Haitian and Cuban dailies. Strong points of CNIP are coverage of social issues such as agrarian reform, commerce, religion, and foreign relations.

Contributors of articles picked up for access include many literary notables and political figures.

Conclusion

Scholars with interest in Caribbean matters will want to have awareness of CNIP. As stated, CNIP offers valuable entry into Haitian and Cuban social and intellectual circles over time frames that are of significant import. CNIP offers a wealth of access to Haitian and Cuban civilization.

NOTES

1. David Geggus, *The Caribbean Collection at the University of Florida Libraries: A Brief Description* (Gainesville: University of Florida Libraries, 1985).

2. Irene Zimmerman, "The Farmington Plan and Florida, 1954," *Florida Libraries* 5, no. 2 (September 1954).

3. See 1998 study and report on UF Latin American Collection at the website of the Association of Research Libraries (http://www.arl.org/collect/grp/uf).

Contributors

Teresa Aguilar Velarde, Banco Interamericano de Desarrollo, Representación de Perú

Roberta Astroff, Pennsylvania State University

B. J. Barickman, University of Arizona

Anne C. Barnhart-Park, Lafayette College

Paul Bary, Tulane University

Claire-Lise Bénaud, University of New Mexico

Adán Benavides, University of Texas at Austin

David Block, Cornell University

Nelly S. González, University of Illinois, Urbana-Champaign

Robert Howes, University of Sussex

Jennifer Joseph, University of the West Indies, St. Augustine

Elmelinda Lara, University of the West Indies, St. Augustine

Sharon Moynahan, University of New Mexico

Guillermo Náñez-Falcón, Tulane University

Richard F. Phillips, University of Florida

Ricardo Rodríguez Pereyra, Universidad Torcuato di Tella

Laura D. Shedenhelm, University of Georgia

Rafael E. Tarragó, University of Minnesota

Eloisa Vargas Sánchez, Red de Información Etnológica Boliviana

Lourdes Vázquez, Rutgers University

Darlene Waller, University of Connecticut

Carlos Alberto Zapata Cárdeñas, Biblioteca Luis Ángel Arango

Conference Program

Saturday, May 26, 2001

9:00 A.M.–9:00 P.M.   Committee Meetings

Sunday, May 27, 2001

8:30–9:30 A.M.   Committee Meetings

9:30–10:15 A.M.   Opening Session

Opening   *Víctor Federico Torres*
                        President, SALALM, 2000–2001
                        Universidad de Puerto Rico

Welcome   *Sherrie Schmidt*
                        Dean of University Libraries
                        Arizona State University

Welcome and   *Orchid Mazurkiewicz*
Announcements   Local Arrangements Chair, 2000–2001
                        Arizona State University

José Toribio Medina   *Cecilia Puerto,* Chair
Award   *Molly Molloy,* Rapporteur
                        New Mexico State University

10:15–11:00 A.M.   Opening of Book Exhibits and Reception

11:00 A.M.–12:45 P.M.   **Theme Panel I: Women, Gender, and Sexuality**
                        Moderator: *David William Foster,* Arizona State University
                        Rapporteur: *Nancy Hallock,* Harvard University

                        Asunción Lavrin, Arizona State University
                        "Gender and the Promise of Self: Women's History in
                        Twentieth-Century Spanish America"

                        Donna Guy, University of Arizona
                        "Gender and Sexuality in Latin America: Past, Present, and
                        Future"

                        K. Lynn Stoner, Arizona State University
                        "Exemplary Militancy and Steadfast Loyalty: The Female
                        Combatant and the Authorization of the Cuban Patriarchal
                        State"

217

2:00–3:45 P.M.

Theme Panel II: Seeing the Other: Representations of Race, Ethnicity, and Gender in Latin American and Caribbean Visual Culture
Moderator: *Darlene Waller,* University of Connecticut
Rapporteur: *Nerea A. Llamas,* University of California, Santa Barbara

Darlene Waller, University of Connecticut
"Ethnicity, Race, and Class in Early Caribbean Postcards: A Preliminary Research Report"

Peter Stern, University of Massachusetts
"Images of 'The Holy Trinity' in 20th-Century Mexican Art"

Anne C. Barnhart-Park, Lafayette College
"Pan-American Identity and Ethnicity: Buscando la América de Rubén Blades"

Library Panel I: Archives and Manuscript Collections of the Southwestern Borderlands
Moderator: *Walter Brem,* Bancroft Library, University of California, Berkeley
Rapporteur: *Myra Appel,* University of California, Davis

Theresa Salazar, Bancroft Library, University of California, Berkeley
"Societies, Families, and Individuals: Searching for Social Relations in the Bancroft Library's Collections"

Eulalia Roel, University of Arizona
"The AGES Project: Bi-National Cooperation in the Digital Age"

Adán Benavides, Benson Latin American Collection, University of Texas at Austin
"The Borderlands, Then and Now: Manuscript and Archival Sources at the University of Texas at Austin"

Walter Brem, Bancroft Library, University of California, Berkeley
"California and the Southwestern Borderlands: Collections and Access"

Library Panel II: From Covers to Content: The Ongoing Challenges in Cataloging
Moderator: *Claire-Lise Bénaud,* University of New Mexico
Rapporteur: *John Wright,* Brigham Young University

Christine Mueller, University of New Mexico
Elizabeth Steinhagen, University of New Mexico
"Pebbles on the Garden Path: Vendor Records in the Work Flow"

Claire-Lise Bénaud, University of New Mexico
Sharon Moynahan, University of New Mexico
"The Covers Are the Story: The Artwork of Ediciones Botas, Mexico"

Laura D. Shedenhelm, University of Georgia
"OCLC, Vendor Records, and Cataloging Triage"

4:10–5:10 P.M.   Committee Meetings

7:00–11:00 P.M.   Libreros Reception

Monday, May 28, 2001

9:00–10:10 A.M.   **Theme Panel III: Archival Sources for Research in Gender and Sexuality**
Moderator: *Hortensia Calvo,* Duke University
Rapporteur: *Roberta Astroff,* Pennsylvania State University

Guillermo Náñez-Falcón, Tulane University
"*Actos prohibidos:* Documenting Sexuality in Colonial Mexico from Documents in the Latin American Library, Tulane University"

Paul Bary, Tulane University
"Sexuality and Gender in Colonial and Nineteenth-Century Mexico: New Uses and Interpretations of Photographs in the Tulane Collection"

Theme Panel IV: The Forging of an Afro-Cuban Identity
Moderator: *Olga Espejo,* University of Miami
Rapporteur: *Joseph Holub,* University of Pennsylvania

Rafael Tarragó, University of Minnesota
"Afro-Cuban Identity and the Black Press in Spanish Cuba, 1878–1898"

Lesbia Varona, University of Miami
"Contribución afro-cubana a la literatura cubana"

Library Panel III: Enhancing Access to Latin American Resources
Moderator: *Nancy Hallock,* Harvard University
Rapporteur: *Sue Norman,* Dickinson College

Richard F. Phillips, University of Florida
"The Caribbean Newspaper Index Project at the University of Florida Libraries"

Cecilia Sercan, Cornell University
"Dublin Core: What? Why? How?"

10:30 A.M.–12:00   **Library Panel IV: Latin American Collections**
Moderator: *Micaela Chávez,* El Colegio de México
Rapporteur: *Bartley Burk,* University of Notre Dame

Nelly S. González, University of Illinois, Urbana-Champaign
"Relevance of Academic Libraries' Hispanic-American
Collections in a Diverse Society"

Carlos Alberto Zapata Cárdenas, Biblioteca Luis Ángel
Arango
"La protección del patrimonio documental regional
colombiano"

Eloisa Vargas Sánchez, Coordinadora Nacional REDETBO
"La Red de Información Etnológica Boliviana REDETBO:
una experiencia en información indígena"

**Library Panel V: Latin American Historical Bibliography:
Access for the Twenty-First Century**
Moderator: *Walter Brem,* Bancroft Library, University of
California, Berkeley
Rapporteur: *Peter Bushnell,* University of Florida

Henry Snyder, Center for Bibliographical Studies, University
of California, Riverside
"Creating a Latin American Union Catalog and Bibliography
to 1850: A Proposal and Plan"

Michael T. Hamerly, John Carter Brown Library
"The Colonial Spanish and Portuguese American Imprint
Cataloguing Projects at the John Carter Brown Library"

**Theme Panel V: Gender Relations, Education, and Politics
in Latin America and the Caribbean**
Moderator: *Peter Stern,* University of Massachusetts
Rapporteur: *Marianne Siegmund,* Brigham Young University

Jennifer Joseph, University of the West Indies, St. Augustine
"Women in Trinidad and Tobago: Role of Education and
Politics"

Elmelinda Lara, University of the West Indies, St. Augustine
"Gender Relations: Domestic Violence in Trinidad and
Tobago"

Lourdes Vázquez, Rutgers University
"The Feminist Movement in Latin America as Part of Our
Collection Design Tapestry"

1:15–3:00 P.M.   **Theme Panel VI: Gender and Cinema**
Moderator: *Adán Griego,* Stanford University
Rapporteur: *Laura D. Shedenhelm,* University of Georgia

David William Foster, Arizona State University
"Hacia un cine queer en América Latina: logros y limitaciones"

José Fuster Retali
"La Virgen y la prostituta: imágenes del deseo masculino en el cine argentino como reflejo del mensaje social"

Angela Carreño, New York University
Lynn Shirey, Harvard University
"Recent Explorations of Gender in Latin American Film"

Library Panel VI: Can We Assure Access to Latin American Newspapers?
Moderator: *Fernando Acosta,* New York Public Library
Rapporteur: *Sarah Leroy,* University of Pittsburgh

David Block, Cornell University
Dan Hazen, Harvard University
Edmundo Flores, Library of Congress
Alfredo Montalvo, Editorial Inca
Denise Hibay, New York Public Library

Library Panel VII: The Changing Reference Environment in the Digital Library
Moderator: *Mina Jane Grothey,* University of New Mexico
Rapporteur: *Catherine Marsicek,* Florida International University

Georgette M. Dorn, Library of Congress
"Hispanic Digital Products"

Trina Carter, University of New Mexico
"Current Status of Virtual ('Live') Reference Services"

Micaela Chávez Villa, El Colegio de México
"Recursos electrónicos en bibliotecas académicas mexicanas"

3:30–4:30 P.M.   Committee Meetings

6:00–8:00 P.M.   Host Reception

Tuesday, May 29, 2001

9:00–10:10 A.M.   **Theme Panel VII: Identity and Social Exclusion**
Moderator: *César Rodríguez,* Yale University
Rapporteur: *Pamela Graham,* Columbia University

Teresa Aguilar Velarde, Banco Interamericano de Desarrollo, Perú
"Identidad afroperuana y exclusión social en el Perú"

Benita Weber Vassallo, Inter-American Development Bank
"The Inter-American Development Bank: Responding to
Social Exclusion Issues in Latin America"

**Theme Panel VIII: Gender and Identity in Latin American
Literature**
Moderator: *Cecilia Puerto,* San Diego State University
Rapporteur: *Darlene Waller,* University of Connecticut

Cynthia Tompkins, Arizona State University
"Las andariegas, de Albalucia Angel, como utopia feminista"

Alvaro Risso, Librería Linardi y Risso
"Rastros de la identidad uruguaya en Jorge Luis Borges"

Film Presentation   *El Pasquín* (José Martín Sulaimán, Mexico, 2000)
                      Commentator: *Micaela Chávez,* El Colegio de México

10:30 A.M.–12:00   **Theme Panel IX: Race and Ethnicity in Brazil**
                      Moderator: *Thomas Marshall,* University of Arizona
                      Rapporteur: *Pamela Howard-Reguindin,* Library of Congress

Roberta Astroff, Pennsylvania State University
"Nipo-Brazilian Return Migration to Japan: A Review Essay
and Annotated Bibliography"

B. J. Barickman, University of Arizona
"And When the Slaveowners Were Not 'White'?: 'Black' and
'Brown' Slaveholders in Early-Nineteenth-Century Bahia"

Theme Panel X: Gay and Lesbian Identity
Moderator: *Tony Harvell,* University of San Diego
Rapporteur: *Geoffrey West,* British Library

Amy Lind, Arizona State University
"Lesbian, Gay, Bisexual and Transgendered Movements in
Latin America: Identity, Power and Politics"

Ricardo Rodríguez Pereyra, Universidad Torcuato di Tella
"Estereotipos gay en la literatura y el cine (Argentina)"

Robert Howes, University of Sussex
"Gay, Lesbian, and Transgendered Serials in Brazil"

**Workshop: Social Movements and Marginalized Groups
on the Internet**
Molly Molloy, New Mexico State University
Rhonda Neugebauer, University of California, Riverside
Marcelino Ugalde, University of Nevada, Reno

1:00–2:45 P.M.   **Theme Panel XI: Violence Against Women on the
                      U.S.-Mexico Border: Activists and Journalists Report on
                      their Experiences**

Moderator: *Molly Molloy,* New Mexico State University
Rapporteur: *Teresa Chapa,* University of North Carolina

Greg Bloom, Editor, Frontera Norte Sur, Center for Latin American Studies, New Mexico State University
Isabel Velazquez, New Mexico State University
Esther Chavez Cano, Casa Amiga Women's Center, Ciudad Juárez

3:00–4:30 P.M.   Town Hall and Closing Session

4:30–6:30 P.M.   Final Executive Board Meeting